310

D1517747

THIS
BOOK-COLLECTING
GAME

Nothing daunts him

A. Edward Newton, the Hobby Rider

THIS
BOOK–COLLECTING
GAME

BY

A. EDWARD NEWTON

AUTHOR OF

"THE AMENITIES OF BOOK-COLLECTING"

WITH ILLUSTRATIONS

BOSTON
LITTLE, BROWN AND COMPANY
1928

TO { AUDREY BABETTE JOSEPHINE CAROLYN } NEWTON

I dedicate this book to four sweet little girls, my cousins:—actually my grand-children, but, thinking that cousins are more becoming to a man of my age and habit, we exchange that name among us.

A. E. N.

My thanks are due to the editors of the *Atlantic Monthly*, the *Ladies' Home Journal*, and the *Saturday Evening Post*, for permission to reprint articles which have appeared in their publications; to the President and my fellow members of The Rowfant Club, for permitting me to use the copy and illustrations appearing in the chapter on "The Format of the English Novel," and to many friends for advice without which this book would be less worthy than it is.

A. E. N.

CONTENTS

I	PRELIMINARY CANTER	1
II	THIS BOOK-COLLECTING GAME	9
III	THE BOOKS OF MY BOYHOOD	43
IV	"WHEN WE WERE VERY YOUNG"	69
V	THE BOOK ITSELF	97
VI	THE BINDING	127
VII	THE AUCTION ROOM	175
VIII	CAVEAT EMPTOR	207
IX	"ABUSES STRIPT AND WHIPT"	233
X	WHAT TO COLLECT—AND WHY	245
XI	AMERICAN LITERATURE	274
XII	CONVERSATION IN THE LIBRARY AT "OAK KNOLL"	294
XIII	HUMOR AND PATHOS OF DR. JOHNSON'S DICTIONARY	309
XIV	THE FORMAT OF THE ENGLISH NOVEL	333
XV	ONE HUNDRED GOOD NOVELS	382
	INDEX	395

LIST OF ILLUSTRATIONS

WITH TWO OR THREE EXCEPTIONS, ALL THE
ILLUSTRATIONS HAVE BEEN MADE FROM
ITEMS IN THE AUTHOR'S LIBRARY

"A. Edward Newton, the Hobby-Rider"..........*Frontispiece*

"Crashing Through"................................. 1

"A Good Sport"..................................... 5

Title-Page of Congreve's First "Novel"................. 6

"Huckleberry Finn".................................. 7

"The Vicar of Wakefield"............................ 13

"Schoolboy Lyrics"................................. 14

Thomas Hardy...................................... 17

"The Last of the Mohicans" (in negligé)............... 20

A Solander Case.................................... 21

Mr. Graham Robertson and Richard.................... 24

The Fool Book-Collector............................. 29

The William L. Clements Library (exterior)............. 36

The William L. Clements Library (interior)............. 37

Title-Page of "Comus"............................... 40

Playroom at "Oak Knoll"............................. 42

"Jessica's First Prayer"............................. 44

Jessica's Temptation................................ 45

"Sandford and Merton".............................. 52

"Rollo's Tour in Europe"............................ 54

Illustration from "Rollo in London".................. 55

"Robinson Crusoe".................................. 61

"The New Robinson Crusoe".......................... 62

The Footprint in the Sand............................ 65

Original Map of Treasure Island...................... 66

"The Day of Doom".................................. 74

Dr. Rosenbach... 79

Cato Major... 83

Goody Twoshoes.. 87

Wynkyn de Worde's "Caxton Device".................... 98

Page from Caxton's "Recuyell de Troye"................101

Page from Caxton's "Game and Playe of Chess"........102

Title-Page of "The History of William Pens Conversion"..108

Dos-à-dos Binding.......................................115

A Page from Morris's Kelmscott Chaucer................120

A Page from Koburger's Nuremberg Chronicle..........121

An Interesting Sampler.................................126

A "Club Binding".......................................127

An Unrestored Grolier Binding........................131

A Grolier Binding......................................132

"Oak Boards"...133

A Henry VIII Binding..................................136

End Papers of a Henry VIII Binding...................137

A Thomas Wotton Binding..............................139

Bound for Henry Prince of Wales.....................141

An Embroidered Binding...............................143

Joyce Collet's Book of Common Prayer.................147

A "Mearne" Cottage-Roof Binding.....................149

Roger Payne..155

An "Edwards of Halifax" Binding.....................160

Gosden Binding..162

A Dutch Silver Binding...............................165

A Finely Chased Silver Binding......................166

A Silver Binding......................................167

A Cobden-Sanderson Binding..........................168

Black Morocco and Silver............................169

A "Riviere" Binding.................................170

A Sangorski and Sutcliffe Binding.......................170

A Trade Binding of 1854............................171

The Doublure....................................173

Christie's Catalogue of Dr. Johnson's Library..........180

The Library at "Oak Knoll"........................185

Goldsmith to Garrick..............................191

Title-Page of "Desperate Remedies"...................203

Title-Page of "The Dynasts"..........................204

A Famous Novel...................................206

A First Folio......................................210

My Only Relic, Dr. Johnson's Teapot...................212

A Fake Map of Bunker Hill...........................220

A Shakespeare Folio in Need of "Restoration"..........224

The Same "Restored"................................225

"Parnassus on Wheels"..............................227

A Page from "Parnassus"............................228

The Ballad of Librolarceny..........................229

"The Eighth Sin"...................................230

Cover Stamps of the Early Editions of "Tess"............231

Title-Page of "Abuses Stript and Whipt"................234

Sundial at "Oak Knoll"..............................245

Thomas James Wise.................................251

Title-Page of "The Compleat Angler"..................258

Key Page to a First "Angler".........................259

The "Angler," Part II...............................261

A Page from White's "Selborne".......................265

"Leary's"...267

"Thersites".......................................269

A Manuscript Page of the "Autobiography of Benvenuto
  Cellini"..271

Walt Whitman..276

Mark Twain...277

Manuscript Fragment of Edgar Allan Poe..............283

"Uncle Tom's Cabin," First Trade Edition.............284

"Uncle Tom's Cabin," Presentation Copy..............285

Bryant's "Poems"...................................290

Franklin's "Autobiography".........................292

Oscar Wilde, from a Caricature by Max Beerbohm......299

"Impressions and Opinions".........................305

George Moore.......................................307

George Moore, Forty Years Ago......................308

Several of Dr. Johnson's Dictionaries...............315

R. B. Adam and Son.................................318

"Pamela" in Binding................................335

A Title-Page of a "Pamela" First...................336

A Title-Page of the Enlarged "Pamela"..............338

"Tom Jones"..339

"Evelina"..340

"Rasselas" in Old Calf.............................342

"Rasselas" in Boards...............................343

"Peregrine Pickle".................................344

"Cranford"...345

Title-Page of First English Edition of "Don Quixote"....347

Frontispiece of Second English Edition of "Don Quixote".349

"Tristram Shandy" in Boards and in Full Levant......350

An "Unpressed" Copy of "The Sentimental Journey"....351

Title-Page of "The Vicar of Wakefield"..............352

Early Tennysons....................................352

"Emma," in Boards..................................353

"Lamia" in Boards..................................354

"Life in London," in Pictorial Boards.................355

"Sketches by Boz".................................357

A Prime "Pickwick"...............................358

"The Way We Live Now"...........................359

"Vanity Fair," in Parts............................363

Comic History of England.........................365

"Mr. Romford's Hounds".........................366

"Jane Eyre"......................................367

A Group of "Three Deckers".......................368

Two Scarce "Three Deckers"......................370

"Literature at Nurse".............................372

"Moby Dick," First American Edition...............375

"Desperate Remedies"............................376

Modern Books in Beautiful Cloth..................378

"The Whale".....................................379

A Trollope in Cloth...............................380

Mr. Micawber....................................381

George Bernard Shaw............................393

"Crashing Through"
dedicated without permission

I

A PRELIMINARY CANTER

Book-collecting. It's a great game. Anybody with ordinary intelligence can play it: there are, indeed, people who think that it takes no brains at all; their opinion may be ignored. No great amount of money is required, unless one becomes very ambitious. It can be played at home or abroad, alone or in company: it can even be played by correspondence. Everyone playing it can make his own rules—and change them during the progress of the game. It is not considered "cricket" to do this in other games.

I have many times been asked what my rules are: the question is easily answered. I have limited myself to a few fine examples of illumination and printing and binding, and generally to the masterpieces of English literature in first editions. This last is a large order: I hitched my wagon to a star fifty years ago, but I did not get up to speed for twenty years. Many collectors have flown higher than I, but none have made a more modest beginning. I own to-day, and value highly, books which cost me fifteen cents, and I well remember when the expenditure of a dollar for a book seemed like extravagance. When I owned a few hundred books I referred to it largely as "my library;" now that I have eight or ten thousand volumes, I know that it is not a library: it is merely a collection of books.

I cannot understand how people can get along without books, and—useful as they are—I do not call a Sears Roebuck Catalogue and a Telephone Directory BOOKS. I am firmly convinced that most people do not know how to live: how should they?—seeing that they march to the tune of "I don't know where I'm going but I'm on my way." The game of life is a good deal harder to play well than is *This Book-Collecting Game*. A good rule is to read as much as one can, but if one must talk, talk about something. Give the idiot who insists upon telling you how many miles he gets out of a gallon of gas, or the golfer who is forever going over a given course in seventy, a wide berth. Someone has said that most friendships are mere confederacies in vice or leagues in folly. It is not so with us: we who play the noble game of authors know that the by-product of book-collecting is FRIENDS.

Thomas J. Wise, the great English collector, has on his bookplate a motto which is characteristic of the man:—

> Books bring me friends where'er on earth I be,
> Solace or solitude—bonds of society.

How many and how variously placed are the friends I
have made through books! If variety is the spice of
life—and it is—the incidents in the life of the book-
collector are many and various. "You are fond of books,
I see," says the visitor, with a leer; as who should say:
I know your guilty secret. "I was brought up with
books and am just crazy about them. I wish you could
see my copy of *A Christmas Carol;* I think it is a first
edition: the illustrations are by Cruikshank" (the il-
literate always think that Cruikshank was Dickens's
premier illustrator) "and is bound in red morocco, with
a portrait of Dickens hand-painted on ivory let into
the cover." Shoot that man into space, painlessly if
you can, but shoot him. "Cut your losses and let your
profits ride" is good advice, even if it does come from
a stockbroker. There are few finer or more innocent
pleasures than TALKING BOOKS TO ONE WHO KNOWS.
There may be joy in heaven—I am told there is—but
the evidence is not conclusive, and I'll take mine
here in my library. And one's mail is so interesting!
I require the services of an able-bodied and nimble-
minded young woman to enable me to cope with mine.
Let me give an illustration.

Some time ago, I received a letter, at the top of which
was an original drawing, which reproduced appears at
the top of this article. It was such an exquisite little
sketch, so full of humorous detail, that it was several
minutes before I gave my attention to the writing underneath it. When I had decoded it—it was written
in a most perplexing hand—this is what I read:—

MY DEAR MR. NEWTON:

Some months ago, Mr. E. R. Gee wrote to me that you wished my permission to use my portrait of Surtees in your forthcoming volume, *The Greatest Book in the World*. Mr. Gee, I believe, notified you of my cordial consent and added that I would be glad to prepare you a special plate suitable for monochrome reproduction. So,—may I ask in the kindliest manner possible, do you consider it entirely amenitous to borrow one's neighbor's things and use them without saying 'thank you?'

Yours for bigger and better amenities,

GORDON ROSS

I was amused and somewhat nettled and delighted. What had happened was this: In the preparation of my paper on Sporting Books I had several times consulted E. R. Gee of New York, the well-known specialist on this fascinating subject. In the course of conversation with him one day, he informed me that he was about to publish a beautiful portrait of Robert Smith Surtees, the creator of the immortal Jack Jorrocks and Pigg and Soapy Sponge, and a host of others. The portrait was indeed a beauty, and wishing to be of service to my friend Gee, I told him that I would, if he wished, reproduce it in my paper on Sporting Books, my idea being to do Mr. Gee and the artist a good turn. I had at the time only just heard of the artist, Gordon Ross, and in the pressure of publication and at the same time getting ready to go abroad, I quite overlooked my indebtedness to him as the artist of the portrait I had reproduced. Immediately I had turned over the manuscript and the illustrations of my book to my publisher,

> I sailed away on the foaming main,
> In the biggest possible hurry,
> For dinner we'd lots of dry champagne,

and lots of other things, and I never gave Mr. Ross or Mr. Gee or their print another thought.

But Mr. Ross is English—that is, Scotch—in a word, British—and a Briton will have his rights. The fact that Mr. Ross has lived and made a distinguished position for himself in New York is, in his judgment, no reason why I should, in his words, borrow his portrait without saying "thank you"—hence his letter.

It has for many years been my habit when in a tight place to "fess up." I wrote Ross and told him the truth: that in the hurry of preparation for my departure it had quite escaped my mind that I should have secured his permission to reproduce his portrait of Surtees; I referred to the pleasure its possession gave me (thank God I had bought and paid for one), and finally I told him that I was delighted that I had been so remiss as it had brought me the exquisite little drawing at the top of his reprimand letter. Finally, I commissioned him to make another and a larger drawing in color of

A Good Sport, or
the minded fence
decorated without permission
to F. E. W.

the same sketch, that I might frame it and hang it among my sporting pictures and use a tiny reproduction of it as a bookplate for my sporting books.

In due course I received another letter from Mr. Ross, also accompanied by another drawing, here reproduced. The letter read: "If I may borrow the literary style of the auctioneers, 'these highly esteemed prints are offered in pairs,' " and much more—in token of complete forgiveness.

Which of the little Ross sketches is the most amusing, the most exquisite? Let the reader decide. They are equally lovely to me, and no friendship is more enduring than one which begins with a little misunderstanding. Love there may be at first sight, but friendship grows more slowly.

To return to books. "I have no repugnances. Shaftesbury is not too genteel for me, nor Jonathan Wild too low." I collect Bibles—and Sporting Books. "I bless my stars for a taste so catholic, so unexclud-

INCOGNITA:
OR,
LOVE
AND
DUTY
RECONCIL'D.
A
NOVEL.

Licens'd Decemb. 22. 1691.

LONDON,
Printed for *Peter Buck*, at the Sign of the *Temple*, near *Temple Bar* in *Fleet-street*, 1692.

A very early, perhaps the earliest, use of the word "novel" in the English sense. It is Congreve's first publication.

This is one of four known copies

ing." Just at the moment the Novel interests me enormously. People have been collecting Poetry and the Drama for years, but the Novel, the last and most popular of the literary forms, has been neglected: its turn will come: it is here now.

A few days ago I bought from Edgar Wells, in New York, a copy of *Incognita, or Love and Duty Reconciled, A*

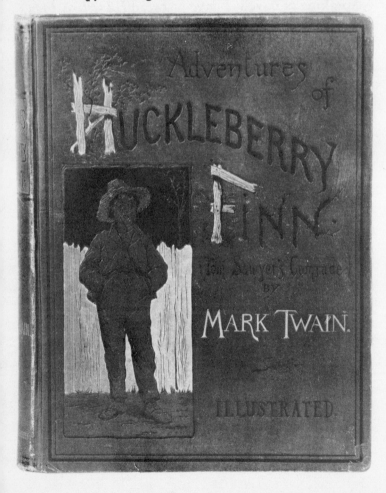

Novel. This is perhaps the earliest instance of the word "novel," used in our sense, on a title-page of an English book. William Congreve wrote it when he was twenty-one. It is very tiny and excessively rare. Dr. Johnson says he would rather praise than read it: bless the Doctor's honest heart! there were no frills about him: what he thought he said.

Speaking of novels. I have just read *Huckleberry Finn*, for the first time. It is a great book: Galsworthy ranks it with *Don Quixote*—and rightly. If I don't live to see the first issue of the first edition of that book sell for a thousand dollars, I shall die prematurely. Now, reader, don't for heaven's sake leap from your chair and seizing pen, ink, and paper, offer me *your* copy of *Huck Finn* for half the money. I said the first issue of the first edition: the one bound in *blue* cloth, yours, probably, is bound in *green:* the one in which page 283 is on a stub; and if you want to know why, ask your bookseller: he will tell you. I'm not teaching book-collecting by correspondence. The sieve of my memory is coarsely meshed: only a few important dates and facts are retained in it, and by the time your letter reaches me I may have forgotten. Ask John T. Winterich: he will know; if I am not mistaken, he has written an article about it. I repeat: *Huckleberry Finn* is a great book. I take no merit for this discovery.

II

THIS BOOK–COLLECTING GAME

First, let me say that our English cousins would not understand this title. "Game" to them means something quite different from what it does to us—to them it suggests something tricky. A London policeman, seeing two or three rather disreputable-looking characters acting suspiciously on a street corner, will approach them with "What's your little game?" He may say "gaime;" in any event, he will tell them to "move h'on" or "be h'off." We, on the other hand, say that a man on leaving college is going into the electrical game, meaning thereby that he has adopted the electrical business as his profession, and that he intends to play it with what skill he has.

I have been playing this book-collecting game for forty years; it is, indeed, the only game I thoroughly enjoy. I remember perfectly how it happened that I began to play it. For a boy, I was a sturdy reader: at school—before I ran away therefrom and never went back—I read Napoleon, having, as a small boy, consumed the Rollo books, *The Swiss Family Robinson*, *Sandford and Merton*, *Robinson Crusoe*, and *Great Expectations*. But Napoleon as portrayed by Abbott enthralled me, and finally I came to have some twenty or thirty volumes about him—quite a lot for a lad. Then one day I awoke from my trance and saw Napoleon—as I still believe him to be—a monster in human form; whereupon I trudged off to Leary's, that famous secondhand bookshop in Philadelphia, and sold the lot, and was ready to begin what I was pleased to think was my intellectual life over again.

Then, just at the proper moment, I fell under the sway of a man old enough to be my father, who, without consciously intending to do so, undertook to direct my reading and suggested that I form a library. "It will be a great delight to you when you are older," he said. "Fine," I replied, "but where shall I begin?" "At the beginning," he said. "With Homer, Pope's translation: the *Iliad;* afterward read the *Odyssey,* which you'll like better." I bought the books and have them still: two volumes, Bohn's edition, in faded green cloth; they are the corner stones of my library. Subsequently, at my mentor's suggestion, I read *The Cloister and the Hearth* and *The Autobiography of Benvenuto Cellini.* These led me to Motley and Prescott; by that time I was twenty, and had read Boswell's *Johnson,* had been in London, and my education—such as it was—was complete. Certainly this education might have been better, but then it might have been worse.

In between what I may have thought was my "heavy reading," I read Dickens, Thackeray, Scott, and Charles Reade. Then the problems of life began to press rather firmly upon my shoulders, but I managed to get some reading done; and someone was good enough to tell me when I bought a book always to get, if possible, a first edition. And when I inquired why, I was told that if I ever wanted to sell my books I might get my money back if I had first editions; whereas, if I had not, I should be pretty sure not to.

Years passed: I bought what books I could; finally got married, bought a home, had children, and came to feel the need of some sort of place in the country for the summer months. It seemed, at the moment, more important to have a place in the country than to have a few hundred first editions, and as it was perfectly clear to me that I could not have both, I decided to part with some of my books. After some discussion and correspondence, carried on through a third party, I decided to sell at auction in New York, and—to save money—to make and print the catalogue myself. And I still have a copy of the slender pamphlet in which were bound up my hopes and fears. There were in all two hundred and forty-six items.

I had made my notes as interesting as I could, and on the afternoon of Monday, May 18, 1896, with my catalogue in my pocket and my heart in my mouth, I climbed up the shabby stairs that led to Bangs and Company's in lower Fifth Avenue, where the sale was to take place. One or two people nodded to me as I entered the room, but no one knew that the books were mine. On the other hand, I knew to a penny what each item cost, and to keep up appearances I bought one or two books that were going for less than they were worth; but I had to be careful, for the sale must net me twenty-five hundred dollars. And it did. As I remember, I ultimately got a check for something like twenty-seven hundred dollars; with which amount I built the cottage in the country in which I still live— with such more substantial additions as I have been able to make as I got a lead on the sheriff.

It was several years before my affairs permitted me to think seriously of again collecting books; meantime I had the mistakes to make that a city man always makes when finally, for good and all, he transfers himself to the country. How we raised every animal

that could be raised—in adversity—and grew everything that refused to grow, until with increase of
fortune we discovered that only the very rich could
afford to milk their own cow and grow their own
vegetables—of what interest is this to any man? Books
are my theme.

A permanent bent had been given to my life and
interests by my first visit to London. Its individuality
was greater forty years ago than to-day: something—
maybe it is democracy—is tending to make most of us
colorless and uninteresting. In an effort to recreate
myself in a less commonplace world, I became a reader
of biography. Of soldiers and soldiering I had had
enough; for politicians, playing their crooked and
sordid games, I had—and still have—a feeling of
abhorrence. The lives of actors and actresses always
promise to be interesting but seldom are. My great
regret is that, as a young man, I was never led to read
Shakespeare, almost to the exclusion of everything
else. But he once seemed too remote for me; and this
feeling led me to neglect the seventeenth century; in
the eighteenth I found the leisure which was lacking
in my own. I became, ex officio, a member of the
Johnson circle. I exchanged—happy exchange—my
perplexities for those of Oliver Goldsmith: what shall
be the name of the new play?—which was to deal a
body blow to the artificial comedies of Congreve, the
plots of which no man can follow without a compass.
How will it be received? Under what circumstances
and difficulties was *The Rivals* produced? And *The
School for Scandal?* I had never seen *The Critic*, but I
could read it; I owned a copy, for I had discovered—

and it was the only discovery I ever made—that almost any book worth reading was worth owning. Quite unconsciously I began to buy books again: once more I was a book-collector.

I have followed the course of many book-collectors. If he be a rich man, he begins by buying subscription books in binding, and if he continues to play the game he will come to hate them. If he be young, he will begin with some modern author, Dickens, or Stevenson, or Kipling, perhaps with Bret Harte; but it makes little difference where one begins, if one keeps on: sooner or later he will wish to own the masterpieces of literature in first editions, and will buy them if he can.

A lovely story—"The Vicar," in old binding

The longing I had for a first *Vicar of Wakefield* is not to be expressed. And a professed lover of Boswell should have a first edition of his great biography, uncut and in boards, especially as a fine copy was then to be had for fifty dollars. A good resolution is never to be satisfied with a poor copy of a book at any price; a superlatively fine copy of a great book is always cheap.

I have referred to book-collecting as a game: it is, and a pleasant one, calling for all the skill you may acquire and as much money as you can afford to spend. If you play it with the "rigour" that Sarah Battle enjoined when playing whist with Charles Lamb, it will take more money than you can afford—then it will prove positively exciting. I shall assume in this paper that if, and when, you stop collecting, should you decide to dispose of your collection, you will have no objection to getting your money back. To do this, you must not ride your hobby too far off the beaten track. Let me explain what I mean.

Let us assume that you have decided to make a collection of Kipling—the greatest English author now living. You may begin where you will, as your purse and opportunity afford. You may decide to buy a copy of *Schoolboy Lyrics*, his first book, if book it may be called,—a tiny pamphlet, in brown or white paper covers, of which fifty copies were printed by his father; it is now worth, or at least sells for, twenty-five hundred dollars,—or you may have to content yourself with a copy of *Echoes*. A boy could hardly do better than start with that excellent story *Captains Courageous*,

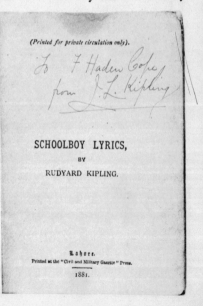

(*Printed for private circulation only*).

To F Haden Coper
from J. L. Kipling

SCHOOLBOY LYRICS,
BY
RUDYARD KIPLING.

Lahore.
Printed at the "Civil and Military Gazette" Press.
1881.

the manuscript of which has recently passed into the Pierpont Morgan Library, and of which three first editions are known: namely, the S. S. McClure edition, of which only five copies were published to secure the copyright, the edition published in New York in 1897 by the Century Company, and the edition published that same year in London; either of these last you can get for five dollars. It would, of course, be nice to have the edition of which only five copies were printed, rather than either the first American or the first English edition; but in any case a good beginning has been made, for these, any of them, are *books*. An article in a magazine is a different matter: it is practically impossible and almost useless to follow an author through the magazines. And, unless it is your purpose to complete your collection and present it to some library or institution, stop with the important books and the important waifs and strays—if this contradictory phrase may be allowed. Otherwise, one's time and money are spent in an exhaustive search for an item hardly worth having when found. Long before the possibilities of Kipling are exhausted, I should turn my attention to some other author of equal distinction of the same period; in the case we are imagining, it would be Thomas Hardy.

Why, do you say? For this reason. Let us suppose an auction sale at which three or four hundred items of one subject are to be disposed of. Kipling does not fit into everyone's collection; not everyone—not even the booksellers, who are certain to be present—knows as much about the subject as a man who has for years specialized upon it, and it may happen that a unique item which may have cost you a lot of money will be knocked down for a song. Another reason: there is such a thing as "sales fatigue." It is difficult for the auctioneer to keep his customers' interest from flagging at a long sale in which there is no variety: variety is the spice of life, and nowhere is it more necessary than in the auction room.

It will be seen that I am at the moment writing from the point of view of the seller; from the buyer's point of view, these long and wearisome sales afford excellent opportunities for strengthening one's collection. And here let it be said that if the average man seeks to make a representative collection of a fairly voluminous author one subject will serve to occupy him for several years; occasionally it will occupy a lifetime. I have in mind the collection of *The Dance of Death*, the most remarkable of its kind ever formed, which was assembled by Miss Susan Minns of Boston. It was sold several years ago by the American Art Association in New York, and in the introduction to the excellent sales catalogue Miss Minns tells how she put the collection together, piece by piece, over many years. In dispersing it she sportily said: "I have had the pleasure of collecting; let others have the same." I applaud the sentiment, but the collection should have been kept together as a monument to the lady's unrivaled knowledge and industry. A bore once asked Oliver Herford what he would like most to see; after a pause he replied: "I should like to see you throw a raw egg into an electric fan." Now, were the question put to me, I should say I should like to see the ordinarily well-informed man, not knowing of Miss

Thomas Hardy, O. M.
After portrait by Augustus John; from original painting
in Fitzwilliam Museum, Cambridge

Minns's hobby, start telling her something about *The Dance of Death*.

To return to Thomas Hardy. His first book was *Desperate Remedies*, published anonymously, by Tinsley Brothers, in three volumes. In those days all novels were published in three volumes, and it was usual for the circulating libraries to buy a certain number of every novel when it came out, few people caring to venture thirty-one shillings and sixpence—the established price—upon a work of fiction, especially if the author were unknown. Hence it is that almost all copies of an author's first book (I am speaking of novels) are known as "ex-library" copies, meaning that a library label has been pasted upon the binding, leaving a stain if removed, and accounting for other damage. From this it will be seen how difficult it is to come across a fine copy in cloth. Bound copies make, of course, a fine appearance on one's shelves, but fastidious collectors have declared for original cloth, or boards with the paper labels, as the case may be, and are prepared to back their fancy to a pretty steep figure. Even as I write there comes to my table a catalogue from Walter M. Hill of Chicago, whose catalogues, by the way, always deserve careful reading. Note how lovingly he describes this item:—

AUSTEN (Jane). Sense and Sensibility; a novel. In three volumes. By a Lady. London, Printed for the author and published by T. Egerton, 1811. First Edition. $900.00

In the original blue boards and with the paper labels, and in perfect state. No foreign element has entered into the physical condition of the copy. A most unusual book in the most desir able and rare state of perfection.

I need it to complete my set. The temptation to buy it is almost irresistible, but one can't have everything. The moment a book is rebound, it must be viewed with suspicion. Half titles are frequently lacking, or, if present, may have been taken from second or later editions. Or it may be that some ignorant bookseller has taken upon himself to add a half title to a book which in its first state had none. Too much is quite as bad as too little; anything more or less than the book in the condition in which its author gave it to the world is not now favorably regarded. And, obviously, rebinding a book, unless it is done carefully, usually means the reduction of margins—and size is a matter of the utmost consideration in buying a book. Binders, all of them, deserve to be hung by the feet until they are dead for the offenses their ancestors in the trade have committed. The nonchalance with which a binder put a book under a knife and removed a substantial fraction of its margins is now recognized as a crime. Every important library contains numbers of rare volumes which, had they been allowed to remain in their original condition, tied up with a bit of string if the leaves were loose, would to-day be priceless; as it is, they may indeed be so, but how much more valuable would they be had they not been subjected to the process of cropping.

Blessings upon the head of Daniel Charles Solander, a botanist of distinction, who after extensive travels became a "Keeper" in the British Museum. He invented the leather case which bears his name. It is a box in the exact shape of a book in which some precious volume may be kept, and which, when placed upon

"The Last of the Mohicans,"
very much in negligé

one's shelves, has the appearance of a book. Such cases are usually made of morocco, sometimes covering asbestos boards, which render them practically fireproof. I almost never have a book bound: the moment one does so, some question arises which could perhaps have been settled if the book had not been tampered with. Many collectors, in binding their books or in having slip cases made for them,—a slip case being a simpler form of case,—have their novels bound in one color, their poetry in another, and so on. This adds variety and beauty to one's books and makes it easier to recognize some particular volume when sought. After Solander's death in 1782, it was sought to honor him in some way, and a small island somewhere in the Pacific was named after him; but a "Solander case" is more frequently referred to than the island, I am quite certain of it.

I have not animadverted upon the collection of books in sets. Let me explain what I mean. Certain sets one must have; no gentleman's library is complete without them: sets of Dickens, and Scott, or Parkman, or Motley, and hundreds of others. These are backbone books—one must have them; but their possession confers upon their owner no more distinction than a pair of pants. There are, however, other books which give perpetual delight; these vary with the wealth and learning of the collector. In my own case a fine copy of Benjamin Franklin's *Cato Major* in original binding, the first classic translated and published in America (in Philadelphia in 1744), would do it; whereas the late Mr.

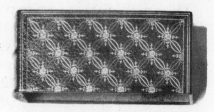

Henry E. Huntington would have had to produce the original manuscript of Franklin's *Autobiography*— and he could have done it, too.

The only "set" of first editions I ever bought, complete in binding, is my set of Trollope. I bought it years ago before the renaissance of this great Victorian had set in. I am glad to have it,—many of the books are practically unobtainable in their original condition,— but it gives me no

A Solander case, made by H. Zucker of Philadelphia

feeling of pride. When, not long ago, Michael Sadleir, an ardent English Trollopean, wrote to ask me a question as to the original binding of one of Trollope's early books, I was obliged to confess that as my set was in binding I could not answer his question. And, by the way, Sadleir has written and Houghton Mifflin & Company have published an excellent book on Trollope, which every reader of this great novelist —and we are legion, to-day—should read and will certainly enjoy.

I like to think that I am responsible in some measure for Trollope's present vogue, both with readers and with collectors. I have always delighted in him because of his humor, and his marvelous pictures of nineteenth-century English life. After his death a quietus was put to his fame by the publication of his *Autobiography*. In it he described the perfunctory way in which he wrote his novels, and, his own generation of readers dying with him, the next would have nothing to do with him. "How can novels so produced be anything but stupid?" it was said. Years ago I wrote a small paper on the genuis of Trollope, being led to do so by the appearance of a silly article in an English magazine to the effect that Trollope was as dead as Cæsar. And about the same time Professor Phelps of Yale wrote in his book on the English novel that "no one would dare call Trollope a genius;" whereupon I rose and said, "I do." To-day Trollopeans are everywhere, even in England. He has more first-rate novels to his credit than any other writer. A complete set of his writings runs to sixty-eight titles, one hundred and thirty-four volumes! Anyone who wishes to spend a delightful evening or two with this novelist will read his *Autobiography*. And would you read an excellent novel? Try *The Eustace Diamonds*.

I sometimes think that the greatest joy that comes from playing this book-collecting game is the delightful acquaintances one makes, which tastes in common soon flower into friendships. Through my interest in William Blake I came to meet and know intimately Graham Robertson—an English authority and collector of that fascinating man. It happened in this way. I was in the British Museum one day, talking to Laurence Binyon; he asked me if I knew Robertson. and I replied "No, but I should like to." "I think I can arrange it," said Binyon; and a few days later I received a letter saying that Mr. Robertson was out of town, but that if I would call at his residence in Knightsbridge his housekeeper would show me his collection of paintings. I did so; saw some wonderful paintings—they are now in the Tate Gallery; and when subsequently I wrote Mr. Robertson, thanking him for his courtesy, I remarked that we had other tastes in common; and I mentioned Gilbert and Sullivan and Irving and Terry. Whereupon I received another letter from Robertson, saying that if I, in addition to being a Blake collector, was a Gilbert and Sullivan and an Irving and Terry enthusiast, he wished I would come down into the country and spend a day with him; that all his best Blakes were in the country, and that he himself had not been in his London house for several years. He said that he would meet me at the railway station; that I could not miss him, as he was a plain-looking man, but that he would be accompanied

Mr. Graham Robertson and his dog Richard

by the finest sheep-dog in England. I went, met Mr.
Robertson without difficulty, spent a happy day with
a most delightful gentleman, and I have never since gone
to England without spending a day in his company,

and his letters to me are a joy. And, of course, I know well Geoffrey Keynes, the splendid young surgeon of "Barts," whose bibliographical studies of Blake would seem to be the last word on the subject—at least the Grolier Club thought so when it brought out its splendid volume.

Let me mention another man, John Burns, England's one time Labor leader, and one of the most brilliant men I ever met. His acquaintance I made in Sawyer's bookshop. The Honorable John is self-educated, but what an education! He has half a dozen degrees from as many universities. What are his interests? Well, in addition to statistics on every conceivable subject, I should say they are politics, London, history, architecture, town planning, and Sir Thomas More, of whom he has the finest collection in the world. He is a seasoned book-hunter, has a wonderful library, and a memory which is bewildering to a man who, like myself, was born with a complete forgettery in place of that useful organ. He does not believe in war, gave up office and five thousand pounds a year for con-science' sake; but, England once in, he did what he could himself: saw his son and only child go—never to come back. And now, with his very charming wife, he lives in semi-retirement, with his books. John Burns, like all good parliamentarians, is very brilliant in re-tort; and there is a good story told of him which I should like here to repeat for the benefit of those who have not heard it. Some time ago, when he was a cabi-net minister and chairman of the board which directs all the functions of the metropolitan city of London, one of his colleagues entered his office, and said, "John, there are two Americans here who want to see as much of London as they can in the shortest possible time."

"And I am expected to show it to them?" said John.

"You are," said his visitor.

"Very well," said John, "I'll take them on to-morrow at ten o'clock." And he did. And he showed them aplenty—not the obvious things, but things of the greatest interest which strangers seldom see. Late in the afternoon the exhausted visitors were treated to tea on the terrace—that famous and delightful function so frequently described in novels. John was as fresh as paint. "And that," he said, pointing with pride, "is our noble river Thames." The two visitors looked and were not impressed.

The man from Canada said, "Mr. Burns, have you ever seen the St. Lawrence River?"

And the man from Missouri added, "Or the Mississippi?"

John replied in a voice of thunder, "Gentlemen, I have seen those rivers. The St. Lawrence River is water, the Mississippi River is muddy water,—that, gentlemen, is liquid history!" As good things have been said, but better—never.

To return to book-collecting. Through book-collecting, I came to meet and know that rare personality, Amy Lowell, and, through her, Professor Palmer of Harvard. The meeting with him came about in this way. I had been spending some weeks visiting friends "down east," and when I got to Boston one hot August day I said to myself, "Well, it's been a pleasant holiday, but it's over now. All my friends will be out of town. Ellery Sedgwick I know is away, and Amy

Lowell will be rusticating somewhere. Nevertheless, I'll go through the motions of calling them up." I was right as to Sedgwick, but wrong as to Miss Lowell. After the usual delays came the rich, well-rounded voice over the telephone (the voice I shall, alas! never hear again): "What brings you to these parts? Certainly you may come to dinner. I'll send the motor for you. You'll find a dear old gentleman in it: Professor Palmer. He's dining with me; he's a book-collector too." "Why, he's the very man I came to Boston to see," I replied. "You did!" cried Miss Lowell. "I supposed you had come to see me! However, come to dinner and I'll show Professor Palmer to you."

Now Professor Palmer not only teaches philosophy —he practises it; his chief claim to distinction, however, is his knowledge of Greek. He has translated Homer's *Odyssey* into a "best seller." "When 'Omer smote 'is blooming lyre," as Kipling says, I wonder what he would have thought had he been told that some three thousand years later, in a world to him unknown, and in a manner to him unsuspected, a fellow by the name of Palmer would sing his songs, in a barbarous tongue, to an audience of over a quarter of a million people.

That evening when Miss Lowell's motor called for us we found Professor Palmer ensconced therein, and I soon discovered that a fine bibliographical evening was in contemplation; for the dear old man had with him a green baize bag, such as Philadelphia lawyers used to carry, full of rare books to show to Miss Lowell, in exchange for which she was to show him her wonderful Keats collection, which is now one of

the treasures of Harvard. There is a fine spirit of
rivalry among collectors, and I said to myself that
there would probably be some exhibition riding of
hobbyhorses, and I had a feeling of satisfaction in the
belief that, although my nag might stumble once or
twice, it would not get altogether out of hand.

That evening was one to be remembered. Miss
Lowell was in fine form: she radiated hospitality as
she welcomed us at the door of her stately mansion
in its park of green velvet, studded with fine old trees
—which I should describe as elms but for a story I
once heard. A little girl was visiting at an English
country house situated in a park famous for its fine
old trees. As she strolled around with her host after
dinner, knowing that she was expected to remark
upon their beauty, she exclaimed, "How beautiful
those old elms are! If they could speak, what would
they say?" To which her host replied quietly, "They
would say, I think, 'We are oaks.' " Anxious to avoid
the chance of a tart correction from Miss Lowell, I
content myself with describing her trees as stately,
and let them go at that.

I soon discovered that poetry was to be the subject
of the evening. Out of Mr. Palmer's green bag came
one rare volume after another: Herrick, and Herbert,
and Blake, and Milton; giants, housed in tiny volumes,
one after another, all to be matched by Miss Lowell.
And as I was not called upon to prove possession, it
was easy enough for me to say, "I have that, too."
Finally I said to Mr. Palmer, "Let us see your Lovelace *Lucasta;* mine is in old sheep." Out of the bag
it came, but, unluckily, in a modern binding. "I have

you both there," said Miss Lowell, displaying, with glee, her copy of the rare little volume; "look at the title-page." We looked, and found thereon the inscription, "*Ex dono authoris*." It was as pretty a game of "authors" as I have ever seen played, and the sport continued till after midnight, at which time it was agreed that I should witness a game of what might be called "solitaire" as played by Mr. Palmer in his library next morning.

My visit to Professor Palmer will ever be remembered; he is a past master in the art of book-collecting, and has, since my first visit to him, given his fine collection of first editions of English poetry to Wellesley College in memory of his wife, the late Alice Freeman Palmer. He accompanied his gift with an excellent catalogue,— a large volume, well printed, and substantially bound,—and he has also printed a slender little volume, *Notes on a Collection of English Poetry*, of which he had thirty copies struck off at the Riverside Press at Cambridge, one of which is

*The Fool Book-Collector
From Barclay, 1570*

before me. Following the title-page is a quotation from Barclay's *The Ship of Fooles*, reading,—

> For this is my minde, this one pleasure have I,
>   Of books to have great plentie,

and more to the same effect.

Then follows, after his explanation of how the collection came to be formed, the considered judgment of so fine a scholar and so eminent a collector that I cannot do better than to quote it: "It is easy to over-estimate the value of old books . . . their shape is often unhandy, their type and paper poor; they usually abound in typographical errors, and they are not supplied with such notes and introductions as enable a reader to stand where the printer stood. . . . But they have a sentimental value as having been used by contemporaries of the author, perhaps by the author himself. . . . In my feeling, the presence of the poet is there, as it cannot be in later issues." He then goes on to say, "The cost of such books is very great and it constantly and rapidly rises. A narrowing supply makes this inevitable. Every time such books are sold a good proportion of them go into some public library, from which they never emerge. Each year, therefore, diminishes the number open to purchase, while the desire to possess them grows with the spread of wealth and refinement. A few rich men have doubled their permanent price in a single year."

We hear overmuch of the prices which collectors are paying for literary and artistic treasures, and occasionally it is suggested that collectors speculate in such material, buying against a rise in price, as it were; nothing could be more silly. Naturally, a man when he pays fifty thousand, ten, five, or even one thousand dollars for an item, wants to feel that he is buying something which will hold its price. And if he hears, as he may, that it has doubled in value, what then?—does he sell? He does not. He will congratulate himself on his purchase; he may speak of it to his friends—and does; and perhaps at his death his estate may be more valuable than was supposed. But the really high prices are paid by very rich men who, in these piping times of profits, spend their money freely to round out and complete, as far as in their power lies, their collections— to what purpose? That it may be more valuable when they give it away—when it reaches the public library or museum which is its final destination. I think of the men who were buying books—recklessly, as was said by the ignorant—twenty years ago. What has become of their books? Harry Widener's have gone to Harvard; the Cochran books have gone to Yale; Mr. Morgan's to New York; Mr. Huntington's to California; Mr. Chapin's to Williams; Mr. Clement's to Michigan; Mr. Folger's to the nation. The list might be continued indefinitely. We cannot take our books with us into the grave—I wish we could.

I am entirely in accord with Professor Palmer's ideas as to the best arrangement of books in their places on the shelves. He says, "Ease of access is the first end of classification," but he prefers, as I do, the chronological rather than the alphabetical arrangement. It offends him to see Crashaw follow Crabbe, or Burns follow Browning: "When I go to a shelf I wish to find there the men who worked together, to see the little imitators gathered about their master mind. We view our poets, then, as living social beings each among his fellows. This is the instinctive order, setting forth relationships even to the casual eye."

As I walked away through Harvard Yard after my delightful visit, my thoughts were of the not very

Reverend Laurence Sterne who somewhere in *Tristram Shandy* says: "Have not the wisest men of all ages had their hobbyhorses, their running horses, their cockle-shells, their drums, their trumpets, their fiddles, their books, or their butterflies, and as long as a man rides his hobbyhorse peacefully and quietly along the King's highway and compels neither you nor me to get up behind him, why should we complain?" Why indeed! But that when one sees a fellow creature toiling along life's highway, going in our direction, should we not give him a lift? Especially if the horse we are riding will safely carry two; and it may happen, when "your brother man" or "gentler sister woman" gets up beside you, that you discover one having like tastes with yourself. If so, I say, the journey's as good as over.

A man without a hobby is to be pitied and avoided: if he is not exactly looking for trouble, he is, at least, willing to meet it halfway; he gets no joy out of life and he has little sympathy for those who do. I don't much care what a man's hobby is: he is a better fellow for having one. The name of Harry Worcester Smith occurs to me; he is a hobby-rider if I know one (he took his hunting stable and a pack of hounds to Ireland and gave good sport). Ask him to put a sentiment in his delightful *Sporting Tour*, in two fine volumes, in which his experiences in the old country are narrated, and he will write: "A sporting life is sometimes checkered but never dull." His presence in your house at breakfast is as exhilarating as champagne at midnight. He never stops to inquire whither you are going and whether you expect to be happy when you get there: he is content to take a chance and join you; for him the destination is not so important as the sense of progress.

Sometimes, when people see the pleasure I get out of my efforts to escape the monotony of life, I am asked: "What hobby shall I ride? What shall I collect?" But to answer this question I have to know what you have in mind when you say "collecting:" whether it be merely for the sake of killing time—of all things in the world the most valuable—or whether, perchance, some one thing, some man or woman, or period in history, or thing accomplished by the sons of Adam, interests you enormously. In that case, *that is it*.

There are rules for collectors, of course, but the exceptions are numerous and brilliant. We are told, for instance, that collectors should begin young, and some, no doubt, do. About a year ago I received a note, written from New York, reading thus: "I have read your books and have enjoyed them very much, hence I do not hesitate to ask you for your autograph. I am now eleven years old. When I get to be a man I am going to have a library like J. P. Morgan." I shrieked for joy, to find, at last, a person not afraid to give Mr. Morgan a run for his money; and in my enthusiasm, after I had answered the letter, I sent it over to Miss Belle da Costa Greene, the librarian of the Morgan Library, saying that after she had worked herself out of a job there was another awaiting her— and such jobs do not grow on trees.

In due course I heard the sequel: how Miss Greene had written my young friend a note telling him that if he seriously intended to form a library like Mr.

Morgan's it was high time he got started, and asking him to call on a particular day and hour. The day and hour came, and the lad; Miss Greene was waiting. The boy was not overcome, as I was when first I entered that noble and beautiful building, filled with some of the greatest bibliographical treasures in the world; but, walking up to Miss Greene, he introduced himself, and, in answer to her question, explained that at present his means would not permit of his buying any books, but that he was making a collection of catalogues of Mitchell Kennerley's Anderson Galleries, and the American Art Association, and that *he had priced copies of the more important sales* of the past year. Miss Greene does not often meet her match, but she did then, and when, to hide her confusion, she asked him if he wanted to see any particular book, he replied, "Yes, I should like to see the first book printed, the Gutenberg Bible." It was brought him, whereupon he at once began to count the lines to discover whether the first pages were of the forty- or the forty-two-line issue. And this at the age of eleven!

On the other hand, Mr. Huntington, who formed the most important library of modern times, did not begin until he was a man of middle age. One reads of an automobile in five seconds getting up to a speed of twenty-five miles: this is nothing to the speed that Mr. Huntington developed.

After a man has rowed his way across a river, it is hardly worth while for him to regret that he has not crossed by the bridge; he has arrived—that is the important thing. But I cannot free my mind from the belief that if I had my life to live over again I should take on "Americana." There is no element of "fad" about it, as there may be about Conrad or Stevenson, for instance. It has come to stay, but it is now too late for me to get up any interest in a badly printed tract describing what is now Virginia, or to go into an ecstasy at the sight of a map, which at a glance one can tell is a gigantic error, simply because I am told it is the first map of what is now North America. But other men, wiser than I, not only can, but do. I spent some hours a year ago in the William L. Clements Library, which is now a part of the University of Michigan, and I have read with interest Mr. Clements's admirable volume describing his books, which accompanied his gift to that university. It is a remarkable book for a business man to write, and it only goes to prove how entirely mistaken are those who think that American business men are without ideals; the very reverse is the fact.

Visit Ann Arbor and see the simple but beautiful temple which contains the books which were, a short time since, the hobby of a busy man of affairs. Read Mr. Clements's modest but scholarly essay in which he says: "All collections must have their beginnings, and in 1903 the foundation of this one was made by the purchase . . . of a library of about a thousand volumes." I would not say that his account of the growth of his collection is as fascinating as a romance, but anyone who cares to read about books relating to the discovery of North America and its development from nothing to that great nation that we call the United States—the greatest romance in the world—will find that a new planet has swum into his ken.

The William L. Clements Library

That the custodian, Randolph Adams, practically grew up in my library suggests that he is a book-lover; his admirable little book, *The Whys and Wherefores of the William L. Clements Library*, *or a Brief Essay on Book Collecting as a Fine Art*, is an excellent treatise written by a scholar whose proper subject is American history. And when I read the excellent reviews that Adams's *History of the Foreign Policy of the United States* is receiving I was thankful that I did what I could to persuade him to become a happy and useful citizen rather than to attempt to make a living by practising what is called "the law," which—I agree with Bernard Shaw—is not a profession, but a conspiracy. I was amazed to learn from Adams that the United

The Great Room of the William L. Clements Library

States had a "foreign policy:" it certainly did not have under Bryan.

I have not suggested that every state in the Union offers a fair field for the collector; that the subject will continue to grow in interest and importance; and that the time will come when books which can now be had for a few dollars will be worth hundreds, perhaps thousands of dollars. I am sure of it. "What books?" you say. Ah! I do not know. Ask the college professors who are working in the subject, or Lathrop Harper of New York, a most reliable guide; ask Dr. Rosenbach, who only a few days ago exchanged a monarch's ransom for a small specimen; ask my friend J. Christian Bay, who is now lecturing on the "Incunabula of

Chicago,"—delicious title,—meaning, thereby, books printed in Chicago before the fire! And then think that there are thousands of men who were not children when that city was still smouldering in ashes. The growth of Chicago is the measure by which we should judge the interest in Americana.

Book-collecting is a great sport; every day new players are joining in the game; we amateurs are playing it against professionals, and sometimes it costs us money, but not so much as one might suppose. To play against Dr. Rosenbach is like trying to break the bank at Monte Carlo; yet even he has sold me items which he would now take off my hands at three or four times what I paid for them. A rare book should, and usually does, advance in value, but it is a good deal more fun to anticipate the rise than to buy it at a high price after it has risen. There are thousands of excellent books by important authors which will never be "collected," for the reason that the first edition was so large. The books to collect are those the success of which was at one time problematical, or those which the subsequent work of an author has made important: these constantly rise in value. Of books of yesterday: de la Mare's *Songs of Childhood*, Masefield's *Salt Water Ballads*, Housman's *Shropshire Lad*, Sheila Kaye-Smith's *Tramping Methodist*, Morley's *Parnassus on Wheels*, keep on advancing in price, to the bewilderment of their authors. How long they will hold their present value, or whether they will go still higher, nobody knows; but it would seem safe to say that an author's first book, if his subsequent work survives the critics, could be bought with impunity. Collectors of modern books now have excellent bibliographies to guide them; these were entirely lacking when I first began to play the game. Some of these are monuments of bibliographical exactness, others are of errors all compact; but, good or bad, as Dr. Johnson says of dictionaries, the worst is better than none.

In the book market I have seen many changes: no longer is London, or indeed England, the only market in which to buy books. For almost a century we have been drawing on that great reservoir, and the level of the supply is permanently lowered; there are now more good booksellers in England than there are good books. There is a glamour, a romance, about prowling around in the bookshops of the old country, but the best picking is now to be had at home, especially in New York City. The book-collector, early in the game, will do well to attract the attention of some good bookseller. This is easy: half a dozen purchases and as many intelligent questions will do it. But he should also study the catalogues, which, once his name gets on the booksellers' lists, will come to him by every mail, and the auction sales should always be kept in mind. It is great fun going to book auctions, and the auctioneers' catalogues are mines of information. In the auction room in New York a great book will always bring what it is worth, and frequently more. Not long ago a copy of Milton's *Comus* brought twenty-one thousand, five hundred dollars. It is always referred to as "Comus," but the title-page of the first edition reads "A Maske." Now I don't mean to say that it is not worth what it fetched, for where will you

A MASKE

PRESENTED

At Ludlow Castle,

1 6 3 4:

On Michaelmasse night, before the

RIGHT HON●RABLE,

IOHN *Earle of Bridgewater*, *Vicount* BRACKLY,
Lord Præsident *of* WALES, And one of
His MAIESTIES moſt honorable
Privie Counſell.

by John Milton!

Eheu quid volui miſero mihi! floribus auſtrum
Perditus ———

LONDON,

Printed for HVMPHREY ROBINSON,
at the ſigne of the *Three Pidgeons* in
Pauls Church-yard. 1 6 3 7.

find another? And if and when you do, it will bring
more. But less famous books, equally scarce, frequently
bring less than they are worth. The fact is,—and I state
it reluctantly,—we collectors do not know our litera-

ture as well as we should; we concentrate our attention too much on star items. This makes the market "spotty," as the stockbrokers say. These are facts to be reckoned with, and one must remember that scarcity alone will not make a book sell at a high price; or, to state the matter another way, it is always unwise to wrench a book out of its natural habitat. A book much sought in Paris, sold at auction in New York, may bring little or nothing.

Let us not neglect the wood for the trees. What a glorious thing is English literature! The man who elects to study it in first editions is riding a noble hobby. Consider its venerable age, its unbroken continuity, its tremendous range. We have the greatest poetry, and drama, and fiction in the world; in essays we yield the palm only to Montaigne, and we have the only biography worth speaking of. What a variety! We book-collectors each of us can ride an animal differing, in some respect, from every other animal; but we are alike in this: that as we put it through its paces and explain its good points to our auditor—when we can find one—we are enjoying life to a degree that a man without a hobby knows nothing of. The exercise keeps the breath of life in us long after we have outlived our usefulness. Whether this be a good thing or not, let our heirs, executors, administrators, and assigns say.

I once knew a Philadelphian, Ferdinand J. Dreer, who retired from business before he was forty to prepare himself for death, which he thought imminent. To occupy his mind he began to collect autographs, and lived to the age of eighty, forming one of the finest collections ever made in this country. At his death he bequeathed his priceless collection to the Historical Society of Pennsylvania, and his name will ever be remembered. May it not be said of the accomplished hobby-rider, as Johnson said of Shakespeare, that "Panting Time toils after him in vain?"

The Play Room at Oak Knoll

III

THE BOOKS OF MY BOYHOOD

SOME time since I sat next to a handsome woman at dinner, and in the course of conversation she made some remark which led me to inquire if she had not once had an Aunt Charlotte. The question made her think for a moment, and then she replied, "Yes, if one can have an aunt who died before one is born; why do you ask?" "Because," I said, "she gave me a book when I was a child, in which she wrote: 'I hope Eddie will grow up to be a fine Christian gentleman.'" It was a wide opening, and in a flash she filled it: "I am glad Aunt Charlotte died before she was disappointed."

I only quote the incident to show what I once was. In my case the child was not the father of the man: much and earnest care went into my bringing up. My sponsors in baptism took their duties very seriously. As they promised, I was made to hear sermons at a tender age, and long before I could read I learned by heart texts from the Bible, collects from the Prayer Book, and bits of poetry—at least that is what it was called—which were designed to stunt the growth of the old Adam which was supposed to reside in every child. I grew up at a time when children, and too often grown-ups, recited. I am horrified to think how often "The Boy Stood on the Burning Deck" in the person of A. E. N., and I never recall the incident without thinking of Dr. Johnson's saying: "Let both little dears recite at the same time; this will make the more noise, which will please them and get it over sooner, which will please me." To this day I can, upon sufficient inducement, recite "Little Samuel Woke," and

> 'Twas God that made the little fly;
> If you pinch it, it will die—

and this I know to be a fact, for I tried, not once, but several times. I fear I was a very bad little boy.

The efforts to make a prig of me, mercifully, failed, but they did make me a sturdy reader, and for this I cannot be too thankful. The first book I remember reading was a thin, small, square volume bound in dark maroon-colored cloth, called *Jessica's First Prayer*, and all recollection of the book had passed completely out of my head until last summer when, prowling about in a parish church in the west of England, I came upon a large and elaborate mural tablet erected To the Glory of God and in Loving Memory of the Author of Jessica's First Prayer. For over half a century the thought of that book had not occurred to me, but when upon my return I

searched for and found the little volume tied up in a bundle with perhaps a dozen other books of my early childhood, I was quite delighted, and taking it up I turned its leaves and looked at the quaint woodcuts with a curious sensation. A few days afterward, meeting my friend Dr. Horace Howard Furness, the eminent Shakespearean, who has read everything and forgets nothing, I asked him about *Jessica's First Prayer* and was not surprised to find that he knew it almost by heart. Someone had read it to him: evidently all little boys of our generation were brought up on the book.

I asked him, too, if he remembered the exquisite little woodcuts which ornamented its pages. "Of course he did."

But in that bundle I found other books; one of them so famous that I stopped whatever I was then reading and devoted some time to them and their history: this is one of the joys of

Jessica's temptation

desultory reading. Have you ever heard of *Sandford and Merton?* Probably yes. Have you ever read it? Probably no. Listen, then, till I tell you about it.

In 1748, in London,—in Wellclose Square to be exact, and Wellclose Square is in Whitechapel,—there was born Thomas Day. His father was a collector of customs, and, dying when his son was only a year old, he left him an estate of twelve hundred pounds a year, out of which was to be paid an annuity of three hundred a year to his mother. From this it will be seen how important male babies were in England at that time, and how unimportant the mothers, who were, indeed, regarded rather as incubators that had served their purpose. In due course young Day went to Charterhouse, and subsequently to Oxford, but he did not take a degree. At Oxford he met and became intimate with Richard Lovell Edgeworth, who was to become the father of the more famous Maria of that ilk.

Young Day was eccentric,—and rich, for a large sum had accumulated during his minority,—but in due course he felt the need for a wife, and looking about him he found no one who filled the requirements which to him appeared necessary. His wife must be well born, beautiful, and virtuous, yet have contempt for dress and polite society; she was not to be a bluestocking, yet she was to have a taste for literature, science, and moral philosophy; she was to be shy and retiring, yet as fearless and intrepid as a Roman mother and under no circumstances was she to indulge herself in "the vapours," which was a retreat into which every eighteenth-century girl retired upon occasion. This might be called a large order, not easily filled, and Day finally decided that it would be best for him to train two virtuous maidens to meet his requirements, setting about the job in a manner that foreshadowed failure.

Gentlemen prefer blondes, but they occasionally marry brunettes, and, not knowing in which direction his fancy would permanently set, Day, for the moment, chose both. "Object matrimony" was his slogan as he presented himself at an orphan asylum at Shrewsbury and there chose an "auburn brunette" of handsome appearance; and he was still of this mind when, a few days later, he visited good Captain Coram's well-known Foundling Hospital in London, and selected a peachy blonde with flaxen hair—both girls being about twelve years of age. However, respectable charities do not hand over the pick of the nest to the keeping of ardent young men without guarantees, but with the help of a barrister named Bicknell, and young Edgeworth, who was married, Day put his name to such agreements as satisfied the authorities that his project was to secure a faultless wife or perish in the attempt. He agreed, in fact, that if he did not marry either girl he would set them up in a reputable business, and if and when either married he would present bride, or brides, with substantial dots: in other words, their "hope chests" were to be well filled.

Edgeworth was an eccentric, too; he became the father of eighteen children out of four wives, married in quick succession. One of the children, Maria, the favorite, was very short, and her he sought to lengthen by stretching her, but after almost killing her he gave it up. She was the eldest of the crop. Is it any wonder that when she took pen in hand to write books, her most successful performance was *The Parent's Assistant?* No doubt she was.

When all the necessary formalities were attended to, young Day took his foundlings, one on either hand, and proceeded to the south of France. He chose France as the place of their education, in order that they might in no wise be contaminated by English-speaking persons, and as neither girl could read or write, he worked in every sense in virgin soil.

How Day endeavored to educate and train the girls; how they quarreled and hated each other and agreed only on one thing, their disgust for their trainer; how they fell ill of the smallpox and other things, and how he nursed them through their illnesses, and the subsequent miseries—all this may be imagined; but the earnest young man was not easily discouraged. His educational methods were original and frequently severe: it was his habit, in order to strengthen the girls' nerves, to discharge pistols, which they believed to be loaded, at their petticoats; while to teach them to bear pain unflinchingly he would drop melting sealing wax upon their bare arms. One is reminded of Teasing Tom in *Patience;* he, it will be remembered,

> Punched his poor little sisters' heads,
> And cayenne-peppered their four-post beds,
> He plastered their hair with cobbler's wax,
> And dropped hot ha'pennies down their backs.

But to leave the Teasing Tom of poetry and return to the Teasing Tom of real life. As the girls grew older and handsomer, Day endeavored to keep from them any idea of their beauty, and repressed as far as he was able their love of dress and any knowledge as to the use of money. It was about the wildest piece of folly a well-meaning man ever engaged in, and the result could have been foreseen. One girl, the blonde, disappeared, and the other, Sarah—otherwise Sabrina, —married, not Day, but his friend Bicknell, receiving from her guardian—for such Day had constituted himself—a wedding gift of five hundred pounds. Indeed, his conduct throughout the whole proceeding was as fine as it was foolish.

But meantime Day was without a wife, and now, looking about in a more normal manner, he met a

Miss Milnes of suitable age and accomplishments, but unluckily, in his view, the possessor of a considerable fortune; this Day insisted should be placed entirely beyond his control, and on these terms they were married and, to the amazement of all, lived happily ever after, the wife adapting herself to her husband in a manner now as out of date as a hoop skirt.

The first year of their married life they spent in Hampstead, but after that time, in order that they might better shun what Day thought the infectious taint of polite society, they determined to settle in the country, and Day acquired a small estate in Essex. Wishing to make some additions to the house, he decided to be his own architect, but as he declined to be troubled about such matters as doors and windows, the result was singularly unsatisfactory. On one occasion, we are told, when a mason suggested that a window be put in a certain room, Day, declining to be interrupted in a book he was reading, instructed the mason to continue building the wall, saying that the window could be put in later. It was Mrs. Day's dressing room, and as the window was never put in, the lady had to make all her toilets by candlelight. But, with all these eccentricities, Thomas Day was a fine man. Thoroughly impractical, he lost money in everything he undertook, but none of his poorer neighbors' wants went unsupplied; food and medicines for the sick and needy were always ready, and he reached one eminently sane conclusion: "The result of all my speculations," he said, "about humanity is that the only way of permanently benefiting mankind is to *give* them employment and make them *earn* money." His farming projects were as unusual as his building operations, and he lost money by everything he did; he gradually separated himself from a considerable part of his fortune, but he gave up his carriage and his wife her maid, and there was no word of complaint.

Such, then, was the man who wrote *Sandford and Merton*, a book which you could now scarcely hire a boy to read, but which was, for almost a century, if not enormously popular, at least enormously read— perhaps we were made to read it. It is the story of a bad little rich boy and a good little poor boy, with parents to match, and a Mr. Barlow who "improves" every occasion with a pious anecdote; Mr. Barlow is, in fact, a sort of prototype of Mr. George in the Rollo books (than which no better books for boys were ever written). Mr. Barlow found tongues in trees, books in the running brooks, and sermons— especially sermons—in everything.

The tale of *Sandford and Merton* drags its tedious length through three volumes (in first edition), being interrupted by countless anecdotes which have no connection whatever with the main story,—if indeed there is a main story,—but which were calculated to instill a love of truth, industry, humanity, and the rest, into the reader. Thus we have the story of Androcles and the Lion, which very naturally leads up to a story of an Elephant, which was one of my favorites. It appears that an elephant once made the acquaintance of a certain tailor, and as it passed the tailor's shop daily on the way to a pond for a drink, it became its habit to stick its trunk in through an open window whereat the tailor was sitting, and he used to feed it cakes or something, until finally the elephant never passed the window without sticking its trunk in to be fed. Well, one day the tailor was in a very bad humor, and instead of feeding the elephant he stuck a needle in its trunk, hurting it severely; whereupon the elephant withdrew its trunk, but, saying nothing, went on its way down the street to the pond; and after it had a good drink it filled its trunk with dirty water, and went back to the tailor and discharged the water all over and nearly drowned him. I especially liked this story, probably for the reason that the moral was not sticking out, as was usually the case—unless it be that it is dangerous to monkey with an elephant, which one would think its size would suggest.

Another story. There was once a man who grew so enormously fat and gouty from lack of exercise and overeating that he was finally forced to consult a physician. The physician listened to him and said he could cure him, but the patient must promise to do exactly as he was told. This he agreed to, whereupon he was deprived of food and placed in a small room, the floor of which was composed of iron plates which could be made very hot. After the man had been locked in the room, the floor was heated, and he, to keep his feet from being burned, was obliged to hop vigorously about, first on one foot and then on the other; in this way he was made to take such exercise as finally cured him of the gout!

One more. Harry Sandford, the good boy, one day so far forgot himself as to fasten with a bent pin to a piece of string a cockchafer, which he whirled about, much to the discomfort of the insect. When it was explained to him that the cockchafer suffered greatly from these proceedings, Harry burst into tears and took the insect home and nursed it, and fed it on green leaves for a fortnight, until it was entirely recovered, whereupon he turned it out to enjoy its liberty. How many times did I ask myself, What and how large is a cockchafer? To my youthful imagination I thought it must be as large as a bird; judge then of my disappointment when I discovered that a cockchafer is a sort of June bug. Never do I see a June bug on its back, vigorously exercising its limbs, without thinking of Harry Sandford. I never liked Harry: in real life, no one, I think, likes a good boy — except perhaps maiden aunts or maiden uncles. Mr. Merton, I am sure, liked Harry because the boy gave him an opportunity to show off. Everyone likes to do that; I do myself — but my opportunities are few.

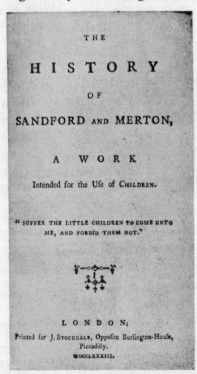

THE

HISTORY

OF

SANDFORD AND MERTON,

A WORK

Intended for the Ufe of CHILDREN.

" SUFFER THE LITTLE CHILDREN TO COME UNTO
ME, AND FORBID THEM NOT."

LONDON:
Printed for J. STOCKDALE, Oppofite Burlington-Houfe,
Piccadilly.
MDCCLXXXIII.

I have said that the first edition of *Sandford and Merton* is in three volumes; they were not published simultaneously. The first volume appeared in 1783; it at once became enormously popular and was read to shreds; hence it is that this volume is very scarce. The second volume came out three years later, and of course the publisher, guided by his success with the first volume, printed a larger edition and reprinted the first volume. The third volume was published in 1789, whereupon the story became the accepted gift book for "all young Gentlemen and Ladies who are good or intend to be good"—to use a phrase of Oliver Goldsmith's.

Before me is the copy I read as a boy; it was given to me on my tenth birthday and has twice been rebound—the first time for my son, the second time for his children—by R. R. Donnelley and Sons Company of Chicago, in an acid-free morocco guaranteed to withstand the ravages of time, if not of children.

But I have several other copies; some years ago I bought a newly rebound set from Maggs Brothers of London. The first volume was the second edition; the second and third volumes were the first edition,—it was the set of commerce,—and every time I looked at it, it pained me. There is no satisfaction in a book that is not "right." So one fine day, when I found a set all first editions,—the first volume presented by the author to (to whom do you think?) Sabrina, now become Sarah Bicknell,—I at once secured it, and thereupon sold my first set at the sale of "The Books of a Busted Bibliophile" for twenty-five dollars; but somehow I missed the book, and when, not long after, I read of a better set in Walter Hill's catalogue for nine dollars, identical with the set I had sold, except that it was in original binding, which made it better, I instantly secured it.

To leave the book and return to its author. Thomas Day was full of good intentions, but his methods of putting them into effect were largely self-defeating. He wanted to enter Parliament, but he could not bring himself to grovel for votes, and how else were votes to be had—then or now? He interested himself in all the questions of the day, in agriculture, in breeding animals; and he came to an untimely death in 1789 just after he had published the last volume of his book. He had always held that any animal could be controlled by kindness; with this idea in mind, although a poor horseman, he attempted to ride an unbroken colt that he had reared, fed, and, as he thought, tamed with his own hand. Mounting the animal, he started on a journey, was thrown, landed on his head, and almost immediately died, whereupon his wife retired to her room and never left it except at night; she

declined ever again to look upon the sun, and in two years the poor lady passed away, dying of a broken heart. So much for *Sandford and Merton*.

I shall not attempt to conceal my enthusiasm for the Rollo books: they were a constant joy to me. With Rollo and the all-knowing Mr. George, in imagination, I was constantly crossing the Atlantic and visiting London and Paris;

and when, ten years later, I actually followed in his footsteps, I found how true was the author's statement, that the Rollo books were intended to instruct as well as to amuse, and that not only the descriptions, but the customs, usages, and modes of life of the countries visited, as well as the character of the incidents and adventures met with, were in most strict accordance with fact. Unaccustomed to foreign travel and with only Rollo's experience to guide me, I, at twenty, crossed the Atlantic, visited London and Paris, the Rhine country, and Switzerland, and got into no difficulties out of which I was unable to extricate myself.

I was letter-perfect in Rollo, and immediately upon my arrival in Liverpool, when at the landing stage a porter took my solitary valise and asking me to what hotel I was going, I, like him, said, "To the best hotel," whereupon I was driven to the Adelphi; and so it was throughout the trip—with this difference, however, that Rollo was traveling with a rich and

wise Mr. George, while I was quite alone. It was *Rollo in London* that prepared me in some measure for the thrill of that great city. With him in my mind, I visited Westminster Abbey and St. Paul's; with him I took a penny steamer on the river and observed that the smokestack had a hinge in it which admitted of its being turned back as the boat passed under a bridge—everything just as it should have been.

And when I was no longer a boy and had not yet become a man I read in a love story, written by a novelist who was later to be a Prime Minister of England, a description of a lad's emotion, which was not unlike my own, upon seeing London Town for the first time. "Ferdinand Armine"—for so the lad was called—"first saw the city from a mail coach as it dashed along its illuminated streets, the guard sounding his bugle with energy." That is the way to make one's entrance into a great city, not, as one does nowadays, by a railway station or sneaking in through a tunnel. "Is this London?" Armine whispered to his tutor; he was assured that it was. Each minute the streets seemed to grow more spacious and brilliant, and the multitude more dense and excited. Beautiful buildings rose before him: palaces, and churches, and streets, suggesting to his inexperienced eye a never-ending triumph. "Is this Charing Cross, sir? Shall we be able to get over?—Is this the fullest part of the town?—Whose house is that?—Northumberland House! —Does the Duke live there?—Who is that?—What is this?—The Admiralty! Oh, let me see the Admiralty! —The Horse Guards!—Oh! where, where?—Let us set our watches by the Horse Guards. The guard of our coach always sets his watch by the Horse Guards. Which is the best clock, the Horse Guards or St. Paul's?—Is that the Treasury? Can we go in? What do they do in Downing Street?—Is this Charing Cross still, or is it Parliament Street? Where does Charing Cross end, and where does Parliament Street begin? Oh, by Jove, I see Westminster Abbey!''

It was in similar mood that I first saw London, and I wish that I could have continued Armine's ecstatic experiences later when he met the object of his affections. How well do I remember the lady! "She had dark and lustrous locks, and a pellucid brow. Only eighteen, yet her figure and bearing was that of a goddess'' (we have Disraeli's word for it), "and her beauty so entrancing that her lover was frequently forced to withdraw, pale and panting with passion, from her presence; only to hear as he leaned against an oak tree under her window the leaves of that same oak murmur in his ear the name of the radiant Henrietta.'' Now that is what I call emotion.

I suppose few people to-day read *Henrietta Temple*, but it was once considered the best love story in the language, and I am not sure that it is not. Maybe it is well to take your *Henrietta Temple* when you are very young—or very old, as the case may be. There are certain books which one must read first in one's youth or not at all. *Lucile* is one of them; and anyone who has not been taught to read Dickens in his youth should go back and grow up over again. Ah! if we could.

As a small boy, how many hours I spent with *Great Expectations!* Children love to be told the same story or have a book read to them which they know by heart. In like manner I read, over and over again, *Great Expectations*—not all of it, but the opening chapters. How often did I go with Pip to the church-yard, there to encounter the convict and be "tilted!" How I despised his uncle, Mr. Pumblechook! I some-times think my present loathing for figures is due to his wretched habit of setting Pip problems in mental arithmetic. Who could be expected to do such a sum as "seven times nine on an empty stomach"—or, indeed, on any stomach at all? How I rejoiced when that miserable man drank the tar-water in mistake for brandy at the Christmas dinner! How sorry I was when the soldiers caught the convict! And how I loved honest Joe Gargery—though I fear I was a little ashamed of him. Could anything be more fascinating than Pip's description to his sister—that termagant—of his first visit to Miss Havisham? And Estella! And Pip's fight with the young man! And the rewarding kiss that Estella permitted Pip to give her! How I wished myself in his place! I have always maintained that the first chapters of *Great Expecta-tions*, up to the time when Pip goes to London, are the best that Dickens ever wrote; the story tails off some-what, I think, and I now feel that its author was at fault in ending the story as he does. But that only shows the immense genius of the man: with all his blunders,—he wrote hundreds of pages that he should have blotted,—Charles Dickens was the greatest nov-elist that ever lived. There is nothing like being certain in matters of taste.

To return to the Rollo books: they were published

in the eighteen-fifties (I suggest that a publisher could do much worse than reprint the entire series) and have been out of print for many years. I once sat next to a charming woman at dinner (I seem always to be sitting next to charming women at dinner, but this is the chief reward for successful amateur authorship—charming women are constantly being sacrificed to us) when, discovering that I had forgotten or had not caught her name when I was presented to her, I asked it. Mrs. Abbott, I was told. "I wonder," I mused, "whether you are any relation to Rollo?" "No, but my husband is; I married my second cousin; his grandfather was Jacob Abbott, who wrote the Rollo books, while my grandfather was his brother John, who wrote the *Life of Napoleon*."

I was "on" in an instant. How well do I remember that so-called *Life!* It was published in two large volumes (what has become of them?) by Harpers, when it was still possible to get excellent woodcut illustrations in books, and these volumes had them. How I devoured this book as a lad! It made *The Count of Monte Cristo* commonplace, as well it might, for what story out of *The Arabian Nights* was ever more sensational than the dullest Life of that remarkable man? And Abbott's *Life* was not dull: no fact ever stood in the biographer's way; he made Napoleon a god, and such for many years he seemed to me—until I came to know better. And there across the table was a man who might have been Rollo's grandson! What distinguished lineage! When an opportunity occurred I told him of a "Rollo Party" I had attended not long before, at which an eminent lawyer and distinguished collector, Hampton L. Carson, had talked about the Rollo books with an enthusiasm which quite carried away his audience. And it was, I think, Amy Lowell's knowledge and love of Rollo which first endeared her to me.

In my bundle of the books of my childhood I found a copy of *The Silver Rifle*, which almost—but not quite —made a hunter of me; a battered *Arabian Nights;* a *Robinson Crusoe*, much the worse for wear; and *The Swiss Family Robinson*, which, as I look at it across the chasm of fifty years, I liked best of all the books I had. This, like its fellow, *Sandford and Merton*, has been twice rebound, the last time in a morocco worthy of its merit, if indeed such leather exists. It was while lunching with Dr. Rosenbach one day that the subject of children's books came up, and he told me of the exhibition of them he was then preparing for the New York Public Library (until that time few people knew that this scholarly old bachelor had the finest collection of early American children's books in private hands). Said I to "Rosy:" "You remember that presentation *Sandford and Merton* you sold me some time back. Well, now sell me another. I want a first edition of *Swiss Family Robinson*." I have seen the Doctor nonplussed, but not often. Finally he said: "I have never seen a first edition of *Swiss Family Robinson;* I ought to have one in my children's collection; I don't believe there ever was a first edition." Then he too waxed enthusiastic over the book, and finally the conversation changed.

Later that very day I wrote to my London friend, Francis Edwards, the excellent bookseller in the Marylebone, High Street, and asked if he had a first edition of *The Swiss Family Robinson*, or if he had ever seen a copy.

In due course I received his reply: neither he nor anyone in his shop had ever seen or heard of a first edition of the book; it must be very rare; if he ever came across one he would report it. A week later a copy of the book was on my desk, with a letter from Edwards stating that the book was in his shop when he had written before; that he had no idea where it came from or what it was worth, but that it must be exceedingly rare; that he was putting merely a nominal price upon it and, if I did not want it, it could be returned. Eagerly I opened the package and found two small volumes bound in old half calf and published by—whom do you suppose?— Mary Jane Godwin at the Juvenile Library, 41 Skinner Street, Snow Hill, Lon-

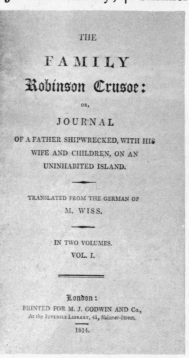

don, 1814. I could scarcely believe my eyes: Shelley's stepmother-in-law, she of the green spectacles, the woman that Charles Lamb hated, and the only one. Knowing what we now know of the composition of the firm of M. J. Godwin and Company in 1816, it is interesting to think that Shelley's money may have financed the translation and publication of the first edition of that famous book. It was in that year that Godwin would neither see nor speak to Shelley, who had just run away with his daughter; he had, however, no objection—indeed quite the reverse —to borrowing money from him, provided that the checks or drafts were not made payable directly to him. In those days the book was called *The Family Robinson Crusoe*.

A few days after this event, Walter Hill, the well-known bookseller of Chicago, was spending a night with me and I gleefully showed him my purchase, and was amazed to hear him say, quite casual-like, "Oh, yes, I know the book; I think I have a copy." Of course, I asked to have a look at it, and upon its arrival I found that the copy I had received from London was the entire book in two volumes, whereas Mr. Hill's copy, in two volumes, was published by John Stockdale, in 1788, but it contained only the first half of the book. So my pretty theories went a-glimmering.

And now we enter upon almost as pretty a bibliographical puzzle as is supplied by Benjamin Franklin's *Autobiography*—than which nothing is more perplex-

THE

NEW ROBINSON CRUSOE;

AN INSTRUCTIVE AND ENTERTAINING

H I S T O R Y,

FOR THE USE OF

CHILDREN OF BOTH SEXES.

TRANSLATED FROM THE FRENCH.

Embellished with Thirty-two beautiful Cuts.

V O L. I.

LONDON:

Printed for JOHN STOCKDALE, opposite Burlington House, Piccadilly.

M DCC LXXXVIII.

Entered at Stationers Hall.

ing. *The Swiss Family Robinson*, as we shall continue to call it, was written in German, late in the eighteenth century, by a David Wyss, a Swiss military chaplain; it was founded on a report of the discovery of a Swiss pastor who had been shipwrecked on an island near New Guinea. The story as it was originally written was intended to be read aloud in the family circle of the writer, but its popularity was such that a publisher was at length sought, and the first part of the narrative was published under a long and complicated German title at Zurich in 1812; one year later, the second and concluding volume was published. It is from this edition that the Godwin translation was made, by whom we do not know. Meantime the attention of a Frenchwoman, a Baroness de Montolieu, had been attracted to the work, and she, in reading the story, considered that it ended too abruptly, whereupon she secured the permission of Professor Wyss, the son of the author, who was now dead, to amend it, and an edition was published in French at Paris in 1824. From that time to this it has been regarded as a French classic, and published frequently. The French, who care nothing for foreign travel, don't give a hoot where Crusoé, as they call him, was wrecked; and in one illustrated edition *ce brave Robinson* is depicted as a Viking living on a coral reef surrounded by kangaroos and other strange animals.

Now that the war is over, I suppose I may safely express my opinion of the French. They are preëminently the selfish nation of the world: as long as all goes right with France, the rest of the world may go hang. We are told that logic is their strong point. "How logical you are this morning," says one Frenchman to another, meeting him in the street—where we should say, "How well you are looking." But their logical and clear thinking stops short at the boundaries of France; outside of France there is—chaos only, and it does not interest them. I observed a curious instance of this recently. Some French newspaper started a discussion as to whether there really had been ten first-class men of letters in the whole world. Finally it was agreed that there had been, and the list was published: it included Homer, Dante, and Shakespeare—the remaining seven were French!

The edition of *The Swiss Family Robinson* which is now current in this country and in England is not the translation published by Godwin, which is indeed very poor, but appears to be a translation from the French which was itself translated from the German. No copy of the book can compare, to my mind, with the little volume in which, more than fifty years ago, I first read the story. It was published by Routledge and Sons, and has fascinating plates in color; but this is mere prejudice, for Harpers have recently published a far better edition, also admirably illustrated, by Louis Rhead, with an introduction by W. D. Howells, who, curiously enough, had never read the book until he did so preparatory to writing the introduction.

I believe most boys prefer *The Swiss Family Robinson* to *Robinson Crusoe*—I know that I did. There is, of course, a certain resemblance in the two books, but Defoe antedated Wyss by a hundred years. Defoe's hero is, of all the ship's company, the only man saved from the wreck; whereas, in Wyss, father, mother, and four

sons are saved. In each case the stranded ship affords
supplies; but the incidents of the Swiss story are more
varied and interesting; no page but has its thrill—for
a boy. Moral reflections are plentiful in both. There is,
of course, no really great moment in the Swiss story
comparable with the discovery of the man's naked footprint in the sand in Defoe; this incident being the first
great bit of what we now call "realism" in a novel—
if *Robinson Crusoe* is a novel, as to which there is much
discussion.

May I digress for a moment? Of course I may—life
is full of digressions. *Treasure Island!* There's a boy's
book if you will. There
is no mushy love stuff
in it, but sheer adven-
ture, and by the time R.
L. S. came to hold a pen,
it was not considered
good form to point a
moral on every page. It
was written to illustrate
a map, and I am the
proud owner of the
original sketch from

*"The print of a man's naked foot
on the shore"*

which the published map was reproduced.

It has an interesting history, which Stevenson himself wrote under the title of "My First Book," in which
he told how his famous romance came to be written.
The original map, which inspired the book, was made
in collaboration with Mr. Lloyd Osbourne, then a
schoolboy with a taste for drawing. Of it Stevenson
says that he "made the map of an island; it was elab-

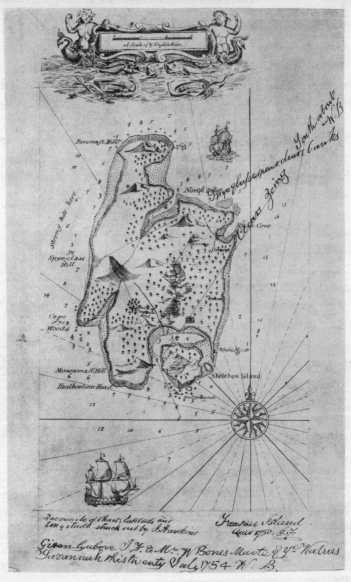

Original map of Treasure Island

orately and (I thought) beautifully coloured; the shape of it took my fancy beyond expression: it contained harbours that pleased me like sonnets: with the unconsciousness of the predestined, I ticketed my performance, 'Treasure Island.'''

Farther on, in the same article, he recounts the sad fate of this first map, and tells how the present map, which is known through reproduction to thousands of his readers, came to be drawn: "The time came when it was decided to publish, and I sent in my manuscript and the map along with it, to Messrs. Cassell. The proofs came, they were corrected, but I heard nothing of the map. I wrote and asked: was told it had never been received, and sat aghast. It is one thing to draw a map at random, set a scale in one corner of it at a venture, and write up a story of the measurements. It is quite another to have to examine a whole book, make an inventory of all the allusions contained in it, and with a pair of compasses, painfully design a map to suit the data. I did it, and the map was drawn again in my father's office, with embellishments of blowing whales and sailing ships, and my father himself brought into service a knack he had of various writing, and elaborately forged the signature of Captain Flint, and the sailing directions of Billy Bones.

The map measures in the drawing sixteen by ten inches, and is beautifully drawn in exact imitation of an old engraved map of the period of the story, with an elaborate vignette at top depicting mermen with dolphins and sea-birds, and further embellished with sailing vessels of the eighteenth century. The "forged" notes of Captain Flint and Billy Bones, as above described, also appear.

At a spot in the island a notation in red ink reads "Bulk of Treasure Here." To the Northeast are the sailing directions of Billy Bones, and below is Captain Flint's note of Treasure Island, dated August 1, 1750, and "Facsimile of Chart; latitude and longitude struck out by J. Hawkins." Under this is written, "Given by above J. F. to Mr. W. Bones, Maite of ye Walrus, Savannah, this twenty July, 1754. W. B."

Some day this map will be very valuable; indeed, it has been suggested that it already is.

My well-read *Swiss Family* is before me, and as I turn its pages the years fall from my shoulders and I am a boy again. How as a boy I longed to be cast on some desert island where I could go out and gather sugar cane which I could suck like a stick of candy! Where monkeys swung from tree to tree, which, attacked with stones, returned the affront with a shower of cocoanuts! Where water turtles big enough to tow a boat—to tow a boat, mind you—were common, whereas the type with which I was familiar simply withdrew itself within itself, when poked with a stick, in a most uninteresting manner. How dull, flat, stale, and unprofitable my youth was, I thought; but actually all the time I was living in fairyland, the fairyland of a book, and now, old man that I am, I have discovered that there is no fairyland except in books, and this fairyland is within the reach of all of us.

IV
"WHEN WE WERE VERY YOUNG"

THE considerate reader—and I hope I shall have no other—will observe in the course of this paper that it does not "date," nor does it "place." I have taken my title, "When We Were Very Young," from a book of charming verses; I might have taken it from another book and called it "Far Away and Long Ago," for the world spins round with what seems to be ever-increasing acceleration, and we seem to be almost as far away from the Battle of Bunker Hill as we are from the Battle of Hastings.

And with this introduction I shall ask you to go back with me as patiently as you can for twenty minutes or so to old New York when it was really new, and to Philadelphia, that clever town built by Quakers, and to Boston, that early took to fishing for a living and to hearing sermons for recreation. We shall go back to these towns when they were very young, when they were spread out pretty thin along the Atlantic coast with great gaps of wilderness in between; a time when we had just about decided that we would be English and nothing else—which is only another way of saying that the French and the Swedes and the Dutch had lost out in the race of colonization. I am very glad of that, for I would not wish to speak any language other than English, which comes to me so naturally.

We were a pious, God-fearing people in those days; we all believed in a personal God of whose appearance we knew nothing, and a personal Devil of whose appearance we knew much, he having been many times painted and described as having horns, hoofs, and tail; and to keep us in a frenzy of fear we employed preachers,—they were as plentiful as blackberries in those days,—who told us what we should and what we should not do, and especially where we should go if we did not do as they told us.

But, if our ancestors were religious, they were also adventurous—they had not left England for that country's good, as has been wittily said of the early settlers of Australia, but to subdue a continent in which they might worship God in their own way, with a Bible in one hand and an axe in another and a gun in another; and, having suffered much for conscience' sake at home, they sought a free country, and immediately proceeded to make it less free than the one they left behind them. This is quite inexplicable—but then, most things are.

Speaking roughly,—very roughly,—three groups settled this country: the Puritans the North, the Quakers the Middle, and the Cavaliers the South; and the Puritans had no sooner settled in New France and re-named it New England than religious controversy and persecution became a matter of continuing occurrence —if the phrase may be permitted. They were as harsh and hard as their climate or the rocky coast on which dashed the waves of the ocean. This quality of harshness was reflected, naturally, in their literature. If any were merry, they were exhorted to sing psalms, and the first book they printed was a metrical paraphrase of the Psalms. They might have done worse—indeed, they soon did. Cotton Mather, one of that long line of eminent Divines, soon published a book on *The Nature, Number and Operations of the Devil;* and another in which he sought to prove that children who were unable to recite his friend John Cotton's catechism without falling into spasms were certainly possessed of the Devil. The full title of his friend's catechism is *Spiritual Milk for Boston Babes in either England, Drawn out of the Breasts of Both Testaments for their Souls' Nourishment*. It is an excessively rare book.

But we must approach this subject of printing in an orderly manner, or we shall get nowhere; and incidentally let me say that the first printing press set up in the New World was not, as we might expect, in Boston or Philadelphia, but in the City of Mexico. The first job of printing done in what is now the United States was a small broadside known as the *Oath of a Free Man*. It was printed in 1638 and is a noble document; it ends with these words, which are calculated to make a politician laugh: "I do solemnly bind myself to give my vote as I shall judge in mine own conscience may best conduce to the public weal, without respect of persons or favor of any man, so help me God." No copy of the first printing is known to exist. An almanac for the year 1639 followed, and one for 1640 followed that, and then in the same year the *Bay Psalm Book*, already referred to. The publication of Bibles in English was a Crown monopoly—that is to say, Robert Barker and his successors in London alone could print Bibles in English, but there was nothing to prevent a sort of sing-song version of the Psalms being made and printed, and that accounts for the existence of the *Bay Psalm Book*.

Stephen Daye it was who first set up and printed in Cambridge, Massachusetts, the Freeman's Oath, the almanacs, and then the *Psalm Book*, and in the same place and at about the same time there were educational beginnings to which subsequently was attached the name of John Harvard. What the Gutenberg Bible is to Europe, the *Bay Psalm Book* is to the United States. The edition is estimated at sixteen hundred copies, out of which eleven only have survived, and of these, six are imperfect. In the American Antiquarian Society, at Worcester, Massachusetts, there is a copy of this famous book in which is a note of Isaiah Thomas, the founder, reading, "After advertising for another copy of this book and making inquiry in many places in New England, I was not able to obtain or even hear of another copy: this copy is, therefore, invaluable and must be preserved with the greatest care. It is in its original binding."

The *Psalm Book* was followed by more almanacs and codes of laws, catechisms, spelling books, and sermons. The *Milk for Babes* appeared in 1656, and was printed in Boston at the press of Samuel Green, and three years later the same printer started something by printing a tract with some such title as *The Heart of New England Rent* at the blasphemies of the present generation, with special reference to the destructive nature of the religion of the sect called Quakers. With this document began a long and virulent controversy: preachers hurled sermons at one another, as Irishmen do brickbats, and, not content with so doing, they had them printed that a wider audience could be reached. It seems curious that the most bitter discussions and the most terrible suffering that man has inflicted upon his fellow man have had invariably as their basis some question concerning what is usually called religion.

You would not bear with me were I to write a paper on the religious and controversial literature of New England, but place must be found for brief reference to one little volume of poems, entitled *The Day of Doom*. This book of religious poetry was first published at Boston about 1664. It has been called, and very properly, "a blazing and sulphurous volume," but it moulded the thought of New England more positively and effectively than any other book of its time. It attributed to the Divine Being a character more loathsome than any to be met with in any literature either Christian or pagan—yet it had for a hundred years a popularity far exceeding any other work in prose or in verse produced in America before the Revolution.

On a recent visit to New England, I meant to run down, if it were possible, an early edition of this work in one of the libraries, but I forgot to do so. My copy is the seventh edition, published in 1751. What has become of the first, or the third, or the fifth? Where are they all? Literally read to pieces, so popular were they. This famous little book, written by Michael Wigglesworth, pastor at Malden and professor of divinity at Harvard, purports to tell how the day of doom came with a crash as of thunder and a flash as of lightning to the horror and consternation of the world. It was Judgment Day, and immediately the good and the evil separated themselves before the judgment seat as though they had rehearsed the act— the Goats on one side and the Sheep on the other. Murderers, thieves, enchanters, witches, idolators,

A best seller of two hundred years ago

whoremongers, those who get rich too fast, haunters of alehouses, "Blasphemers lewd and Swearers shrewd," to the left. "On the other hand, the Sheep do stand." The proceedings are ghastly: weepings and wailings and gnashings of teeth are heard as the Goats are hurried into everlasting fire. Finally a band of little children draw near—those who never had a chance to do evil, but were "straitway carried from the womb to the tomb." What is to be their fate? The Judge is moved to compassion,—at least that is what it is called in the poem,—and thus addresses the children:—

"I do confess your crime is less—
    though every sin's a crime;
But a crime it is, therefore in bliss
    you may not hope to dwell,
But unto you I shall allow
    the easiest room in hell."

Think of it: but listen! The Sheep are singing; they rejoice:—

"To see all those that were their foes
    thus sent to punishment
Then do they sing unto their King
    a song of endless Praise;
They praise his name, and do proclaim
    that just are all his ways!"

I have not, I think, painted in too lurid colors the literature of New England, and it will, at once, be seen that work of this gruesome character will not stand comparison with that which was being produced in England at the same time; the lyrics of Herrick or the work of Mr. Lemuel Gulliver, for example.

But human nature is human nature; not every day is Judgment Day, thank God, nor is it a New England Sunday; may we not suppose that occasionally on a week-day, perchance, a longing might be expressed for some reading in a lighter vein than the poems of Michael Wigglesworth or the sermons of Cotton Mather? Yes, there was such a longing, but before relating how it was satisfied let me say a word about the first Bible printed in this country. Thomas Aitken, a Scotch printer settled in Philadelphia, printed the first Bible in English after the Revolutionary War, by which we had freed ourselves from countless annoying little restrictions upon our trade and commerce, amongst which the printing of Bibles was the least. Few, except students, have read a little book published in London in 1765, entitled *An Act for Granting and Applying Certain Stamp Duties and Other Duties in the British Colonies and Plantations in America*. It is commonly called *The Stamp Act*, and in a volume of sixty or more pages recites how "upon every Skin or piece of Vellum or Sheet or Piece of Paper on which shall be engrossed or written or printed any Grant, Deed, or other Instrument whatever, there shall be a stamp of two shillings or a greater sum. And on a pack of cards the sum of one shilling. . . . And for every pair of dice, ten shillings." And when all these duties were found to be unworkable and were repealed, it was followed by what the historians call the "Five Intolerable Acts," including one to regulate and suppress commerce.

But there was no law against printing Bibles in a foreign language, and if the translation of the Scriptures by John Eliot be not in a foreign language, then I am unable to tell a foreign language when I see one.

I shall not attempt to enlarge upon the title of John Eliot's Indian Bible, as it is usually called—not only because I cannot, but because I fear very few of my readers understand the dialect of the Indians spoken in Massachusetts in the year 1663. I admit that the book is not handsome, but it was a noble venture on the part of Eliot and also of the printer. Of course the consent of the Crown had first to be secured, but there was no difficulty about this, and finally appeared from the press of Samuel Green and Marmaduke Johnson the famous book with an unpronounceable name, a small quarto of six hundred unnumbered pages. It was printed on good paper, from new type set in double columns, and by general consent the finest known copy is in the Morgan Library; we should have been disappointed not to have found it there. There are, however, a good many other copies existing; it was not thumbed out of existence as so many early Bibles were. I suspect that the Sitting Bulls and Rains-in-the-Face of the time cared little for it and I doubt whether the fine copy that was sent to King Charles II, then reigning in England, withdrew his attention for long from the frail beauties of his court, although he had expressed a desire to see the famous book, and one of the earliest copies was presented to him by the Governor of Massachusetts for the time being.

Other Bibles and fragments of Bibles in the language of the Indians of Massachusetts were printed by Eliot from time to time, but the great item of this character remains to be mentioned,—Richard Baxter's *Call to the Unconverted*,—of which Evans's bibliography of early American imprints says, "No copy of the 1664 edition is known to exist." But to the delight of Dr. Rosenbach a copy was discovered not long ago in the library of the Royal Society in London and sent to the auction room, where it was, of course, purchased by him for the sum of six thousand and eight hundred pounds,—about thirty-four thousand dollars,—he acting for Mr. Huntington. This was the last important work to which the pious John Eliot's name is attached.

Of course the discovery of the unique book, its sale, and the high price it fetched, made an interesting news story and was told in various ways in the newspapers all over the world, with this result, among many others: one day there walked into the Rosenbach establishment in Philadelphia, from New England, an old clergyman who had read of the transaction and was thrilled by what he thought was the discovery of another copy of the identical book in his own house. But for every great book unexpectedly bringing fame and wealth to its owner there are ten thousand disappointments. The copy which the old gentleman had brought to Philadelphia was an English reprint published a few years ago in Hartford, and was not worth the paper and twine in which it was wrapped. For a few days, a few weeks, perhaps, its owner had deluded himself with the idea that he had a book worth thirty-four thousand dollars, and he almost fainted when he was told that his book was quite worthless.

No bookseller has ever before occupied the position which is now admittedly Dr. Rosenbach's: he is the first bookseller in the world to-day. I could, I am quite sure, prove this statement, but, in the words of Dr. Johnson, I shall expect it to be accepted without proof. And now let me tell you another story of this remarkable man. Some time ago he, being in London, discovered in the auction room another famous book: a copy of Philip Pain's *Daily Meditations*, printed in Cambridge in 1668. It was the first volume of poems, so called, published in this country. Dr. Rosenbach said nothing; listened, but heard nothing. None of the booksellers in London said a word about the book, and it seemed evident that they thought the imprint, "Marmaduke Johnson, Cambridge, 1668," meant Cambridge, England. Was it possible they were all napping?

*Dr. Rosenbach leaving London, loaded down
with priceless books*

Seymour de Ricci, the great French bibliographer, was in London, and him "Rosy" took into his confidence. Said he to De Ricci: "This *Daily Meditations* is the first volume of poems published in America: it is unique and worth anywhere from five to ten thousand pounds. I shall buy it for Mr. Huntington, but if I bid on the book myself it may be that the talent will smell a rat, for everyone knows, or ought to, that Marmaduke Johnson was a great colonial printer. Now what I want you to do is this. When the book comes up at the sale, I shall glance at it and yawn and pass it on; I shall not bid. Let someone else start the bidding, and when I hold my pencil like this" (suiting the action to the word), "you commence bidding and keep on."

What happened? Well, the bidding began at five pounds, and in about a minute De Ricci had the book for fifty-one pounds, and there was great chagrin when it was discovered that "Rosy" had again put one over the most astute group of book-buyers in the world. And Mr. Huntington enriched his library with a unique item for fifty-one pounds—plus the usual ten per cent.

It was 1678—ten years—before another volume of poetry was published in the colonies. Then Anne Dudley Bradstreet published a reprint of a book, which first saw the light in London in 1650, its English title being *The Tenth Muse lately sprung up in America;* but its title in the colonial edition was *Several Poems, Compiled with Great variety of Wit and Learning by a Gentlewoman in New England.* A copy of this from Dr. Rosenbach's personal library is before me as I write, and I am bound to say that it does not entirely belie its title.

I shall not detain you with the poet who called himself "The Simple Cobbler of Agawam," now Ipswich, where the hooked rugs come from, but pass on to what may with justice be called the first printing of an English classic in America. Having in mind the temper, or rather the temperament, of the colonists, it is not hard to guess that the book was Bunyan's *Pilgrim's Progress*. A copy of this famous book had found its way to Boston, an enterprising printer had put it in type, and it was being circulated in New England as early as 1681. Would you like to see a copy of this rare book? Only one is known to exist; it was formerly George Brinley's; it is now in the Huntington Library, near Los Angeles.

Three books there are the popularity of which makes them practically unobtainable to-day in first editions. Bunyan's *Pilgrim's Progress* is one; *The New England Primer*, with its rhymed alphabet beginning, "In Adam's fall we sinned all," down to "Zaccheus he did climb a tree, his Lord to see," is another; and the third is the *Divine Songs* of Isaac Watts. Of this last my friend Wilbur Macey Stone says there were no less than two hundred and fifty editions—*editions*, mind you—published in Great Britain and over three hundred editions in America. Rhyme embalms reason as nothing else does, and the proof, if proof were necessary, of the immense vitality of Bunyan is that he wrote in prose. Before me is a copy of the *Pilgrim's Progress, the Second Part*, "published in Boston, New England, by John Draper for Charles Harrison, over against the Brazen-Head in Cornhil in 1744." It is the first edition of the second part published in America, and is the property of Professor Tinker of Yale. What does Tinker mean, he a Churchman, with this Dissenter in his library, this wolf in his fold? I think I shall not return it to him.

Speaking of classics, it is usually said that the first classic published in America is Cicero's *Cato Major*, published by Franklin in Philadelphia in 1744. Franklin himself is our authority for the statement that it is the first "translation" of a classic in this Western world, and adds the hope that it may be followed by others performed with equal judgment and success, and be a happy omen that Philadelphia shall become the seat of the American Muses. This is usually understood as meaning, "edition" of a classic, but Franklin, of course, knew that already S. Keimer, his first employer, in Second Street, Philadelphia, had as early as 1729 published *Epictetus, His Morals*. A seemingly unique copy at the Brinley sale brought seven dollars; now that these vanities are better appreciated, seven thousand would seem to be a fairer price.

And now that we have come to the early Philadelphia printers, let me refer to George Wither's *Abuses Stript and Whipt*. The title has always fascinated me, although I did not know until I began the study of early printing that these verses had made their appearance in Philadelphia as early as the year 1688. The title—no doubt it was that—intrigued those austere Puritans and Quakers, who took their pleasures so sadly; one can, in imagination, hear some old Puritan complain that there were still abuses to be script and

M. T. CICERO's
CATO MAJOR,

OR HIS

DISCOURSE

OF

OLD-AGE:

With Explanatory NOTES.

PHILADELPHIA:

Printed and Sold by B. FRANKLIN,
MDCCXLIV.

Cato Major. A desirable Franklin imprint

neighbors to be whipt, and that he would much like to take on the job. With this volume are published some of the lucubrations of Sir Francis Bacon—his first appearance in the New World. This book came from the press of William Bradford. But two copies are known—one of them in the safe-keeping of our own Dr. Montgomery of the Historical Society of Pennsylvania.

I wonder whether I may not now attempt to draw some sort of mental picture of the intellectual and social life of our ancestors—whether they were Puritan or Quaker or Cavalier. The social life of the Puritans calls for little comment; it was bound up with the intellectual, and they got what kick they could, if a slang phrase be permitted, from hearing terrible tirades against all manner of things, under the guise of sermons, and appeals to the Almighty for mercy for one's self and a quick judgment upon one's neighbors, which were called prayers; and worst of all, perhaps, was the horrible cacophony, having neither key nor direction, which was song—these were the conditions under which that fine thing, the New England conscience, developed. Down almost to our own time, the word "theatre" was taboo; there came finally to be a playhouse in Boston where excellent theatrical performances were given, but the "Hub" preferred to call it the "Museum."

I would not be understood as slurring the New England conscience—my regret is that it no longer functions. Our Anglo-Saxon ancestors were good substantial folk who brought to this country sound minds in strong bodies and a fine sense of decency and order. Settling along the border of a great continent, they passed down to their children the traditions of the race from which they sprang; these traditions gave intellectual color to a hinterland of enormous extent, until finally it was washed out by an influx of foreigners who know nothing of our literature or our language and care less. We have, I am afraid, closed our doors too late: the evil of a mixed population might, perhaps, have been dealt with by an enlightened aristocracy, but by a democracy—never.

To get back to a pleasanter subject. Some years ago there was a dinner of the New England Society in New York City; the speakers lauded the New England fathers; they praised their virtue, their integrity, their skill at overcoming obstacles, their ability to withstand the rigors of the New England climate. At last Joseph Choate, that accomplished gentleman, excellent lawyer, and exquisite wit, was asked to say something —whereupon he rose and, among other things, said that he agreed that it took a rugged character to withstand the horrors of a New England winter, but that he, for his part, toasted the character of the *New England mothers*, for they had stood the rigors of the New England winters and the *New England fathers*, too. I would rather be the author of one good jest than have written a political platform: it takes more brains, and it lasts longer. But—I don't know—most political platforms are very funny.

I was motoring through New England "down east" last summer, and not far from Barre, in Massachusetts, passed a recently completed brick building, beautifully patterned after a colonial model, obviously a public building of some sort. Inquiring of my host what it was, he told me it was a library. "But who will use it?" I exclaimed. "There seem to be very few people hereabout." There were a few houses, to be sure, but not enough, one would suppose, to call for a fine library. "Oh," said my friend, "we are a very intellectual people up here; we have not yet been contaminated by the foreigners of Boston. Why, Barre, which we are just approaching, has a village improvement society which is fifty years old. You'll see"—and we did: one of the sweetest, most orderly hamlets in the land, I should say, with a lovely common right in the middle of it. Meantime the man at the wheel was chanting an old saying:—

"Barre for beauty,
Petersham for pride,
If it hadn't been for codfish
Dana would have died."

for salt codfish is a staple article of food during the long winter in New England.

People speak of Franklin as the first civilized American; he was not: he was only one of many: there were many more civilized Americans one hundred years ago, in proportion to our population, than there are to-day. Isaiah Thomas, of whom we, in Philadelphia, know little, was one of them. He, like Franklin, was a printer, a publisher, and a philanthropist, and his enduring monument is the American Antiquarian Society in Worcester, to which, at his death, he bequeathed his private library, then one of the best in the country. Think of this great man, for such he was, publishing, in 1787, *The History of Little Goody Two-shoes*. The first English edition was published in 1766,

First Worcester edition of Goody Twoshoes, 1787

and if *Goody Twoshoes* is not from the pen of Oliver Goldsmith, it should have been.

South of Philadelphia, the Church of England, the establishment of Charles II and Anne and the Georges, functioned rather as a part of the social order of things than as a form of religion. Burnings for heresy and witchcraft were unknown, and, as the apparel oft bespeaks the man, one's religious bias was made clear by one's costume: it was austere in New England, drab in Pennsylvania, and pleasing in the aristocratic South; and a glance at the literature of those three separate communities will show that there were three, —no, two, for south of Philadelphia printing hardly existed—schools of literature. Pennsylvania was a hot-house in which every variety of religion flourished, from the Quaker of England to the Mennonite, Dunker, and Shaker of the Rhine country. Intolerance and suspicion were the bonds that united them. But these sects did not function in Philadelphia; mercifully they trekked westward. Philadelphia was Quaker and Church of England—aristocratic, in other words; and from these came a demand for belles-lettres, and where there is a demand, a supply is not unusual.

One of the great books of the world, More's *Utopia*, written, as the title-page assures us, By Sir Thomas Moore (*sic*), Lord Chancellor of England, was printed and sold in Philadelphia by James Chattin in Church Alley in 1753. The copy which I have had the pleasure of examining was purchased for the "Wilmington (Delaware) Library and Young Men's Association" for two shillings and sixpence—an excellent investment of half-a-crown. Pope's *Essay on Man* was "printed and sold by W. Dunlap at the newest Printing Office in Market Street" in 1762.

It would be interesting to know which appeared first, Goldsmith's *Traveller*, from the press of Aitken, or Johnson's *Rasselas*, published by Robert Bell; they both appeared in the same year, 1768. The authors were friends and, in some sort, rivals, and we may, if we will, fancy a pleasant contest of wits between the two men upon hearing of the literary activities of "the Plantations." Professor Tinker calls attention to the fact that Bell, the publisher of *Rasselas*, so calls the story for the first time on any title-page, and *Rasselas* it has since remained. Bell used the imprint "America," instead of the usual one, "Philadelphia," and he also employed the phrase "printed for every purchaser," which pleased Dr. Johnson because it suggested to him that the printer expected that the book would be scattered among the people. Tinker adds in his pretty little history of this volume that when William White, who subsequently became the first Bishop of Pennsylvania, met Dr. Johnson in 1771, he told him that there was an American edition of the *Rasselas*, and promised to send him a copy upon his return to Philadelphia, which he did, notwithstanding the fact that Johnson, complaining of the behavior of the colonists over the Stamp Act, had very rudely remarked that if he had been Prime Minister he would have sent a man-of-war to level Boston or New York to the ground. But White, in telling the story, adds, "I have heard from him sentiments which convince me that he would not have done as he said." Johnson's bark was always worse than his bite.

Aitken—who, it may be remembered, published the first English Bible in America, with the permission and endorsement of Congress, in 1782—published in 1773 from his shop in Front Street, opposite the London Coffee House, Blair's *Grave*, to which was added *An Elegy Written in a Country Churchyard*, by Mr. Gray. The Bible, Blair's *Grave*, and the *Country Churchyard* seem to suggest a gravity of mind not so conspicuous in William Menzie, who published, the year before, Goldsmith's *Vicar of Wakefield*. That lovely book was eagerly pounced upon and read to pieces; only three copies of this edition are known, according to George P. Philes, the eminent authority upon Americana.

All the world knows that Franklin always thought and spoke of himself as a printer, and it is not always

realized how early in his career his interests were
diverted into other and more important channels. His
first employer in Philadelphia was Keimer, the publisher of *Epictetus*, but his stay with him was short,
as was his stay as a journeyman printer in London.
After his return to Philadelphia, he devoted his
energies to his trade for a time, but before his fortieth
year he had taken into partnership David Hall, in
order that he might retire from business, enjoy his
leisure, and philosophize in his own way. At the
time of his retirement, Franklin's career as one of the
great men of the world had not yet begun, but his
disappearance as a printer left the coast clear for
Robert Bell, a Scotchman who came to this country
about 1766 by way of Ireland. He first became an
auctioneer and then a publisher. An early venture was
Robertson's *Charles V;* this was followed by Blackstone's *Commentaries* in four octavo volumes (1772).
Thomas Paine, who has never been appreciated as he
deserves,—for with his pen he enormously assisted the
cause of the colonists,—entered his employ, and Bell
it was who published his famous pamphlet, *Common
Sense*. This work had an enormous sale; it appeared in
1776, at a time when there was great scarcity of paper,
and all the broken quires in Bell's warehouse were
collected and culled for the first edition.

Bell was a thoroughgoing Whig, zealously support-
ing the liberties of this country; moreover, he was a
man of taste and judgment, and honest even to his own
disadvantage, as his tract on the *Free Sale of Books*
abundantly proves. Apparently the General Assembly
was about to take some step looking to the limiting

to one man the right to sell books by public vendue or auction. This, Bell says, would be injurious to the arts, science, learning, and manufactures of Pennsylvania, and he begs that their sale may remain free,— "free and unconfined as the circumambient air," he puts it,—and especially he prays that he may not be appointed to this monopoly, notwithstanding the many claims that he might set up to a preference. And he further calls attention to the fact that "the Revolution was accomplished not to diminish, but to increase the freedom of every individual. The fine and unadulterated excellence of republics forbids the possibility of monopoly." How naïve all this sounds to-day when everything is "in chains," from the theatre to the corner store.

In 1777 Bell turned his attention to *Paradise Lost*. This seems to me a magnificent venture. Consider conditions in Philadelphia in 1777: they were in a "commotion," to use Bell's own word. The Declaration of Independence had been signed at the State House the summer before; the battle of Germantown had been fought and lost; Washington was at Valley Forge with his starving and naked army; Cornwallis was in control of Philadelphia, and Howe had his fleet in the Delaware; yet here was a self-contained man doing business as usual—or trying to. But why *Paradise Lost*—the famous epic of which Dr. Johnson once remarked that, however magnificent it is, no man ever wished it longer. It was indicative, I think, of the good taste of our ancestors. We had no fleet; Britannia ruled the waves; there was no way of getting good books, any books, from London; here, then, was an opportunity for the enterprise of Robert Bell. And he produced a very creditable piece of bookmaking: the type, ink, paper, and printing are excellent, and there is a very decent frontispiece of Milton, engraved by one J. Norman after the Faithorne portrait, with the famous lines of Dryden under it—on the whole, the volume would be no discredit to a London publisher, yet this book was produced in Philadelphia one hundred and fifty years ago, during one of the most significant wars in history.

What shall I say of James Thomson's *Seasons*, but that no poem of equal length in English has ever been so popular. The same reason that prompted Bell to print an edition of *Paradise Lost* led him in that same year to print a *Seasons*, and once again J. Norman is called to supply a frontispiece. In this volume the publisher tells us that his shop is in Third Street next door to St. Paul's Church: we can now locate him without difficulty.

The first edition of *The School for Scandal*, perhaps the most brilliant comedy in our language, was a pirated edition published in Dublin in 1779. Ten years later it was printed by Prichard and Hall in Philadelphia, in Market Street, between Second and Front. The title-page states that the play has been performed with universal applause at the theatres in New York, Pennsylvania, and Maryland, from a manuscript copy in the possession of John Henry, joint manager of the Old American Company.

The first theatrical performance given in America was in a small loft in Philadelphia, in August 1744; the play was Addison's *Cato*. It might be described as an amateur performance. The first American playbill known to be in existence announces a performance of *The Orphan* at The Theatre in Nassau Street, New York, on Monday, March 26, 1750, at precisely half an hour after six o'clock. The playbill also announces the sale of a parcel of ironmongery, a quantity of cordial waters, and a dwelling house in Wall Street near the City Hall, inquiries for which are to be directed to Catherine Beekman, widow. (That was the time to buy real estate in New York.) There is also to be sold a negro fellow who understands all sorts of country work, having been brought up to it, and a likely negro wench. Mrs. Mary Lloyd's book, *Meditations on Divine Subjects*, was announced as "soon to appear," and there are current quotations on flour, beef, molasses, port wine, and rum. The price of New England rum was two shillings and fourpence a gallon, whereas the best West India product brought as much as three shillings and eightpence a gallon. But at either price, in those happy days, a man could afford to raise a thirst and a family at the same time; to-day he must make his choice—he cannot do both. This, however, is a digression. The first performance of Shakespeare by a regular theatrical troupe, which came from England and performed *The Merchant of Venice*, took place in Williamsburg, Virginia, on September 5, 1752. From that time to the present the theatre has been the most popular of our amusements. The first Shakespeare published in the New World—Johnson's edition, by the way—was published in Philadelphia by Bioren and Madan in 1795. It was in eight volumes, the first of which has for a frontispiece a portrait of the dramatist engraved by R. Field from the Chandos picture.

We must retrace our steps a little. Burns's *Poems Chiefly in the Scottish Dialect* appeared in Philadelphia, printed for and sold by Peter Stewart and George Hyde, on the west side of Second Street, nine doors above Chestnut, in 1788, and Byron when his time came was almost as popular in this country as in England. The first American edition of *English Bards and Scotch Reviewers* appeared in Charleston, South Carolina, in conjunction with Brannon and Morford, 118 Chestnut Street, Philadelphia—J. Maxwell, the printer, also a Philadelphian. What we should now call a blurb calls attention to the fact that "many years have passed since the English press has given us a performance so replete with genius, good sense, and spirited animadversion."

Byron, Scott, Tom Moore, and other popular authors were reprinted in Philadelphia almost as soon as their books came out in London, Moses Thomas being by now the leading publisher or pirate, for by now there was little credit and less risk in book-printing. There were no copyright laws; for many years our publishers battened and fattened on the English author, much to his disgust. We took our good where we found it; so did our friends across the water, but they found little. They took what we had—a pocket handkerchief; we robbed a bank: our morality was the same.

Here and there our publications in book form ante-dated the English. Charles Lamb's *Mr. H.*, "as it was performed at the Philadelphia theatre," was printed by

Mr. Carey, 122 Market Street, in 1813: the first English edition followed five years later; a note informs us that "copyright is secured according to an Act of Congress"—we wonder how. A copy of this book brought fifteen hundred dollars in the auction rooms of the American Art Association, as recently as February 1927. Lamb's *Elia*, the second series, appeared with the imprint of Carey Lea and Carey, Philadelphia, 1825; the English edition of the same book in 1833; and the Philadelphia edition contains six essays not then reprinted. Thackeray's first book, *The Yellowplush Papers*, was printed by Carey and Hart in Philadelphia some years before a book of his had appeared in London; and the list could be continued.

By the end of the first quarter of the nineteenth century, Philadelphia began to lose to New York its publishing supremacy. Wilder and Campbell, in publishing in 1824 Thomas Medwin's *Journal of Conversations* with Byron at Pisa, announced their aim to make their establishment a focus at which most foreign publications could be found, or the channel through which they might be procured. New York, with its magnificent harbor only a few miles from the sea, gradually became an entrance to and an exit from a great continent. Publishing is not manufacturing on a great scale, as we now understand it; the thing most necessary to success is to keep in close touch with the primary makers of books, the authors; this could best be done in and from New York. This, together with the rise of the New England school, Emerson, Hawthorne, Lowell, Holmes, and the rest, who published in Boston, completed the discomfiture of our Philadelphia publishers. For a decade or two—until the Civil War—our bookstores were the best in the land; rich planters from the South invariably stopped in Philadelphia to replenish their libraries. John Pennington's shop in Seventh Street, near Walnut, was a rendezvous for book-lovers from all over the country; and Moses Pollock, in Commerce Street below Fifth, had another well-known establishment. Pollock was the uncle of our own Dr. Rosenbach, and it is said that he once sold a book for sixteen dollars that he lived to see bring sixteen hundred at auction. That confirmed in him his growing belief that the best way to keep a shop was always to buy and never to sell. As he was a bachelor, he required little on which to live, and in his later years there was nothing he hated so much as a customer.

When I was a boy, there was Porter and Coates, who—at 816 and subsequently at 900 Chestnut— maintained a magnificent store; there was Claxton, Remsen and Haffelfinger; and last, but by no means least, there was J. B. Lippincott and Company—both of these firms having establishments on Market Street. The firm of Lippincott still maintains a fine publishing house on Washington Square, but our glory as a publishing and bookselling centre has departed. One thing alone we boast—the great Curtis Company, with its famous magazines which are the envy and the despair of the whole publishing world.

V

THE BOOK ITSELF

IT may be supposed that anyone concerned with this volume knows that what are called books to-day were originally "rolls,"—hence the Rolls or Record Office, —but if anyone will read or attempt to read a "roll," and then a book, he will see what an improvement upon a "roll" the book is. Books were originally of parchment, then of vellum,—there is small difference between the two,—and then of paper. Volumes have been written about the discovery of and the art of making paper, and then came the art of printing from movable metal types. It has recently been shown in an excellent book, *The Invention of Printing in China*, by Thomas Francis Carter of Columbia University, that the art of printing was known in China much earlier than in Europe, but by general consent Gutenberg is accredited with the art of printing as we know it, about 1450; anyway, we will start there with the Gutenberg Bible.

Every time one of these great books comes upon the market, there is a great furore; the last one to be sold at auction was the Melk copy, which at the Anderson Galleries in New York, on February 15, 1926, brought the record price of one hundred and six thousand dollars. Dr. Rosenbach paid it, and immediately sold the volume to Mrs. Harkness, who presented it to Yale University: it was a noble gift.

One peculiarity of this great book is that it has neither a colophon nor a title-page; both of these important developments in the printed book came later. If I were asked what a colophon is, and how it

¶ Imprynted at London in Fleteſtrete/by Wynkyn de Worde/dwellynge at the ſygne of the Sonne/and fynyſſhed in the yere of our lozde god. M.CCCC. xxxiij. The.xxvij.daye of Maye.

The last page of a famous book, Wynkyn de Worde's "Caxton device,"
has never been fully explained. The initials,W.C.,are certainly Caxton's,
but what is the meaning of the cypher? Nobody knows

came to get its name, I should reply that a colophon
is a note, either printed or written on the last page
of a book, giving the title of the book, sometimes the
name of the author or printer, and the date or place

of publication: in brief, very much such information as one now finds, or expects to find, upon a title-page. Occasionally the word "Alleluia" is added, suggesting thankfulness that the job is completed. It gets its name from an ancient city in Asia Minor, where, it is claimed, Homer was born; it was, in its day, governed by a rich aristocracy which provided a famous troop of horse that was kept to make the final and most important charge in battle: hence it is the last or final piece of writing or printing in a book.

The colophon is one of the many subjects on which Alfred W. Pollard, former Keeper of the Printed Books in the British Museum, has written learnedly. It requires only a moment's thought to realize the importance of the colophon and the title-page, and anyone who has observed the fate of any large book knocking about the house—a Bible, a dictionary, a directory, even a telephone book—will understand how easy it is for a big, heavy book to lose its first and last pages. Such has always been the fate of heavy books throughout the ages. This sometimes makes it difficult to tell at a glance what the book is.

We think we live in a progressive age, and we do, but the awakening of the world after the so-called Dark Ages, the discovery of the art of printing, and the discovery of America gave the world a tremendous fillip. The art of printing swept over Europe like wildfire. In Germany, Italy, France, and the Low Countries, the urge to print was enormous; only England was backward, for a reason which will presently be explained. Types were cut and cast, and set in Latin, Greek, and Hebrew, besides the languages common in the countries in which the books were produced. It is computed that in less than fifty years— by 1500, to be exact—about thirty-eight thousand separate books or editions had been produced: these books are called Incunabula. This is a plural Latin noun meaning, variously, cradle or birthplace: hence, the beginning of anything. It is a generally recognized European word, although the French word *incunables*, meaning the same thing, is now coming into use. Having in mind its original meaning, it should perhaps have been limited to books printed in any or all countries before 1475, say, but the habit of speaking in round numbers prevailed, and it is understood to refer to any book printed before the year 1500. The most important book on the subject of incunabula is a great bibliography in Latin, first published a century ago in Stuttgart by Ludwig Hain. About sixteen thousand books or editions are mentioned by him, and there is a supplement listing seven thousand additional titles. One frequently sees this work referred to in old book catalogues, as mentioned or not mentioned by Hain; an asterisk (*) before the title means that Hain has personally seen the volume referred to. An entirely new work on this subject, undertaken with the approval of the German Government, but suspended by the World War, is again going forward.

Very frequently incunabula have no title-page or colophon, and give no information as to what the book is or when, where, or by whom it was printed: hence the extreme difficulty of dealing with the subject; but scholars are able to determine much by careful

morn Be tymes / the kynge pryant assemblidz alle the
troians for to here the answer of Anthenor/the whiche
saydz to the kynge otherwyse than he hadz founden / ma-
kyng a longe sermone for to couere wyth hys felonnye
where he spack longe of the puyssance of the grekes &
of theyr trouthe m theyr promesses / Andz how they
hadz holden the tryews that they hadz maadz lyyng to
fore the Cyte . Andz hadz ben faythfully gouernedz with
oute brekyng of them . Andz after spake he of the ffe-
blenes of the troians andz of the grete daungers that
they were Inne . Andz m thys concludedz that forthon
hit were prouffitable to seke peas andz that they come
therto . Andz saydz hyt coude not be / But yf they gaf a
grete quantyte of goldz andz syluer vnto the grekes for
to restore to them the grete domages andz losses that they
haddz m the warre / Andz after auysedz the kynge andz
the other eche m hym self / for to employe hym m thys
thynge wyth oute ony sparynge / Andz for as moche
saydz Anthenor as J can not knowe at thys tyme alle
theyr wylle / J woldz that ye woldz late Eneas goo
wyth me vnto them for to knowe better theyr wylle
andz to thende that they beleupdz vs better / Every man
alowedz the wordes of Anthenor . Andz than wente he
andz Eneas vnto the grekes / andz wyth hem the kynge
Cassilpus .

    Han the counceyll was fynysshydz andz alle
    doon / the kynge Pryant entrydz m to hys cham-
    bre and began to wepe right strongly as he that
apperceyuydz well the trayson / Andz playnedz sore
the deth of hys soñes andz also the grete domage that he
Bare / Andz yet that worste is that he muste bye hys

*A page from Caxton's "Recuyell de Troye." The first
book printed in English at Bruges in 1471*

The thyrd chapitre of the first tractate treteth Wherfore
the playe Was founden and maad   Capitulo iij

The causes Wherfore this playe Was founden ben iij
᛫ The first Was for to correcte and repreue the kyng
for Whan this kyng enylmerodach sawe this playe / And
the pawns knyghtes and gentilmen of his court playe
Wyth the phylosopher ᛫ he merueylled gretly of the beaulte
and nouelte of the playe ᛫ And desired to playe agaynst
the philosopher. The philosopher answerd and sayd to hym
that hit myght not be don / but yf he first lernyd the play
The kyng sayd hit Was reson and that he Wold put hym
to the payn to lerne hit /   Than the phylosopher began to

*A page from Caxton's "Game and Playe of Chesse," the first English
book with an illustration*

study of the types employed and close observation of the watermarks in the paper.

England was slow to make use of the discovery of the art of printing, but this should not be understood as implying any lack of interest or scholarship in Britain; for the great books of the world were printed in Greek or in Latin, which were then what might be called universal languages, while the Italian, French, German, and English languages were but little known outside their respective countries, and in many cases not too well in them. French was the language of the court and of the law courts in England until well into the fourteenth century, and traces of old French survive in our own law courts to this day. Caxton printed the first book in the English language—if English it may be called—*The Recuyell of the Historyes of Troye*, in Bruges in 1471; and his second book, the first with an illustration, *The Game and Playe of Chesse*, not long after. His first book printed in England, *The Dictes and Sayings of the Philosophers*, was printed at Westminster in 1477; this was the first English book with a colophon, and the copy in the Rylands Library in Manchester supplies the month and the day—it was the eighteenth of November. *The Recuyell of the Historyes of Troye* and other specimens of Caxton's printing, while fascinating to the English or American collector, are distinctly inferior, as examples of printing, to the work of the Continental presses. As late as 1539, when a Great Bible was desired in English, it was printed, or at least begun, in Paris, while the first complete English Bible was printed by Froschover at Zurich in Switzerland in 1535.

In a book intended for the use of one who is beginning to collect books, or who is willing to read about them, it is hardly worth while to spend much time over *How to Tell a Caxton*. We are not likely to run across Caxtons, except in the vault of the Brothers Rosenbach in New York, and then we can tell them by the price. Nor shall I devote much time to incunabula in general. The catholic collector may wish to have a few examples of early printing, and it is still possible to secure good examples of Bibles, Prayer Books, and the like, without totally wrecking one's bank account; but the modern collector gets a very slight thrill over a mediæval treatise on Theology, Jurisprudence, Philosophy, and Philology,—indeed his opinions on these subjects are not fit to print,—and it is with these subjects that the earliest books chiefly concern themselves. To-day we devote our attention to what may be called human interest: books written for and read by men not very unlike ourselves.

A hundred years ago, this book-collecting game was played in a very different manner: it was then almost exclusively the recreation of a gentleman—and a gentleman might be described as one who had no steady occupation. He probably had had a classical education and read Latin and Greek with comparative ease, and he would have thought it beneath his dignity to devote very much time or thought to a book printed in English, except to Caxton's and those of his immediate successors.

Reader, have you, perchance, a copy of Dibdin's *Bibliographical Decameron* at hand? It is a magnificent book in three volumes, usually finely bound in old straight-grained red morocco, and it was once a book which no gentleman's library should be without. To-day it is—well, it is not a "plug," but very nearly. The text itself is unreadable, but the notes in fine print, and chiefly in Volume III, give the book such vitality as it has. Turn to page forty-nine and read the long account of the "Roxburghe Fight," as it pleases the would-be facetious author to call the Roxburghe Sale, one of the greatest sales in the history of book-collecting. It would be a pious thing for someone to lift this story from out of the immense amount of verbiage in which it is em-bedded, and print it in a pamphlet in type which can be read by the naked eye.

The sale took place in the dining room of John, late Duke of Roxburghe, on the north side of St. James's Square. Dibdin describes the events of the great day, June 17, 1812, as though he were an eyewitness of a battle—which indeed it was. The star item was a Boc-caccio of 1471. Two great nobles contended for the prize. The bidding began by a gentleman from the coun-try bidding one hundred guineas; someone said five hundred; Earl Spencer made it a thousand; and the Mar-quis of Blandford added ten. To every bid made by Earl Spencer, the noble Marquis adds, imperturbably, ten, until the amazing sum of two thousand, two hundred and fifty guineas is bid by the Earl, to which is added the usual ten of the Marquis; and the hammer falls. Whereupon the noble Earl says, "I bow to you," and retires. "We are good friends still," remarks Blandford, extending his hand. "Perfectly," says the defeated Earl. This was a great game, played by giants, but my point is this: not a man present at that sale could by the utmost stretch of his imagination comprehend how any very keen bibliographical interest could be aroused by a Shakespeare folio or a quarto; yet to-day such a price as the famous Boccaccio fetched is paid at every important auction sale for items then entirely neglected.

I have been led into a digression. To return to the printed book: the quick perfection of the type, ink, paper, and all that we mean by the word "format" of the early book, is bewildering to one who has watched the development of other arts and sciences. The colophon soon gave way to the title-page; the earliest book in English with a title-page is said to be *A Passing Godle Lityll Boke Necessarye and Behovefull agenst the Pestilens*. It was printed about 1486 by William de Machlinia, a contemporary of Caxton. In due course the title-page developed; woodcut borders came into use, in the centre of which was the printed title, and then perhaps the printer's device. Some of these devices were very beautiful and remain unsurpassed to the present time. These printers' marks were originally placed on the last page of the book under the colophon; subsequently they appeared as an ornament below the title of the book on the title-page, where they have ever since remained.

After a time it was discovered that large mortised frames or borders made of wood easily became warped or broken, and these then gave way to engravings on copper, and from these engraved title-pages it was only another step, and a logical one, to the engraved frontispiece. Early in the sixteenth century, such great masters as Dürer and Holbein did not think it beneath their dignity to design borders for title-pages (the title of the Great Bible of Henry VIII is said to be from a design of the latter), and it is generally conceded that engraved titles reached the height of excellence at the Plantin-Moretus Press at Antwerp. To the book-lover, this wonderful old printing establishment—still preserved and now a public museum—is one of the most interesting places in the world.

But one cannot always believe what one sees on a title-page. Early editors and printers were often in peril of their lives. Authority did not look kindly on the dissemination of learning: it preferred to tell the common people what they should believe, and so for one reason or another fictitious names were not infrequently employed to disguise real ones. The so-called Matthews Bible was really the work of John Rogers, who perished nevertheless during the reign of Queen Mary; and "printed in Paradise and to be bought where it is sold" appears on the title of a book printed during the period of the Commonwealth.

In the early days of bookmaking, designs for title-pages and portraits were used over and over again; any effigy of a man with a fine crop of whiskers would serve as the portrait of a philosopher, and such cuts were used many times over various names, not infrequently in the same volume. My attention was kindly drawn by an unknown correspondent in the City of Mexico to the fact that the border designed for the title-page of the Edward VI Prayer Book (1549) was deemed suitable for at least three other books, one of which was a *Dialectica of Aristotel*, printed in the City of Mexico in 1554; and this may be as good a place as any to observe that the first printing press set up in the New World was in that same city.

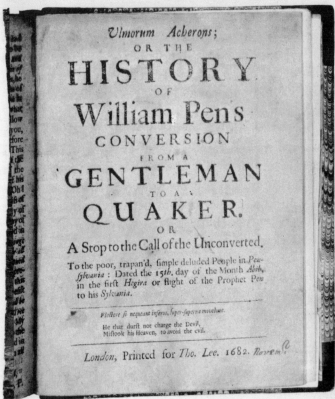

I am not sufficiently familiar with the title-pages of books printed elsewhere than in England to say to what extent humorous or joking title-pages were usual on the Continent, but in England such titles were not uncommon. One such title occurs to me, as applicable not alone to the year in which it was printed, 1642 (the figure six was set upside down, so that the date reads 1942), but to England after the Great War. The title is *The Virgins Complaint, for the losse of their Sweet-Hearts by these present Wars. And their own long solicitude and keeping their Virginities against their wills.*

No one can long interest himself in the study of old books without discovering that a "watermark" frequently plays an important part in identifying a book which, without it, might be difficult to place. There is, curiously enough, no article on this subject in the *Encyclopedia Britannica*. A watermark is a device, an initial, a date, trade-mark, or emblem, woven into a sheet of paper during the period of its manufacture. It is made from a design, usually of wire, and set into the screen on which the paper pulp, later to become a sheet of paper, is deposited. By holding the paper up to the light it can be seen quite clearly, the paper being a trifle thinner where the watermark is.

The study of the invention of paper, its manufacture and watermarks, is a fascinating one. Probably no man living knows more about it than Dard Hunter of Chillicothe, Ohio. He has written a fascinating—and now very scarce—volume on the subject, entitled *Old Papermaking*, and the watermarks of the old papermakers. Incidentally, Mr. Hunter is the most interesting bookmaker in this, perhaps in any, country. Speaking of himself and his work, he says:—

"I was reared in the midst of paper, type, and ink, and my earliest recollection is watching my father set type and print on an old hand press. I have seen through the press upwards of two hundred different books, but none of them ever pleased me. The Italian book printers of the fifteenth and sixteenth centuries have never been excelled: their paper, even after four hundred years (look at the page of a Gutenberg Bible), shows a richness of tone and texture which modern papermakers have never equaled. So I went to Italy and studied the art of making paper; then I went to Vienna and studied type design at the oldest Institute of Graphic Arts in the world, and subsequently to London and studied toolmaking at the Royal Technical College. When I came home I built a small mill with my own hand, thatched it with rye straw grown on my own small farm, and equipped this miniature mill with appliances such as had been used by fifteenth-century papermakers. An old creaky wooden water wheel reduced the linen and cotton rags to a fibrous pulp, from which I made each sheet of paper separately in a hand mould. I next set up a small type foundry, and, with no other tools or utensils than those that would have been used four hundred years ago, I cut the letter punches in steel, struck the matrices in copper, and cast the type in a hand mould. When there was sufficient water to turn the water wheel, I was able to make about seventy-five sheets of paper a day. When there was no water I made type. The whole undertaking revealed to me the interest there is in papermaking and watermarking."

The equipment, the moulds, the letter punches, matrices, type, tools, and copies of the two books made from them, are now in the Smithsonian Institution, Washington, D. C., and a label on the case in which they are displayed reads: "In the history of printing these are the first books to have been made in their entirety by the labor of one man." Someone has written of this remarkable man that, although he will never become rich, he has the unique distinction of writing his name on an absolutely white page in the history of bookmaking.

In connection with the printed book, there remain several matters to be touched upon before we turn over the printed sheets to the binder. We have referred to the colophon and the title-page; there remains to be mentioned the half title or bastard title, as it was sometimes called. This is a brief synopsis of the title, and immediately precedes it. It is usually placed in the centre of the upper half of the page, and the page following it is always left blank. Practically all books now have half titles, and no book is complete without one; and, unless the volume be very rare indeed, no collector will place in his collection a book which, requiring a half title, lacks it. Only the careful study of the signatures, the comparison of one copy with another, or the use of a carefully compiled bibliography, will show what book has or should have a half title. It is always to be remembered that book-collecting is a sport, a game. One does not have to own a first edition of Johnson's *Vanity of Human Wishes;* one can lead a noble, upright life without it, even if one cannot be quite happy; but if one has it, it must be perfect. It was published in 1749 without a half title, whereas his *Life of Savage*, published in 1744, has a half title. In neither case does one know why or have to find out.

I have used the word "signature." A signature is a mark designed to assist the binder in getting the proper following of the page of a book. It was not, according to William Blades, an invention of the printer: it was, he says, quite as necessary for the scribe to mark the sequence of the sheets he wrote as for the typographer to mark the order of those he printed, for whether the page be written or printed it is equally necessary for the binder to have a clue as to the order in which one page follows the other. At first, the signature was written at the foot of every printed page; there is said to be an example of this in an uncut copy of Caxton's *Recuyell* in the Royal Library at Windsor; but after a time printed signatures came into use, and he further defines them as "signs or marks placed beneath certain pages to distinguish the sections sometimes called quires or gatherings which they print." To-day they serve another and most important purpose: they enable the careful bibliographer to ascertain whether or not any pages of a book are missing.

The collation of a book, especially an old book, is by no means easy, and the art of collation should be— and is—mastered by every bibliographer worthy of the name. And here is a reason why one should always, if possible, secure a book in its original condition, in boards or cloth, as issued. Some time ago my friend Geoffrey Keynes asked me if I would collate for comparison some Jane Austens I had in original boards. I replied that I could not, but that I would get Mabel Zahn to do it for me. I sent her my books, and then for good measure I borrowed a "bound" set, firsts too, and had them collated as well—with what result? Not one of my books in original condition was wrong; not a single book in the bound set was right. I never attempt the job of collation myself: it is one of the many things you can well employ someone to do for you. It is a part of the drudgery of the game, very like cleaning

your own gun, which usually goes off and kills someone—especially if it is not loaded.

May we not now assume that our book is safely
printed, and folded, and collated in sheets or in sections, or in quires,—as the English say,—and ready for
the binder? I think so. So far we have done little or
nothing ourselves: we have only defined, and not too
exactly, some of the words we shall have occasion to
use as we grow more skillful in this book-collecting
game.

The first books were large, very large, but the world
has never yet agreed upon just what name to apply to
a large or a very large book. "Folio," "elephant folio,"
"double elephant," and "atlas folio" are loose terms
and mean "large"—but how large? To be exact one
must state the size of the book in inches—or, on the
Continent, in centimetres.

In an English periodical, I read not long ago that it
was high time papermakers all over the world got together and agreed on a standard-size sheet so that,
folded twice, it would be a quarto, four times an octavo,
and so on. Such a suggestion is absurd. This can never
be done, for the size of a sheet of paper will in the
future, as in the past, depend on many things: on the
conditions under which it is made, its quality, and the
particular purpose for which it is intended, to mention
only three. There is competition among papermakers,
and the man who makes a desirable paper cheapest per
pound will get the business; it is his business to make
paper, not to give a book a name, indicating a size,
after it is printed and bound. No, if we are to have
reform and intelligibility in the name of a book (mean-

ing its size), publishers must agree that all books smaller than a certain size and larger than another certain size are to be known as—what you will, irrespective of the number of times the sheet which makes up the volume is folded; and after a time—and it will be a long time— such silly names as those we now have will disappear.

What idea does a cataloguer living in Exeter, England, say, intend to convey to a man living in Chicago by saying that a book is a "small foolscap octavo;" and what in heaven's name is the difference between an "octavo" and a "crown octavo" and a "royal octavo?" To call a "quarto" large or small does not help matters much; what we must have is a lot of words— new words, if need be—which will convey to a man's mind the idea that a book within certain limits of size —within a certain bracket, as our income blanks have it—is always called by a certain name.

"I am for whole volumes in folio," Shakespeare makes one of his characters exclaim, and he is, if I remember rightly, about to write a sonnet. This would be quite all right if the sheet on which the sonnet was printed, when folded once (which is what a folio is), were originally no larger than the sheet on which I am now writing; but, in general, sonnets when printed in folio find few readers.

Our position in this country in regard to the names for the sizes of books is more difficult even than is that of the English, for we buy very largely from their catalogues, and they buy little or nothing from ours, and our nomenclature is entirely different from theirs. With us a duodecimo (12mo.) is a book about the size of an ordinary novel—a book, say seven and one-half inches high by five inches wide; an octavo (8vo.) is a book about nine and one-half inches by six and one-half inches. Before me is a catalogue —and an excellent one —from the business of my dear old friend James Tregaskis, in which a twin, or *dos-à-dos*, binding—in this case a small Testament and a Prayer Book bound together, with their positions reversed, a binding difficult to describe but not unusual— is called a duodecimo.

A dos-à-dos binding

I know the size of the little nugget they are describing, for I have one exactly like it. It is bound in white satin and is elaborately embroidered in colored silk and metal thread. The unskilled collector ordering this article from the catalogue will be greatly surprised to receive a tiny book, only four inches high by two inches wide. Yet Tregaskis is only using the accepted English terminology, for the item in question came from the Huth collection and was shown some years ago at the exhibition of bindings at the Burlington Fine Arts Club, and it was there, as I happen to know, described as a duodecimo. So much for difficulties which inhere in the use of words intended to indicate size.

And in this connection publishers would be well advised to heed Dr. Johnson's saying: "Sir, no man reads long with a folio on his table. Books that you may carry to the fireside and hold readily in your hand are the most useful after all."

We shall now concern ourselves, briefly, with printing. It is, I think, generally agreed that the first books printed were designed to look as though they had been written with the pen; how could it be otherwise? But it was only a short time before everyone who knew enough to read knew that the text or script he was reading was printed, not written. The printed book was not long looked upon as a miracle; print shops sprang up everywhere, and books, sacred and profane, were printed; artists of distinction began to design type, type that should no longer imitate writing with a pen, but should have a character of its own. Volumes, whole libraries, have been written on the subject, some of them very beautiful, some very technical, and others that I find rather exasperating, for I believe that the first requisite of a printed word or a printed page is, or should be, its readability.

The world goes round and round rather than on and on, in some things, and printing is one of them. Many of the books printed before 1500 are as beautiful as, perhaps more beautiful than, any that have been printed since. We in this country do not, I think, sufficiently understand or admire the great typographical marvels of the past; in the first place, we see very few of them except in the great public libraries—and it is chilling work standing with aching feet on the cold, hard floors of museums peering into glass cases at books which too frequently give no clue as to what they are. For this reason I think that an unimportant book on the table of a friend, or in your own library, is of greater interest than some great and priceless tome in a mausoleum, which is what too many libraries are. There are all sorts of libraries: the world's best is the British Museum; the world's worst—and greatest, too, no doubt—the Bibliothèque Nationale in Paris.

But books, not libraries, is my theme. In general, early printed books in English are very bad; Caxtons, if fascinating and priceless, are not beautiful. The first folio of Shakespeare, one of the great books of the world, is an ugly book—and almost as full of blunders as it is of beauties.

Great progress was made in the printer's art in the fifty years following the appearance of the "First Folio," as it is always called; then they began to print badly again; and just as printing became very bad indeed, new life was infused into the art by John Baskerville. I dare not retard the progress of this paper by any details of the life of this great printer. His edition of Virgil, and his Milton, in the words of Macaulay, astonished all the librarians of Europe by their beauty, as did also his little Horace. Baskerville, in the phrase of to-day, put Birmingham on the map; his types are beautiful, and he was very particular in the important matters of paper and ink.

Next in merit, in England, are the productions of the two Charles Whittinghams,—uncle and nephew,— the founders of the far-famed Chiswick Press, which still functions to-day. And no paper on printing would be even passable without reference to the great Oxford

University Press, founded in 1468, and still going strong —stronger than ever to-day, under the able direction of my friends Humphrey Milford and R. W. Chapman, the secretary thereof.

We now come, in this hasty sketch, upon the name of William Morris: poet, artist, manufacturer, socialist, and last, not least, printer. By 1890, printing had again fallen from high estate; it needed for its revival just such a superb enthusiast as Morris. His achievement was a noble one: toward the end of a busy life, in 1890, he started the Kelmscott Press, which before his death, in 1896, gave new direction to the art with which his name is inseparable. I bow to Morris as the man responsible for the renaissance of printing; but, personally, I do not much like his work. In his note on his *Aims in Founding the Kelmscott Press*, he says: "I began printing books with the hope of producing some which would have a definite claim to beauty, while at the same time they should be easy to read and should not dazzle the eye, or trouble the intellect of the reader by eccentricity of form in the letters." In his aim, he was not, in my judgment, entirely successful. His books are *not* easy to read, and they *do* dazzle the eye. A page of a book is not a picture, something to be merely looked upon—it is something that should be read. Readability is, after all, the supreme test of a page of text, and no one, I think, can long read a Kelmscott Press book with pleasure. In this respect his followers and disciples have been more successful than the master; but this does not make the value of his work less. He worked with immense enthusiasm, designed several founts of type and an immense number of ornamental

letters and borders and the like; and his supreme
achievement in printing is his Chaucer. Is it? Authorities differ. I once heard a lover of old books speak of it as
vulgar, and I understood what he meant. It is in no respect a finer book than the *Nuremberg Chronicle*, printed by
Koburger in 1493; indeed, it is not so fine, for, whereas
the *Chronicle* was a natural flowering, the Morris Chaucer
is an exotic. Is it not a reflection on our judgment that
the newer work is appraised at a thousand dollars and
the older and much scarcer book at half that sum?
Forget the price, and compare the two books.

It is not pleasant to say anything in detraction of
Morris, and I am sorry that I am not through with the
subject, but I must set over against him the name of
another man who in a humble way began to work in
the same field—if I may call it the same field—when
the broad Atlantic lay between them. I refer, of course,
to Thomas Mosher of Portland, Maine.

It is curious to remember that the two men who
have so influenced the style of the modern book,
William Morris and Thomas Mosher, began their
work, quite independently of each other, in the same
year, 1890. It is now almost forty years ago that I
bought, immediately upon its appearance, the first
Kelmscott Press book, *The Story of the Glittering Plain*.
I bought it from E. D. North, who was then with
Scribner's, because it interested me rather than because I thought it beautiful. The book created a
sensation at the time: it was hailed as a great achievement. Mosher's first book, whatever it was, created no
comment. He, so far as I know, made no pronounce-
ment; he merely went to work, and with the limited

A page, and a very beautiful page, from Morris's Kelmscott Chaucer

Secunda etas mūdi   Foliū   XI

Ecunda etas mūdi principiū a Noe habuit post diluuiū: qd fuit vniuersale p totū Anno sexcē
tesimo vite Noe a principio aūt mundi bm he. Millesimosexingentesimoquinquagesimosexto.
Sed bm.lxx. interptes quos Beda et Ysido. approbāt his mille ducenti ז. xlij. ז durat vsqz
ad abraham bm he. 292. annis. Sed bm.lxx. 842. annis. Ante diluuiū vo p.100. annos
Dominus apparuit Noe id ē quingentesimo anno vite Noe.

Oe diuini honoris et iusticie amator fi
liusLamech. ingenio mitis ז integer in
uenit grām corā dno. Cū cogitatio bo
minū pna erat ad malū. Oīm tpe oīes in vram
rectā reducere satagebat. Cūq˜ instaret finis vni
uerse carnis precepit ei dns vt faceret arcam de li
gnis leuigatis bituminatā intus et extra. que sit
trecētoz cubitoz geometroz longitudinis. Oro
sius ז post eū Augusti. ז Hugo. Cubitū geome
tricū sex cubitos vsuales facere dicūt: quā pticaz
noiant. Sit itaqz trecētoz pticaz lōgitudis: qn
ginganta latitudinis ז triginta altitudinis. i. a fun
do vsqz ad tabulatū sb tignis. Et i cubito cōsum
mab illā. In q̄ māsiūculas cenacla fenestrā ז osti
um i latere deorsum facies. Noe igit post cētus ז
tr. ānos ad arcā fabricatā. q̄ p solatio vite erant
necēria cōportauit. Cūctoruq̄ aialiū ad buādū ge
nus eoz masclos sil ז feminas piter introduxit.
Ipe deniqz ז filij eiˀ vxoz ז vxores filioz primo
die mē aprilˀ ingressus ē. Facto diluuio cū dns
oēm carne deleuit. Noe cū suis saluatˀ ē. Stetit
qz arca sup altissimos mōtes armenie. Qui loc̄
egressor vocaſ. Egressi vo grās egerūt. Et alta
re facto: deo sacrificabant.

Oe signū federis qd vo inter me et vos ז ad
homnē aniā. Gn.ix.

A Keus pluuialis siue Iris licet dicatur bie sex
vel quatuor colores. ʒn duos colores principa
liter habet. q duo iudicia repñtant. aq̄us diluuiū
pteritū figurat ne amplˀ timeaſ. igneus futuri iu
diciū signat per ignem vt certitudinaliter expecteſ

Illo diluuij Anno prima seculi etas terminata ē
ab Adaz vsqz ad diluuiū inclusiue. Etas scda ince
pit q̄ ז ad abrahe natiuitatē vsqz perdurat.

Oe vna cū filijs ז vxore ac filioz vxorib˜ er
archa egresso: ʒfestim altare edificatore cūctˀ
pecoribˀ volatilibusqz mūdis holocausta dno obˀ
tulit. Et eˀ odore suauitatˀ odoratˀ ē˜ dns. Pro
pter qd eidem dns benedixit ac filijs suis dicens.

A typical page from Koburger's Nuremberg Chronicle, 1493

means at his disposal—and they were extremely limited in Portland, Maine, in the early nineties—produced books which were beautiful in type and format, were easy to read and easy to hold; moreover, they had this great merit: they were published at a price which put them within reach of all. Mosher did not prate about art for the masses or the beauty of democracy, and then produce books which only rich men could buy; but by the sheer force of his good taste and good judgment he got the results he set out to secure. He was never a printer himself, but he had ideas and ideals, and he was able to impress them upon others; with the passage of time he came to command the best types, paper, and ink that could be had, and he used them like the artist that he was.

I have before me as I write two of the catalogues which, before the war, he used to issue annually. One is dated 1906: it is a slender catalogue of sixty-eight pages; the cover is of dark blue paper printed in an allover design in dark green, while in a small panel in the upper left-hand corner, in vermilion, is the title *The Mosher Books*, and the date. I have called it a catalogue: it is more—it is an anthology. Even more beautiful is the pamphlet issued four years later: it is now a booklet of eighty pages; the cover is old rose with the printing in two shades of the same color. Nothing could be more daintily simple than these brochures which were intended for gratuitous distribution. But I have only suggested their greatest, their most enduring charm. Never before or since, I believe, has a man made such a delicate appeal to the reader and the book-lover. With exquisite quotations in verse and in prose, from every source under the wide and starry sky, he called attention to the literary merit of his wares, saying just enough about type and size and binding to enable one to order by letter—for practically he sold only by mail.

Occasionally, not often,—not often enough,—someone went to Portland and asked where his shop or printery or office was, and practically no one knew. When he was at the height of his fame, known all over the world, someone went to Portland, registered at the hotel, and then asked where he could find T. B. Mosher. The clerk didn't know, had never heard of him, but he would inquire; after a time he returned, saying nobody knew; if he had ever lived in Portland he must be dead. A prophet is not without honor, and so forth.

Mosher's books have another merit which one looks for in vain elsewhere. I refer to their literary quality. I don't think he ever printed a book merely because it would sell, although I have no doubt that many people bought his books because he printed them—and they never regretted doing so. His selective taste was as unerring as his knowledge of the practical side of his business. He made the best literature of all time and of all countries popular, if so be a book may be called popular which in a nation of a hundred millions sells in hundreds only. But mass production was not for him.

Simplicity—what may be called readability—he kept ever before him. Whether a Mosher book was of large format or small, bound this way or that, one could always tell it at a glance—or could until every printer and publisher in the country copied more or less his style. Morris has his disciples,—Rudge, Rogers, Nash, Updike, Goudy,—but no less a debt is owed Mosher by those who may be called commercial publishers, and it is these who disseminate the taste of the nation; indeed, it seems to me our printers owe as much to Mosher as to Morris. Mosher may have thought of himself as democratic; he would have laughed to have heard himself called an aristocrat of publishers; but he was an aristocrat in his mind and in his method. All of us who love books, inside and out, are and will ever be in debt to Thomas Bird Mosher. I feel no hesitation in speaking of him. I never saw him, and I had only one letter from him, and that was when, some ten years ago, I wrote in the *Atlantic Monthly* a few lines of appreciation of the work he was doing in the making of fine books. I am glad I did; I am glad I spoke while yet he was alive; after his death, to say what I thought would merely have been to join in the chorus.

Some of the best writing brains of this country are functioning in the art of advertising. A cigarette advertiser has said, "There is a little Turkish in all good cigarettes, but"—some cigarette or other—"is all Turkish." In like manner, I should say that there is a little Mosher in all well-printed books, but the best-printed books are all Mosher. Bruce Rogers remarked to a lecturer who had paid a tribute to Mosher in the Grolier Club one evening, "I would rather have done his work than mine." It was generously said, but Bruce Rogers can afford to let others look after his fame: it is secure. But there is, I fear, some danger—because Mosher was a publisher and not a printer and because, as a publisher, he paid few or small royalties—that his real service to the book-lover will be forgotten.

Comparisons are always odious. There is glory enough for all. Both men are dead, but their work still lives after them; both in England and in this country we have not one supreme, but many excellent printers —and this is as it should be. It is absurd to suppose that if you want a finely printed book it must, necessarily, come from the press of so-and-so. There are many excellent printers. Edward Stern & Company, Inc., of Philadelphia, for example, who did this book, do not pose especially as "art printers," but they do good, conscientious work, of which this book is an example. The method by which it is printed—"the aquatone process"—makes the use of ugly, smelly, highly glazed inserts unnecessary for the printing of "half-tone" illustrations. It is the first—certainly one of the first commercial books to be printed in this manner, and will be far-reaching in its effect. The lines of Tennyson occur to me:—

> Most can raise the flowers now,
> For all have got the seed.

And the seed was planted by William Morris in England and by Thomas Bird Mosher in this country.

An interesting sampler

VI
THE BINDING

BINDING is an English rather than an American art, or craft, and it is—or was—a French or Italian rather than an English one. We Americans are a practical and inventive people; we can erect a substantial and magnificent building, or drill for and set a hundred miles of telegraph poles in an incredibly short time, or build a complicated piece of machinery that will add, or subtract, or multiply, or divide, a lot of figures faultlessly, while our friends abroad are putting a point to a lead pencil preparatory to making a calculation which will afterwards have to be "proved"—but we can hardly bind a book. Why this is so will be clear after a moment's thought. The system by which an old and complicated trade is learned is not ours. In the European sense, we have no apprentices and we do not develop craftsmen. If there happens to be a good binder in any of our large cities, the chances are ten to one that he is an old German or an old Frenchman, possibly an old Englishman, who is eking out an existence doing binding for the few of us who appreciate good work, are content to wait a long time for it, and to pay a very considerable price for it when done.

Some years ago a number of gentlemen in New York, members of the Grolier Club,—instigated, it would seem, by Robert Hoe,—brought to this country a group of expert Frenchmen skilled in their respective arts and established what was called the Club Bindery. Magnificent specimens of their work, undoubtedly the finest ever done in this country, were dispersed at the Hoe Sale in 1911, but money was lost in the enterprise

A "club binding" on a presentation copy of Goldsmith's "Traveller"

and the movement came to nothing. After painful vicissitudes, what was left of the effort went to Garden City and was swallowed up in the organization of Doubleday, Page and Company. There are several excellent what might be called trade binders in New York, but no one of the standing of Riviere and Son or Sangorski and Sutcliffe of London. At the moment of writing, a noble gesture is being made in Chicago by R. R. Donnelley and Sons, whose efforts should be supported, as their work is excellent, but in general it may be said that we do not bind in this country.

Another and very good reason why the binder's art has never flourished in this country is that never, until quite recently, has it been "protected." Until the last tariff act was passed, the date of the book carried the binding: that is to say, a book published over twenty years, or a book in a foreign language, came in duty free, no matter how magnificently and recently it was bound. It was quite usual for booksellers in London or in Paris to assemble a set of books, published at any time prior to 1900, say, bind it handsomely in calf or morocco, and send the set into this country quite free of duty. By the last tariff bill an effort was made to protect the American binder: the book or set of books, minus the cost of binding, is now valued at a proper sum and comes in duty free only if published over twenty years; and binding, if done within twenty years, is valued at an additional sum and is subject to a duty of thirty per cent on old books and twenty-five per cent on new.

It is a clumsy and unsatisfactory method, but our ingenuity has not contrived a better, and it affords some measure of protection to our binders; and if we are to remain a protectionist country—and I hope that we may—there is no reason why American bookbinders should not be expected to make some sort of headway against the European bookbinder, who pays perhaps seventy per cent less wages than our own. The free-trader will say, let the work be done where it can be done the cheapest and the best, but our great industries were not built up in that way. All were "infant indus-tries" in my boyhood, and look at them to-day—the admiration and the envy of the whole world.

This paper does not pretend to be a technical essay on the binder's art: it consists merely of the more or less casual observations of a book-collector who is deeply interested in all that goes into the making of a book from the moment when it is conceived by the author to the time when, "out of print and scarce," it is sought by the collector.

Bindings may perhaps be considered in two classes: first, those which were intended primarily for the pro-tection and identification of the book which they cover, and which cost at the time of manufacture only a few shillings; and others which, although they were de-signed to cover, protect, and identify books, were also works of art, in metal or leather or velvet, encrusted, it may be, with precious stones, or ornamented with curiously wrought carvings or some other elaborate decoration, not infrequently designed as gifts from one crowned head to another. The amateur who would study these must visit time and again the great museums or libraries abroad: the British Museum, the Bodleian at Oxford, and the Rylands Library at Manchester. The

A fine, unrestored Grolier binding

Pierpont Morgan Library also has some magnificent bindings, and there are some fine modern French examples in the Spencer Collection in the New York Public Library; and at least one gentleman in New York has a superb private collection; but in general it may be said that we know nothing about bindings in this country and that one is hardly likely to come upon anything better than indifferent specimens in the course of his wanderings through the bookshops of either New York, London, or Paris. In Italy one may possibly find a few,

A fine Grolier binding from the collection of Templeton Crocker, Esq.

An early binding in "oak boards"

and if one buys them he will have to pay an export tax, and may, indeed, be prevented from taking them out of the country altogether. The study of museum bindings, then, may be considered as beyond the scope of this paper: I have only one example which deserves to be called a "museum piece"—a fine, unrestored Grolier with an unexceptionable provenance. The large and characteristic "Grolier" here shown is from the collection of Templeton Crocker. We shall now briefly consider the less important examples of binding which may be seen at any good bookshop in New York or London.

The first English bindings available to the collector are those which date from the time of Henry VIII; these at the time of binding cost only a few pence. They are for the most part books which are simply but substantially sewed and placed between oak boards covered with leather. A binding "in boards" means, to-day, a binding of the cheapest and flimsiest character, however artistic it may be, either with or without a cloth spine; but originally the term meant just what it said: that the book had oak or other wood boards covered with leather, with clasps of metal or with "ties" of leather to keep the book closed. With the passage of time, wood boards, being heavy and clumsy and given to warping, gave way to pasteboard: that is to say, sheets of paper were pasted together, and when a "board" of sufficient thickness was thus obtained it was allowed to dry under pressure, and became "pasteboard." This was subsequently covered with leather, sometimes with silk or velvet, gradually ornamented and elaborated until the bindings became very magnificent indeed. They may have borne the title of the book only, or more likely the coat of arms of their owner—for any man or woman of sufficient wealth and position to own a book almost certainly had "arms."

Before considering bookbinding as a comparatively modern art, it may be well, in imagination, to examine a few old books curiously bound in boards and otherwise. I have one: Boethius's *De Consolatione Philosophiæ*. It is an English manuscript of the fifteenth century on vellum; the binding is contemporary, and consists of oak boards covered with deerskin let into another piece of deerskin, which completely surrounds it and terminates in a large knot; a lead clasp fastens the outer cover. This book was intended to be carried at the waist, and the knot prevented it from slipping from under the belt of the wearer. We are chiefly familiar with binding of this character from descriptions and illustrations in old books. The British Museum possesses several such on books of a religious character, but this is a "lay" book, and there are several recipes in English against colic written on one of the flyleaves at the end. Owing to the character of the leather, neither title nor arms are stamped thereon. And this may be as good a place as any to say that in olden times books very frequently had their titles lettered by hand, not on their backs,—or, more correctly speaking, on their "spines," —but on their fore edge. In such cases, the books when placed on shelves had their front edges exposed in order that their titles might be easily read—exactly opposite to the way we put our books on our shelves to-day. There were a large number of books so displayed in the treasure room of Messrs. Maggs Brothers when I was last in London.

I have another curious old manuscript written in Arabic, "according to the African fashion,"—whatever that fashion may be,—which is also enclosed, merely wrapped, in the skin seemingly of a goat, the hair of which still remains on the inside. The pages of the book seem never to have been fastened together. It

is accompanied by eight pages of manuscript, written in a fine hand by a former owner, a Dr. Codington, fully describing it; but I confess never to have read it with care. What I most sought was a date, and this, seemingly, is lacking.

My next example is a book bound for King Henry VIII, bearing his "arms." In this the boards are of oak, covered with

A Henry VIII binding

a dark brown calf; the centre panels of both covers bear the royal arms of the King, surrounded by a garter, stamped "in blind:" that is to say, without gold. In compartments on either side of the arms are four badges: the Tudor rose, the castle, the pomegranate, and the fleur-de-lis; while in a rectangular

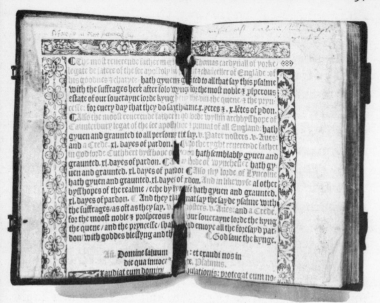

The end papers of a Henry VIII binding

border around the whole, in Gothic letters, is a Latin motto. The book is a copy of Pliny the Younger, and it has a special point of interest in that the binder used, for the front and back end papers, what may have been a unique example of an English Catholic Indulgence, granted by Thomas Wolsey when Cardinal of York. The upper part of this indulgence is printed in red and black Gothic letters, and is in English. The lower part is in Latin, and unfortunately of this lower part only half is intact; the other half has been torn away. It commences: "The most reuerende father in god Thomas cardynall of yorke legate de latere of the fee apoſtolyke . . . chanceller of Englade: of his goodnes & charyte hath gyuen . . . to all that ſay this pſalme with the ſuffrages here after folowynge, for the moſt

noble & pſperous eſtate of our ſouerayne lorde kyng
. . . the VIII: the quene . . . for euery day that they
do ſay th same,'' etc.

Many fragments of curious and priceless books have
been rescued from oblivion by taking to pieces very
carefully the printed sheets of paper or vellum out of
which was made the pasteboard for the binding of books;
and a great scholar like Wilberforce Eames of the New
York Public Library, who has been the recipient of
every honor which the learned of the world can show,
is frequently able to tell from careful study of the text,
the type, and the watermarks of the paper, whether or
not the scraps thus rescued have value.

There seems to be little doubt that leather-bound
books, ornamented with gold tooling, were brought
first to Venice from the East, and thence made their
way throughout Europe. France—that is to say, Paris
—early became, and has ever remained, the place where
the binder's art has flourished as nowhere else. The
work of the great French binders—Nicholas Eve and
Clovis, Le Gascon, Padeloup, and Derome—has never
been approached by the binders of other countries, but
their work was usually intended only for king, courtier,
or courtesan at the time of its execution, and to-day
genuine specimens of their work are practically unobtainable. But English bindings have, nevertheless, an
interest for us, even if they are not the very best, and
these alone we shall consider.

The first English binder of whom we have any
definite record is Thomas Berthelet, Royal Printer and
Binder to Henry VIII. One of his bills for binding is in
the British Museum, as is also a warrant signed by the

King ordering it to be paid. Berthelet bound books in satin and velvet, but he seems to have preferred leather, —calf,—white, black, or colored, and "gorgeously gilted," as he says, after the "Venecian fascion." It is pleasant to know that the bill was promptly paid—as binders' bills should always be. In amount it was "one hundred seventeen pounds sixpence and one halfpenny sterlyng:" a considerable sum in the year 1541. In the opinion of Cyril Davenport,—not always a reliable guide,—Berthelet also bound books for Queen Mary, Edward, and Elizabeth, the latter employing goldsmiths and expert needlewomen in elaborately ornamenting the books bound for her, some magnificent specimens of which are in the British Museum.

My only example of Elizabethan binding is a small book, curiously enough entitled *De Amore Conjugali*, bound in dark brown calf, ornamented with double lines, enclosing the badge of the Queen; a falcon crowned; on the dexter side of the mound a rose tree impressed in gold. The falcon was the crest of the Earl of Wiltshire, father of Anne Bullen.

An English Grolier. Thomas Wotton

About this time there lived in or near London an interesting bibliophile, Thomas Wotton. He was born in 1521 at Bocton Place in Kent, and came to be looked upon as a patron of learning and the fine arts. He had a fine collection of books, and he adopted Grolier's motto as his own, and many of the books bound for him bear the legend THOMAE WOTTONI ET AMICORUM. Hence he is frequently referred to as the English Grolier. Queen Elizabeth offered him knighthood, which he declined, and this title was subsequently conferred by James upon his son Henry, of whom Izaak Walton wrote the life. I am able to reproduce a binding from his library through the courtesy of my friend Templeton Crocker of San Francisco, who, hearing that I was interested in English bindings, very kindly sent me a choice selection that I might have the pleasure of studying them in my own library.

Authors, book-lovers, and collectors should try—hard as it may be—to keep a warm spot in their hearts for James I (VI of Scotland): he had all our failings and a lot which were peculiarly his own. I forgive him his *Counterblaste to Tobacco* on account of his *Basilikon Doron* addressed "to his Dearest Son Henry the Prince," over the manuscript of which, in the British Museum, I have several times pored until I feared the attendants suspected me of designs upon it. It is bound in very dark purple velvet, and the ornaments are cut out of thin gold finished by an engraver; above the royal coat of arms are the initials "J. R." The authorities say that this book was bound in Scotland, and that Scottish bindings of early date, like this, are very rare. Books bound for King James, after his coming to

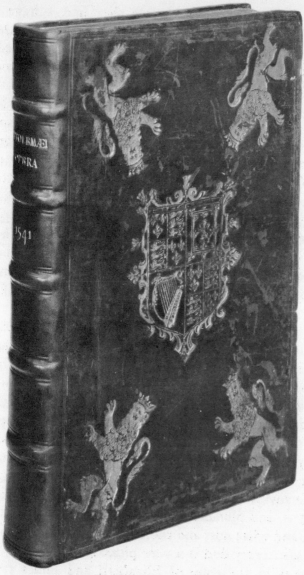

Bound for Henry Prince of Wales

THIS BOOK-COLLECTING GAME

England, are not rare, nor are they fine. I have a citron-colored example, which is characteristic of the period. In the centre are the royal arms, crowned, surrounded with a garter bearing the motto, HONI SOIT QUI MAL Y PENSE. Each corner is composed of an elaborate design, while the semé—that is to say, the field—is dotted with roses, a form of ornamentation more used for James I than for any other sovereign. English binding at this period was merely a copy of the French, and it is interesting to see a fine French style coarsely copied by an English or a Scotch binder, lacking both taste and skill. My James I example formerly belonged to Horace Walpole, and has his bookplate therein; as has also my example of binding for that splendid bibliophile, George II, who, according to Walpole, was made ill by the mere sight of a book.

Henry, Prince of Wales,—it will be remembered that he was little more than a lad when he died,—has been severely criticized for having so many of his books rebound. In 1609, his father purchased for him the library of his tutor, Lord Lumley, an antiquarian of Elizabeth's time, who had what was then considered, with one exception, the most valuable private library in England. But, in justification of Henry's act, it may well be that the Lumley books were in need of binding; in any event, Prince Henry had them bound with his arms, and plumes, and Scotch thistles, and Tudor roses, and what not; and those of us who own a book from his library find it a very pleasant possession.

It was in the time of Elizabeth and James that embroidered bindings became the fashion, and these

A superb embroidered binding, time of James the First

bindings, seemingly so delicate, have indeed resisted the wear and tear of the centuries surprisingly well. It may be that their apparent delicacy was their protection; in any event, there are some magnificent specimens in the British Museum. It was the age of needlework, and the magnificent old mansions which are the glory of the English countryside are full of embroidery attributed to the Queen of Scots and Queen Bess; indeed, had they produced all that is attributed to them, they must have stitched away their entire lifetimes to the total exclusion of the game of politics which we know they played: one lady losing and the other keeping her head as an exhibit of her skill—and the lack of it.

I hope I am not given to boasting, but I think my own example of embroidered binding at least as fine as any I have seen in any library. It covers a Bible of 1607; both sides and the back of the book are encrusted with gold and silver thread, while the story of the Garden of Eden and the fall of Adam are told in a picture of colored silks; at the bottom of each side is an inscription, "A Dreame." The back is divided into four panels, filled with trees, birds, insects, and the like, and the gilded edges are gauffered. For whom was this obviously royal binding made? I do not know. Reference has already been made to the style of binding affected by James's son, Prince Henry. His younger brother's—Charles the First's—reign was too troubled for him to give as much attention to his books and bindings as his early impulses would suggest.

A word here must be said upon that elusive subject, the bindings of the nuns of Little Gidding. The name is a fascinating one, but what we want to know is, did they bind or didn't they? And, if so, what? Nobody knows. It would be pleasant to think of a group of pretty English nuns stitching away at the embroidery covers of the innumerable Prayer Books and Bibles and dos-à-doses that have come down to us from the seventeenth century, but there is no warrant for it, auctioneers' and booksellers' catalogues to the contrary notwithstanding.

Nicholas Ferrar—who, with the Collets, was the founder of the English Protestant Nunnery of Little Gidding—was born in 1592. Up to his twenty-first year he led a secluded life, occupied by incessant study. In 1613 he left England to recruit his health by foreign travel, and remained abroad for six years. Returning home, he for a short time was in Parliament, but he could not give his heart either to business or to politics. In 1625, when the plague was raging in London, Ferrar and his mother, a most devout lady, left town and took refuge with his brother-in-law, John Collet, at Bourne. Some little time before, his mother had purchased the manor of Little Gidding, Huntingdonshire; and now first the church, which had been used as a barn, and afterwards the manor house were put in order, and the whole clan of Ferrars and Collets—the Collet family numbered fourteen children —took up their residence there, to live a life of prayer and praise and recreative work under the ordering and management of Ferrar. The "nuns" were his nieces. Each of them took charge of the housekeeping by turns; all the ladies, moreover, besides teaching in a little school, were "trained surgeons" and they wore "black stuff gowns all of one pattern, and always the same."

It was one of Ferrar's principles that everyone should learn a trade, and the trade practised at Little Gidding was that of bookbinding. "An ingenious bookbinder" was entertained to instruct the whole family in the art of binding, gilding, and lettering. Visitors were welcome if they chose to come, but nothing was allowed to interrupt the regular course of daily life within the house itself. On this charming but slender foundation, apparently, has arisen the legend that there are books about that are the work of the nuns of Little Gidding. The nearest thing that I ever saw to a Little Gidding binding—to know it— is a large *Book of Common Prayer, the Psalms and Bible*, which bears the inscription of Joyce Collet, one of the nieces, which was used as the family Bible, on the blank leaves of which is a manuscript record of the births and deaths in the family from 1683 to 1719. It is a superb book bound in crimson velvet with a rose-stamped border, but it can hardly be the work of amateurs, such as the Little Gidding ladies appear to have been. I am able to illustrate the binding of this book also by reason of the courtesy of Mr. Crocker, and I wish that I could be certain that it is what it purports to be—a "Little Gidding binding." Beverly Chew, whom I once consulted on this subject, told me that he had never, to his knowledge, seen a book that was the work of the Little Gidding nuns.

I once received a letter from an anonymous correspondent, setting me right as to what kings were and what were not *in* "the best fashionable society."

The Book of Common Prayer, the Psalms, and Bible.
Joyce Collet's copy, from the Crocker Collection

Queen Victoria, I was told, herself remarked one day, when she was about fifty, that she heard with surprise that she was not *in;* nor was James I. Charles I, the "Martyr," had too many troubles for him to discover whether he was *in* or not, but Charles II was *in*, undoubtedly; the first three Georges were not. George IV, as Prince Regent, undoubtedly, "led" London society—whither, let us not inquire. The Prince Consort was laughed at by society. King Edward always led, King George V never; the present Prince of Wales leads it. Perhaps he may have thought he was leading the best American society during his stay, a year or two ago, on Long Island: be this as it may. Curiously enough, the kings that were *in* all patronized the binder except George III. He was a great collector—of books, if he dissipated somewhat his Empire.

With the return of Charles II from his "travels"—as he wittily referred to his exile—the art of the binder flourished in England as it had never done before, and as I feel it has not done since. The supreme name in English binding is that of Samuel Mearne. Among the documents in the Record Office is one reading: "Charles the Second by the Grace of God, King of England, etc. . . . know yee that wee are credibly informed our beloved subject Samuel Mearne of London, stationer, hath in the art or misterie of binding bookes . . . . certain knowledge . . . and wee doe by these presents . . . appoint him, the said Samuel Mearne, the booke-binder of us," etc. Napoleon once remarked that he had found the crown of France in the gutter; that he had picked it up and put it on his head. Samuel Mearne might have paraphrased this remark. But unluckily we know very little about Mearne: his name does not appear in the *Dictionary of National Biography*, and the best authority on English bindings,

A "Mearne" cottageroof binding

Gordon Duff, in a paper entitled *The Great Mearne Myth*, says: "Samuel Mearne was a politician—a bookseller and publisher, not a craftsman. He was a 'Searcher' for Charles II, for scandalous books—not scandalous in our sense, but books that taught Popish practice or false doctrine, in favor of, or maybe it was against, infant baptism." Like our own bootleggers, he is said to have seized merchandise to destroy it and then sold it to his own profit. He died in 1683 and was succeeded by his son as Bookbinder, Bookseller, and Stationer to King Charles; the son lived only a short time, and was succeeded in office by William Churchill; but no authority has ever spoken of him as a binder.

A binder was, in those days, an humble craftsman; it took very little capital to become one; and John Bagford, to whom we are indebted for what little we know about Mearne, refers to a man named Suckerman as uncommonly skilled in gilding; maybe it is to Suckerman that we are indebted for what are commonly called Mearne bindings. John Bagford was a shoemaker and leather merchant, who had a turn for collecting; anything that related to a book—prints, broadsides, title-pages, designs for binding, and information relative thereto, anything and everything— he packed into the sixty-four folio volumes, a sort of glorified scrapbook, which is now in the British Museum.

But whoever is to be credited with what are called Mearne bindings used the finest leathers then obtainable; and, however he may have been influenced by the French binders of the period, he invented or perfected one important and distinguished contribution to the binder's art: I refer, of course, to the "cottage design." Mearne bindings—as I shall continue to call them—fall naturally into three classes: the "rectangular," in which there is a panel formed by the lines conforming to the volume itself, usually with important centre ornamentation and further decoration at the angles; the "allover," in which, as the name implies, a geometrical or conventional design entirely covers both sides of the book; and the "cottage," which usually consists of a rectangular panel, in which the upper and lower lines are made to take a gable shape, as in a cottage roof. In these bindings it was usual to avoid the sharp apex of the gables by breaking them inwards, and perhaps leading them into the elaborate centre ornament, so that the "cottage" effect is not immediately noticed. But to describe a binding in mere words is like attempting to suggest the beauty of color or a perfume: they must be seen and carefully studied before their full beauty is apparent; and, as in every other form of art, the more one knows the more one enjoys a fine example.

One specimen of Samuel Mearne—I bought it from Pickering and Chatto for a Mearne—covers a copy of Butler's *Hudibras*. It is described as being a fine example of contemporary English red morocco, super extra gilt, with royal arms on sides and royal cypher, C. R., with much more of lesser interest. Butler's *Hudibras* (pretty dull to-day, if truth be told—except for a lot of phrases which are now part and parcel of our daily talk) was Charles the Second's favorite poem. We are told

> He never ate, nor drank nor slept,
> But Hudibras still near him kept;
> Nor would he go to Church or so
> But Hudibras must with him go.

Curiously enough, Mearne, according to the records, bound innumerable Bibles and Prayer Books in his best manner for the roisterous King. Did we not know that Charles II spent much of his time with and his money upon the ladies, one might suppose that his favorite occupation was the pious one of giving away these books, bound with his arms, and it is quite in character that when he went to church a *Hudibras* went with him to while away a tedious sermon. The school of Mearne, however, continued until it was finally absorbed in that of a binder who was second only in influence to Mearne—Roger Payne; and here we come upon a character, if you will.

With Roger Payne we enter at last upon a period of which something is definitely known. He was born at Windsor in 1739, and for a short time worked for Thomas Osborne, the bookseller, who had the distinction of having been knocked down by Dr. Johnson with a copy of his Dictionary, if a legend is true, but no doubt Johnson more correctly told the story to Boswell when he said: "Sir, Osborne was impertinent to me and I beat him." Through the kindness of another bookseller, "Honest Tom Payne" (but no relation to Tom Paine, the author of *The Age of Reason* to whom we Americans owe so much), Roger Payne was set up in business as a bookbinder, and with his brother and later with another man, Richard Wier, and Wier's wife, became the leading binder of the metropolis. He worked assiduously, giving his personal attention to the commissions entrusted to his care, and he was scrupulously honest; but he was a drunkard and lived in misery in an alley just off St. Martin's Lane.

I have a small example of his binding, and I never understood how he came by his great reputation until, several years ago, through the kindness of Dr. Henry Guppy, the Librarian of the Rylands Library, I had an opportunity of carefully examining some fine examples of his work, bound for his great patron, John Earl Spencer: these are indeed superb. While to some extent influenced by his predecessors,—as all binders since his time have been,—Payne, in a large measure, took his own line and kept it. His best work was usually done in straight-grained morocco, of either dark blue, bright red, and olive, or citron color. The sides of his books were frequently almost plain, while the spine was elaborately tooled, and quite frequently there was more gilding on the *doublure*, or lining inside the book, than on the outside; Payne did not make his display for the casual. His ornamental devices were small circlets, crescents, stars, acorns, roses, dots, and running vines and tiny leaves; yet with this seemingly meagre assortment of irons he succeeded in producing some of the most beautiful of semi-modern English bindings. His end papers were usually "stayned" by himself, to match or contrast with the cover of the binding; and an amusing feature of a transaction with Payne was the receipt of a characteristic bill. Collectors try, and almost in vain, to get a fine binding and a fine bill. They do not now often come together: if the bill is interesting, the binding is not, and vice versa. I have a fine, if small, example of his work, genuine without a doubt, and a fine bill; but alas! they do not mate together—the bill refers to another book. I paid dear old Jimmy Tregaskis fifty-odd pounds for it, many years ago. It sets forth in great detail what was done and the itemized cost thereof.

Payne's chief patrons were Earl Spencer, the Duke of Devonshire, and the Reverend Clayton Cracherode, the famous bibliophile who at his death bequeathed his books to the British Museum. There they may be studied with delight, but undoubtedly his master-piece was the *Æschylus*, bound for Earl Spencer, and now with the "original and diverting bill"—as Dibdin calls it—in the great Rylands Library in Manchester. If you, reader, ever have an opportunity of examining it, don't miss it; it is one of the finest bindings ever executed in England, and it cost the noble Earl just sixteen pounds, seven shillings!

The last years of Payne's life were tragic: ruined by drink and dissipation, he was kept alive by the charity of his friends and former patrons, who buried him, when dead, in the churchyard of St. Martin's-in-the-Fields. I secured a curious portrait of him at the sale of the library of my friend Beverly Chew. It was published after his death, and shows him at work in his shop, with his unkempt hair, his curiously elon-gated visage—a picture of misery and distress. Re-prints of this portrait, slightly colored, are common; the original was published by S. Harding, 127 Pall Mall, March 1, 1800.

Suckerman (Mearne's gilder) is not an English name; Payne, as I have said, is the first English binder

ROGERUS PAYNE,

Natus Vindesor: MDCCXXXIX. denatus Londin: MDCCLXXXXVII.

Effigiemhanc graphicam solertis BIBLIOPEGI Μνημόσυνον meritis BIBLIOPOLA dedit.

Etch.ᵈ   by S. Harding, Nᵒ 127, Pall Mall, March ᵗ 1800.

Sumptibus Thomæ Payne.

of whom anything is known. The names of other famous English binders—Baumgarten, Kalthoeber, Staggemeier, Hayday, Riviere, Zaehnsdorf, Sangorski, and Sutcliffe—seem to bear out the statement with which I began this paper: that binding is a continental rather than an English art.

Who was "Edwards of Halifax," the next important English binder? Was he a binder? Was he a craftsman himself? Or did he keep a shop and give his name to a certain type of binding? I have searched the books and I have asked the question, but without result; occasionally a London bookseller has cleared his throat as if to say something wise—and then changed his mind. If I am able to throw some light on the subject it is because Arthur Swann, who long functioned as an auctioneer, now become a bookseller—and a good one —sent to England and secured from several sources a batch of data which I have digested.

The founder of the firm of Edwards and Sons was William Edwards, a bookseller and binder, who set up his business in a stable in Halifax in Yorkshire, in 1763. He had three sons, but it was the father who originated the bindings which bear the name. He settled two sons, James and John, in business in London, in 1784, under the name of Edwards and Sons. The establishment was in Pall Mall; it specialized in fine books, and James became "opulent." He it was who, in 1785, took out a patent for the famous vellum bindings with which the name Edwards is associated. Like our own Dr. Rosenbach, he became a distinguished collector as well as a bookseller, and his great possession was a book known as the Bedford

Missal. It is claimed that this is the most beautiful
book in the world—in any event, it ranks with the
famous Book of Kells, and is a book with a history.
It was made for John, Duke of Bedford, and his wife
Anne, John being the son of King Henry IV of England.
Presented by the Duchess to King Henry VI on
Christmas Eve in the year 1430, it later became the
property of Henry II of France—and so on. It is a book
twelve inches high, eight inches wide, and about
three inches thick. It is, of course, a manuscript, but
it is not a missal, nor is it a Book of Hours, nor any
other recognized service book; its special beauty lies
in the magnificence and number of its illustrations.

This great book came up for sale at auction in 1786,
and George III sent his librarian, Mr. Nicoll, to
examine it, and on receiving his glowing report
expressed the intention of buying it.

"It will bring a high price, Your Majesty," said
the librarian.

"How high?" asked the King.

"Two hundred guineas," was the reply.

"Two hundred guineas for a book!" exclaimed the
Queen, putting down her knitting, and raising her
hands with horror at the idea.

"Still I'll have it," said the King, "but as the
Queen thinks two hundred guineas enough, I'll not
go higher." And he didn't, but Edwards did: he bid
two hundred and three guineas, and got the book.

Edwards sold his stock and retired from business in
1805, married, purchased Harrow Grove, a famous old
manor house not far from St. Albans, which had been
the country residence of several Archbishops of Can-

terbury; but he kept the Bedford Missal. Ten years later, being in poor health, his library was removed to a house in George Street, Hanover Square, and sold at auction on April 5, 1815, the famous book being bought by the Marquis of Blandford for six hundred and eighty-seven guineas; but the Marquis, like other extravagant book-buyers, having no ready money, had to borrow five hundred pounds with the book pledged, and it remained in pawn, so to speak, for eighteen years, when it was again sold at auction for eleven hundred guineas; and it is now in the British Museum, where I examined it last summer, with an attendant standing by to turn its leaves.

This is a long digression; we shall now return to the business in Halifax. When the founder died, he was succeeded by his son Thomas, who united with book-selling the sale of patent medicines—as was not unusual at that time. He specialized, however, in bindings, and became famous for books with fore-edge paintings, books bound in "Etruscan" calf, and books bound in transparent vellum, for which a patent was in the family. All of these appear to have been produced in Halifax. Slater seems to think that James Edwards took out a patent for fore-edge painting: this is a mistake. This same process was employed by others, and it was a development of painting a title or otherwise decorating the fore edge of a book. It consists of fanning or spreading out the leaves of a book, and, having fastened them securely, of painting the edges in such a manner that the picture will show only when the book is open, as it was when the work was done; when closed, the painting will disappear.

A hundred years ago, this form of decoration was very popular; it is a pretty if rather petty art, and whoever practised it must have been kept busy painting characteristic English scenes, peaceful landscapes of the countryside, a river perhaps, with a bridge or a church or a castle in the background. I have a nice example, bought twenty or more years ago: it is on a copy of Gray's *Poems*, bound in the straight-grained crimson morocco of a century ago, and the view is of Stoke Poges churchyard. The book was printed in 1800, and the binding has the stamp on the edge (not inside), BOUND BY TAYLOR & HESSEY. We have no reason to believe that they were binders, but we do know that they had a shop at 93 Fleet Street, as from that address they published *Endymion* for Keats and *Elia* for Charles Lamb. It used to be said that this was a difficult art (which I never believed) and that it was a lost art (which I doubted); but quite recently the market has been flooded with books in nice old straight-grained morocco bindings, and having seemingly new and pretty fore-edge paintings under the gold. If the art was lost, it is evident that someone has found it and is doing very well with it. If a bookseller, seeking to sell a genuine old example,—if indeed there are any left,—tells you that the new are inferior to the old, just laugh at him.

The patent granted to James Edwards was for a method of rendering vellum transparent so that a painting on the underneath side shows through. On account of its color and surface, vellum soils easily. A book bound in vellum, in Edwards's manner, with its decoration in water color or in India ink on the

A fine example of an "Edwards of Halifax" binding

underside of the vellum, may be easily cleaned without injury to the decoration. I sold several fine examples of these bindings at the sale of "The Books of a Busted Bibliophile" in New York, in December 1926, for about half what they cost me in London ten or fifteen years ago, so little intelligent interest is taken in bindings in this country. I still have one of the finest bindings in this manner that I have ever seen, with the exception of the Prayer Book with the arms of Charlotte, Queen Consort of George III, thereon, now in the British Museum.

James Edwards was a gentleman, and he lived on terms of intimacy with all the great book-collectors of his day, including the noble Earl Spencer, the founder of what is now the Rylands Library in Manchester. Edwards died in 1816, at the age of fifty-nine, and was buried in a coffin made of the wood of his bookcases in Harrow Church. On the north wall of the chancel is a tablet to his memory; I saw it two years ago. It has a long inscription, ending with the text: "Mark the perfect man, and behold the upright: for the end of that man is peace." And, be it remembered, the man was a bookseller. Let us have more such booksellers: the more the better.

One more name remains to be mentioned, and we are with the binders of yesterday: Thomas Gosden, the sporting bookbinder, as he was known to his friends. You will search the English reference books in vain for anything more than a footnote in regard to this interesting character, but the late William Loring Andrews of New York made a special study of him and published it in a charmingly illustrated book, *An English Nineteenth-Century Sportsman and Bibliophile.*

On his business card Gosden described himself as a bookbinder, publisher, and print-seller, but he was more than this: he was an excellent sportsman with rod and gun, and an ardent antiquarian. He spent a great deal of his time poking about in churches and graveyards, making drawings of tombs and tablets, and—if the truth must be told—making them not overwell. I have several of his drawings; one of the stone covering the grave of Dr. Johnson in the Poets' Corner of Westminster Abbey, and another of the tomb of Isaac Watts. These are simple in character, and from the evident lack of skill shown in these and others that I have seen, which are grotesquely out of drawing, I am quite certain that he did not himself design or draw the exquisite little tools, of flies and fish and reels and rods and baskets, to say nothing of sportsmen themselves, very much in miniature, as he is sometimes said to have done. Nor is it necessary that he should: he created a style—that is enough.

An excellent example of Gosden binding

Examples of Gosden bindings cover almost invariably books on some form of sport; they are not now too easy to come upon, owing perhaps to the fact that there is a group of collectors in New York, led by David Wagstaff, who have been buying them assiduously for some years. I have one, *Anecdotes on the Origin and Antiquity of Horse-Racing*, which he himself published from his address in Bedford Street (it was his own copy with his bookplate), and several on angling, which seems to have been his favorite recreation. One of his most common bindings is also one of his best: it is a copy of Walton's *Angler*, bound in dark green calf; on one side of it is a portrait of old Izaak, and on the other a portrait of his friend and disciple, Cotton, while above and below are emblems of the sport with which these names will ever be associated. The sides appear invariably to have been stamped in blind, and I am of the opinion that one large brass stamp was used to crush the design into the leather; the back is tooled partly in gilt and partly in blind. Loring Andrews says that this binding is found so frequently that he is of the opinion that it was used upon an entire edition of the *Angler;* but he adds—and I agree with him—that it is quite as satisfactory as one entirely tooled by hand.

Either necessity or choice made it necessary for Gosden to change his business location at least three times; he is known to have had a shop in Piccadilly, in St. Martin's Lane, and Bedford Street, Covent Garden. It was from this address that he published an engraving of the famous sporting picture, "The Jovial Fox Hunters." The original painting is now in the possession of my friend, Harry Worcester Smith, who, among his many other sporting distinctions, not long ago rode a steeplechase against professionals—and won; thus repeating at the age of sixty a distinction which he first achieved at thirty. Needless to say, he keeps himself—as all sportsmen should—in the pink of condition: the cup that cheers as well as inebriates and the delight of strong cigars after dinner are joys that are not his.

To return to Thomas Gosden: he seems never to have heard—or if he heard, he forgot—the old adage, "Keep your shop and your shop will keep you." He came to a sticky end; he neglected his business, became a bankrupt, and, dying suddenly, was buried in the churchyard of St. Clement Danes. He will ever be held in affectionate remembrance by all collectors of sporting books.

But Thomas Gosden, interesting figure though he was, can hardly be said to have left any impress upon the art of the binder—that distinction belongs to the man we call Samuel Mearne and to Roger Payne. Payne's influence, indeed, is present to-day, although it may for a moment have been eclipsed by the overelaborated style with which the names of Sangorski and Sutcliffe are identified; happily there is promise of return to the simplicity of Payne and his immediate successors. Payne died in 1797; his followers were Hering, Kalthoeber, and Lewis. Hering, who worked for Payne, inherited his tools and imitated his manner, but he was not as particular as Payne in the selection of his leathers, and his work lacks distinction, as the work of a copyist always lacks the character of the master. Charles Lewis's work I like better, and I am able to show a fine and characteristic specimen from the collection of my friend Mr. Frank B. Bemis, of Boston, whose motto, perhaps unconsciously adopted, is: "Only the best need apply."

About the middle of the nineteenth century there flourished in London a commercial binder: that is to

A Dutch silver binding

A finely chased silver binding

say, he was largely employed by the trade, whose bindings possess the merit of simplicity and delicacy, yet with hardly a trace of decoration. Excellent sewing, forwarding, and lettering; the use of very thin boards, making, nevertheless, covers which lie very flat —these are the sterling qualities with which the name of Francis Bedford is associated. Read between the lines at the bottom of the inside cover of a book bound in plain crushed Levant morocco, and if you read—and you may need a magnifying glass—the name of F. Bedford, you may be sure that the book is well bound; if "washed," that the job has been well done. Who he was, who his successor is, I have been unable to discover. Living in Daylesford, a hamlet in Pennsylvania, so far from the seat of knowledge, information that is commonplace in London is here difficult to secure. To-day the best English binders are Messrs. Riviere and Son, Zaehnsdorf, and Sangorski and Sutcliffe. The first two are noted for good sound work in crushed Levant morocco; the latter for a type of binding much affected by collectors who value bindings more than books. I refer, of course, to those overelaborated covers, which are nevertheless works of art—only I have the feeling that they are somewhat out of place on a book. It has been said, and truly, that books cannot live without bindings; in like manner, I should like to suggest that Sangorski and Sutcliffe bindings are so beautiful that they do not require books— they are themselves works of art.

Another example of silver binding

There remain to be mentioned an abomination known as tree calf, an invention of one Clarke, sometime a partner of Francis Bedford, I believe, and the beautiful Dutch and German silver bindings usually found on books of devotional character. These, like the Sangorski and Sutcliffe examples, always seem to be more bric-a-brac than books, but collectors will wish specimens of all, and good examples are becoming very scarce. Beverly Chew had some fine examples, which at his death were bequeathed to the Grolier Club.

A word may be permitted on the subject of books bound in vellum, a fashion that came back with

William Morris and his Kelmscott Press. Anyone who wishes books bound in vellum "with ties" may have them—they are not for me. They are impossible to hold and to read, and should one lay one down to fill

one's pipe,—and a book and a pipe should go together, — lo and behold, the binding is curled up beyond recognition. I may be told that the ties will prevent warping. True, but who wishes to tie a book closed as he puts it down? And did William Morris forget that "ties" never last? Hardly an important sixteenth-century book but had its ties or clasps. Where are the ties now? Almost invariably they have disappeared.

Fine example of
Cobden-Sanderson binding

One other great binder, perhaps the greatest, remains to be named, Thomas J. Cobden-Sanderson. He was, I venture to say, the last and the greatest of the Victorian craftsmen, as Morris was the first and best advertised. It was Mrs. Morris who suggested to Cobden-Sanderson the idea of becoming a binder after he had nearly killed himself with uncongenial legal work. He was a small, insignificant-looking man (I once sat next to him at dinner, but he was so shy that

I could get nothing out of him), and was the husband of a militant suffragette (doubtless his wife had scared him so that he lost the power of speech), but he was a great binder. He served an apprenticeship under De Coverley, whom he quickly excelled, and his naturally fine taste was improved by his careful study of the masters of his art, French as well as English. His finest bindings are signed by himself and dated; subsequently he established the Doves Bindery, and in 1900—after the Kelmscott Press had ceased producing —the Doves Press. Of this press, the finest example is said to be the Bible in five quarto volumes. Personally I do not care for it: I have the old-fashioned idea that a book should be made to read, and I doubt if the Doves Press Bible can be read.

I should decline to call a book "bound" if in boards, or in boards with a cloth spine, or bound in any manner less substantial than cloth. But perhaps I am wrong, for as the paper out of which the book is made is simply wood pulp, which will

A Bible in black morocco with silver ornaments

A "Riviere" binding on first edition of the Rubaiyat

A Sangorski and Sutcliffe binding on a first Rubaiyat

disintegrate with time, it is hardly worth while to put a durable binding upon it. But fifty or seventy-five years ago, when rag paper was yet used,—not necessarily linen rags,—which is practically nonex-istent to-day, books were sometimes very beautifully and substan-tially bound in cloth. I am able to show several examples of such bind-ings, one of which is upon a book bearing the imprint of Dayton and Wentworth, Boston, 1854; the gold stamping on this book is almost as bright as the day of issue.

A trade binding of seventy-five years ago

I am sometimes asked, "Can you give me the name of a good binder? I have a set of"—something or other—"which is falling to pieces; the binding is broken at the hinges, and I should like to have it rebound." My reply invariably is: Unless the set is valuable—which usually it is not—the best thing is to tie it up with a piece of string and put it on the top or bottom shelf of your bookcase and forget it. If you bind it, it will cost you more, probably, than if you went into a bookshop and bought a new—and a better—set. Our commercial machine-made bindings are fairly good, but they are bound in quantities; good binders cannot afford to bother with odd jobs of binding, unless they are well paid; the cost of material is high, and good labor is scarce. And if it is a waste of money to have a set of any but the finest books rebound, it is frequently to reduce your highly prized volume by eighty per cent of its value to put it in the binder's hands. This statement requires explanation.

We may suppose that one has picked up a very valuable book upon a stall for a few shillings. The book is in tatters; it may lack one or both covers; it may, in short, be such a volume as one has either to bind or to throw away. In that case, go to the best binder you know, and carefully—very explicitly—tell him what you wish done: the book must be very carefully collated; not a fraction of its size is to be lost; the edges are to be gold on the rough; and it is to be put in a plain crushed Levant morocco jacket, and lettered so-and-so. Then you will have saved an old book, and every time you see it you will feel a certain satisfaction—and wish the book were in its original condition.

The temptation to bind is almost irresistible, but it should be overcome. It is, I admit, difficult: one looks at one's books in shabby, "shaken" cloth covers, from which perhaps library labels have been unskillfully removed, and thinks how much better they would look if decked in full or half leather with, perchance, some little ornament or emblem or mark of ownership which the book would then carry to its dying day. But this impulse should be resisted; the books must be allowed to remain as they are. I have a rival, Morris

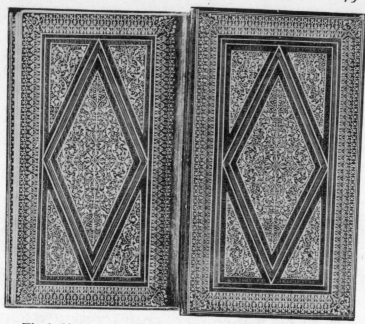

*The doublure, or inside leathers of a finely bound book: when the
doublure is very elaborate, as in this case, the outside of
the book is frequently very plain*

L. Parrish. He specializes in the moderns: in Carroll,
of which he has several hundred items, and in Trollope, Meredith, Hardy, and a lot of others and—wise
man that he is—he won't touch a rebound volume
at any price. He is a patient man and can afford to
wait. It is not much fun to go to your shelves and get
down a book to show to a friend, and then have to
apologize for its being "in binding." Mr. Parrish is so
extreme in his views as not even to approve of Solander
cases. He keeps his books in cases with glass doors,
inside which are dark shades on rollers to keep the
light from fading the original cloth covers. Any book
which has been in a lending library from which a

label has been "skillfully removed" should be carefully examined before placing it upon one's shelves.
And any bound book, no matter how thin it may be,
should have its title lettered on its spine; nothing is
more annoying than to look for a book on a shelf,
having no clue to its identity except its size and color.
Is it the volume you are looking for? No; you take
down another and another—muttering things the
while which will not bear repeating.

A word may be said in regard to the effect of coal
gas and illuminating gas on books in old bindings.
They are most harmful, and unless great care is taken
it will be only a few years before the leather shows
signs of disintegration, especially at the "hinge," and
presently the binding will fall to pieces. To keep
bindings in good condition, it is well to have them
treated occasionally by an expert; or, if one is so
minded, he can secure the necessary preservatives from
any good binder. Messrs. Zaehnsdorf, of London,
make and sell an excellent compound known as
Hutchin's "Curator Preservative," also a "Leather
Veneer," which is said to give excellent results, but
I have never found it wise to compete with a craftsman. Unless one is very neat and dextrous, like my
friend William Macey Stone, one is apt to make a mess
of things; indeed, I should, I think, prefer to be my
own dentist and have an expert look after my books.

No reader of this book will know better than the
writer how imperfect it is: the subject is a difficult one,
and opinions may differ, but I have endeavored to
make only such statements as I could substantiate and
illustrate with examples either from my own collection or from the much finer collections of several
friends, to whom I am greatly indebted.

VII

THE AUCTION ROOM

THERE are a lot of proverbs and cant phrases designed to tell you what kind of man the other fellow is. One immediately occurs to me: "A man is known by the company he keeps." But if one wants to know what kind of fellow he himself is, he can hardly do better than watch himself function in the auction room: the result will hardly be pleasing.

The first time I went to an auction in the private house of an acquaintance I outbid a man I didn't like for several items I had no use for, including a filthy and dilapidated refrigerator and a bedstead so large that I could not get it into the room which I had in mind when I bought it. Then it was that I discovered that I was of a mean, covetous, and acquisitive disposition. What my wife said of that refrigerator I shall not print, and I can see that bedstead now, across a chasm of years: it was a huge black-walnut affair, with festoons of flowers, fruit, and thorn pieces cut out and glued upon the headboard in a style which we now disdainfully call "early Victorian." The refrigerator I gave to the colored man hired to haul it, and the mattresses which came with the bed, for excellent reasons, were burned. The services of a carpenter with a saw were required before the bedstead, a monstrosity, could be brought into the house, and finally we had a supply of fine and expensive kindling. And to this day, when I see some poor wretch—as he invariably seems to be—bidding against me for something I don't in the least need, I feel an evil spirit rising within me, and hardly need the encouraging voice and smile of the auctioneer urging me on to something very like destruction. To me the auction room is a flame and I am a moth—and how I singe my wings!

Theoretically and superficially, an auction sale—whether it be of a railroad sold under foreclosure of a mortgage from the steps of some county court house or of a lot of rugs disposed of under the blaze of artificial light between dark velvet curtains—is about the fairest way of buying and selling any given piece of merchandise there is; but actually, *Caveat emptor*. Things are not always what they seem. In old times a bell was rung announcing that the sale was about to begin, but if the auctioneer—who wanted to begin and end the sale in favor of some particular bidder—rang the bell in his pocket so that it was not heard, and knocked down the property before most people knew that the sale was on, what then? And what is to prevent a "knock-out" and a dozen other forms of iniquity? "There are tricks in all trades," and the auction game is fuller of tricks than most: I know what I know and it has cost me something to learn.

For what information we have of the first book auctions, we are indebted to John Lawler, sometime chief book-cataloguer of the ancient firm of Sotheby's. He, with tireless patience and rare knowledge, compiled a little book on the subject, from which we learn that the first auctioneer in England was William Cooper, a bookseller living in 1676, at the Sign of the Pelican in Little Britain. Little Britain is a district just back of St. Bartholomew's Hospital in London. In Cooper's preface to his first catalogue, he says: "It

hath not been usual here in England to make sale of
books by way of auction *or who will give most for them*,
but it hath been practiced in other countries to the
advantage of both buyers and sellers . . . and it is
hoped that this way will not be unacceptable to
Scholars." The catalogue in which this statement
appeared was that of Doctor Lazarus Seaman, a
prominent theologian of the City of London, whose
library of fifteen or twenty thousand volumes fetched
a total of about three thousand pounds. It is hardly
worth our while to comment upon those halcyon
days—"those halcyon days, that golden age is gone"
—when an Indian Bible of John Eliot could be had for
nineteen shillings and the Homer of 1488 for nine.

But if Cooper was the first, and Millington the
most important of the early auctioneers, John Dunton
—author, printer, bookseller, auctioneer, and traveler—
was the most interesting. He was born in 1659 and his
autobiography, *The Life and Errors of John Dunton*, will
well repay reading. Should not the Life of every man
be called his Life and Errors? It was the late Clement
Shorter, the ardent book-collector and editor of the
Sphere, who first called my attention to this curious
book, which is very little known. Dunton learned to
love women and books at the same time—in his fourteenth year—and he early adventured with both. He
claims to have published six hundred books, which is,
of course, nonsense; but he published a great many, and
if he held no auction sales in England, he held many
in Ireland. When a depression fell upon the book trade
at home, he promptly sailed for Boston, leaving his
wife Elizabeth—whom he affectionately called "Iris"

—behind him. "Absence endears a wife" was one of his maxims: many men have unconsciously adopted it. In Boston—where, he says, five hundred pounds was owing him—he was well received, and he visited the eminent divines that were then sprouting vigorously in the rocky soil of New England. But he does not appear to have collected the money,—or if he did, he spent it,—for on his return home he was sought by bailiffs, and to escape arrest kept within doors for almost a year, finally escaping to Holland and what is now Germany. But this is a digression.

In 1764, Henry Fielding's library was sold; books filled with his autograph notes brought but a few shillings each, and five volumes of legal manuscripts in his own handwriting only thirteen shillings. Contrast such prices with the thousand and odd pounds which the novelist's agreement with Andrew Millar for the copyright of *Tom Jones* brought a few years ago, and what would Fielding have said had he been told that the day would come when a man would pay Charles Sessler three thousand dollars for a copy of his immortal novel in boards uncut?

Skip we the intervening sales until 1781, when the noble library of Topham Beauclerk was disposed of. A copy of the sale catalogue is before me; it lists over thirty thousand volumes "in most languages and upon almost every branch of Science and Polite Literature." Beauclerk, it will be remembered, was a great-grandson of Charles II, out of Nell Gwyn, as the stud books say; but it was for his learning and charm and wit that Dr. Johnson hobnobbed with him, and went with him and Bennet Langton on the famous outing that Boswell records. I love the story. It will be remembered that the philosopher was once awakened about three in the morning by two men knocking at his door; they had been dining together at a nearby tavern. Johnson thought he was being attacked by burglars and came downstairs armed with a heavy poker, but upon discovering that they were his friends, and learning that they wanted him to join them, he became good-humored at once, and, dressing, sallied forth upon a "frisk." They went to Covent Garden, where Johnson offered his services to the greengrocers and fruiterers, which were declined; then they went to a tavern and had a bowl of bishop; afterward they got a boat and had a row upon the river, and finally it was suggested that they join the ladies, but Johnson would go no further and scolded his friends for deserting him to go and sit with a set of wretched "unideaed" girls.

Beauclerk was only forty when he died, and Johnson was disconsolate at his passing. "Poor, dear Beauclerk," he wrote to Boswell, "his wit, his folly, his acuteness, and his maliciousness, his merriment and reasoning, are now over: such another will not often be found." I was quite overjoyed when, some years ago, I stumbled upon several volumes from Beauclerk's library and a priced copy of his sale catalogue. Books from a man's library invariably bring you close to the man himself; I felt that I had been one of the company on the river. It took forty-nine days to dispose of the library and it would take almost as long to locate any sought-for item in the catalogue, owing to the violent and arbitrary method of arrangement, which to some

A

CATALOGUE

OF THE VALUABLE

Library of Books,

Of the late learned

SAMUEL JOHNSON,

Esq; LL. D.

DECEASED,

Which will be Sold by Auction,

(By ORDER of the EXECUTORS)

By Mr. CHRISTIE,

At his Great Room in Pall Mall,

On WEDNESDAY, FEBRUARY 16, 1785,

AND THREE FOLLOWING DAYS.

To be Viewed on Monday and Tuesday preceding the
Sale, which will begin each Day at 12 o'Clock.

Catalogues may be had as above.

extent continues in English book-auction catalogues to this very day.

My next catalogue is that of the library of "Books of the late learned Samuel Johnson, Esq., LL.D, which was sold by Mr. Christie in his Great Room in Pall Mall on Wednesday, February 16, 1785, and three following days." The copy before me formerly belonged to General Oglethorpe, a friend of Dr. Johnson's; at the sale of his effects it passed to Samuel Lysons, the antiquarian, and subsequently it became the property of the eminent Johnsonian scholar and collector, Colonel Grant, at whose sale, in May 1900, it fetched twenty-five pounds, ten shillings.

I made a facsimile reprint of a copy of the sale catalogue of Dr. Johnson's library several years ago—not of my copy, but another one, the property of my friend Colonel Ralph Isham. Isham's catalogue is more interesting than mine, if it has a less distinguished provenance, for the reason that in his copy not only are the prices the books fetched marked in ink, but the names of the buyers are given also. May I quote from the foreword I published as an introduction to the little volume? It was written in the attic room of Dr. Johnson's house in Gough Square, the room in which the Dictionary was written.

THE CATALOGUE OF DR. JOHNSON'S LIBRARY!

Our book-collecting, then, all comes to this. A man spends freely of his time, his money, and his energy—and dies. And ere he is cold in his grave, enter his executors with power to act and sell under the hammer of the auctioneer the books which once were part and parcel of the man himself. Certainly the disposal of a man's library should be undertaken as reverently as the disposal of his "corps," which in some sort his library is.

Of those who attended the sale, how many kept their catalogues? Perhaps only a handful escaped immediate destruction; certainly only one or two persons could have been sufficiently interested to indicate in ink the prices which the items fetched and the people who paid them, and then put the catalogue away so carefully that it is preserved to us. One cannot say with any certainty that this is the worst book catalogue ever made, but the mere sight of it, I am told, made my friend Mitchell Kennerley, he of the Anderson Galleries in New York, so ill that—but never mind: let us agree that the books were not "overcatalogued."

There were not a great many volumes: about three thousand in all. What has become of them? What has become of the little volume which someone saw with the inscription, "This was dear Tetty's book?" Tetty was the Doctor's wife, it will be remembered. What book was it? What was the condition of the First Folio of Shakespeare that it brought only one pound, two shillings? Doubtless it was imperfect; perhaps it was disfigured by its owner's notes! What would not one give to own it? Was the Burton's *Anatomy of Melancholy* the identical copy that served as an alarm clock and got the Doctor out of bed two hours earlier than he wished to rise? My copy—and mine is a first edition in pristine condition—puts me to sleep as quickly as an opiate: that is what I keep it for.

It was a very miscellaneous collection of books that the Doctor gathered about him. He did not treat them well, it will be remembered, but "tore their hearts out." When he sought to borrow a book from Garrick, who had a very pretty taste in books and binding, he shuddered. But he could give excellent advice on the subject of book-collecting, as he did on everything else.

Let us allow our imagination to play for a moment and fancy that this library, dispersed a hundred and forty years ago, could be reassembled and resold to-day at Mitchell Kennerley's Anderson Galleries, in New York, and that the items in bundles were separated and properly described and catalogued—as he would certainly do the job. What competition there would be! What prices these books would fetch! What "great room" would hold the throng? Kit Morley would write another "What Am I Bid?

Said the Auctioneer" poem and I should be a bankrupt: things are better as they are. I am glad this library was "disseverated" (it is Gabriel Wells's word) when it was.

The last old auction catalogue that I shall refer to is that of James Boswell, Junior. James Boswell, the biographer, died in 1795. We know that he was a hoarding animal and that in the preparation of his *Life of Johnson* he had accumulated a great mass of letters, journals, data of all kinds, which it was his intention should be kept forever in the archives at his ancestral home at Auchinleck; but in some way the legend arose that at his death all, or almost all, of this material was immediately destroyed. All the great Johnsonians—Croker and Hill and Sir Leslie Stephen, even that impeccable scholar R. W. Chapman —seem to have been of this opinion; but little by little items of interest have been seeping into the market; some came from the sale of his son's library, which was sold at auction "by Mr. Sotheby at his house in Wellington Street, Strand, in 1825." His catalogue is before me, but, owing to the archaic method of listing books by sizes, it is not too easy to refer to. Moreover, an item, "Tracts Poetical 10 volumes," may mean anything or nothing; and there are many such entries. Birkbeck Hill is our authority for the statement that Boswell's descendants were much ashamed of their ancestor's intimacy with the Lexicographer and determined to ignore it as much as possible. Immediately upon the death of Boswell, the biographer, his fine portrait of Johnson by Reynolds was sent into the lumber room, and Hill himself, a hundred years later, was refused admission to Auchinleck when he called.

In an interesting paper he tells how, when Boswell's daughter heard that he was publishing what she called "another addition of the Life of Johnson" (*sic*) containing some new material, she wrote and asked him whence it came.

This may be as good a place as any to refer to the fact that an immense amount of Boswell material came unexpectedly to the surface in Dublin, a year or two ago, and was secured after much negotiation by Ralph Isham, who promises that it shall be published when it has been digested and edited. I should like to tell the whole story of this interesting discovery, but it is not mine to tell: suffice to say that it is the most important literary find that has occurred in many years.

Old catalogues are very provocative. Reynold's portrait of Johnson, which had on Boswell's death been removed from his living apartments in disgrace, brought at the auction sale of his son in London seventy-six pounds, thirteen shillings; while a portrait of Boswell himself, a three-quarter length (I wonder what it was), brought eleven pounds, six. In all, about one hundred and fifty Johnson items were sold at this sale; and doubtless a large number of pieces which now adorn the library of my friend, R. B. Adam of Buffalo, must originally have been the property of Boswell Junior, but I have not had the patience to track them down. One would like to know the present whereabouts of the original draft for the "Plan" of the Dictionary entirely in Johnson's handwriting, which brought seventeen shillings and sixpence; it was bought by "Thorpe," who was a large buyer; and it is interesting to see that seven holograph

The "Oak Knoll" Library

prayers brought nine guineas for the lot, one of which finally passed into the "Oak Knoll" Library, as did also the first edition of Boswell's *Johnson*, with an inscription: "To James Boswell, Esq. Junior from his affectionate Father, The Authour." At Boswell's sale it brought one pound, sixteen shillings, and ten years later when John Murray (Byron's Murray) bought it, before he had it extra-illustrated, he paid—as a note in his handwriting records—two pounds, ten!

But to return to the auction room. One of the most intriguing books I know of on the subject of auction prices was published in 1901 by the late William Harris Arnold, under the caption, *A Record of Books and Letters*. First, let it be said that Mr. Arnold was never a rich, but always a very astute man. About the year 1895 he decided that he would seriously and systematically purchase all the fine books, within certain limits, that he could afford, in the belief that, should he ever desire to sell them, he could do so at a profit; but his chief profit, as he told me, was to be the pleasure of the chase. He began by a systematic study of booksellers' and auction catalogues; he worked at his hobby night and day, and after six years he stopped as suddenly as he began and disposed of his books "at auction, or who will give most for them?" He bought both English and American first editions, and published the result of his venture in two handsome and now scarce volumes, entitled, respectively, *A Record of Books and Letters* and *A Record of First Editions* (of American authors), printed at the Marion Press, Jamaica. The books were sold in the winter and spring of 1901, by Messrs. Bangs and Company, the then fashionable New York auctioneers. I have said that Mr. Arnold was very astute: he was, but he would have been even more astute had he not disposed of either of his collections, notwithstanding the fact that he immediately began collecting another library which was not dispersed until after his death. His *Records* are before me as I write. They are, practically, reprints of the sale catalogues, very handsomely printed, giving in parallel columns the cost of each item in red ink with the price it fetched at auction in black. A finer volume to place in your wife's hands, if and when she complains of the prices you are paying for books, never before existed. The totals run: cost for the English authors, $10,066.05; selling price, $19,743.50. For a picked list of Americans: cost, $3508.16; selling price, $7363.17. Or a total profit of $13,532.46, which was certainly very gratifying as the result of a game which was entered into rather for the pleasure of the chase and for its cultural value than with the idea of making a profit.

There are a lot of concerns selling bonds (which are not too easily disposed of, should you wish to turn them into money) who advertise pretty freely, "Twenty years"—or more or less—"without loss to any investor." A good conscientious bookseller could say the same thing, provided his customer bought enough books and was satisfied to average. In no other sport can you eat your cake and have it with anything like the same certainty as in this book-collecting game.

Mr. Arnold's list begins, as so many of our American catalogues begin, with the entry: "Andrews, W. L.; *A Short Historical Sketch of the Art of Book Binding.*" It cost him a dollar and a half, and he got thirty-four dollars for it: this might be called a flying start. The first nine items in his *Record* were "Andrews," and the total cost was ninety-one dollars, with a selling price of three hundred and ninety. "Andrews" books were then very fashionable; they would not fetch as much to-day—for there are fashions in book-collecting as in everything else. Mr. Arnold did almost equally well with his Keats. A presentation copy of the *Poems*, with an inscription in the poet's hand,—"My dear Giovanni, I hope your eyes will soon be well enough to read this with pleasure and ease,"—cost him seventy-one dollars and brought five hundred; but what would it bring to-day? As I write these lines, a copy in boards, without any inscription, "back somewhat worn, small piece missing," brought last night at the American Art Association the amazing price of thirty-three hundred dollars, and perhaps by the time these lines are read this figure will be exceeded. Mr. Arnold's *Tom Jones*, in original calf, cost him twenty-eight dollars and sold for thirty-three; it was not a scarce book then, but five hundred dollars would not be an excessive price to-day. The eighteenth century is coming into its own.

He had a copy of what was then termed the "second" edition of Goldsmith's *Deserted Village* (1770), morocco bound, gilt on the rough, "the only copy known." Whenever one comes across the phrase, "the only copy known," it is well to consult Wise, if his valuable catalogue is available and the item is within his range —as it is, in this instance. And this is what he says, with omissions: "The first edition, privately printed; the origin of this edition still remains obscure: if a note made by Bishop Percy may be relied upon—and it probably may—the pamphlet was produced before the close of 1769. The succeeding edition in quarto did not appear until May, 1770. Of the duodecimo, seven by four and one-half inches, only five examples have as yet been traced." Mr. Wise's copy is uncut; it would be, of course. For this little nugget Mr. Arnold paid thirty-three dollars, and sold it for one hundred and ninety. Years ago I paid a London bookseller thirty pounds for mine, and a copy sold recently for four hundred and fifty dollars. Mr. Arnold had a copy of Dr. Johnson's Dictionary in boards, uncut; he paid something over fifteen dollars for it, and sold it for seventy-six; some years later I bought the same identical book from A. J. Bowden for thirty-eight.

The name of Bowden carries me back many years: he was a remarkable man. Born in England, he came to this country with better mental equipment than any man then playing the rare-book game. He had knowledge, a wonderful memory, was integrity itself, and he had courage and skill, but he had a sad failing: when most needed, he was not to be found. Everyone trusted his judgment, but no one could, with safety, entrust him with his commissions; for this reason he frequently played a lone hand—and sometimes he played it well.

He would buy a book for five dollars, sell it for fifty, then take a drink, and then another—drink, not book. His great coup was in Philadelphia in 1890, when I first came to know him. In that year there was an auction sale of some personal effects of the Washington family, including the family Bible of Martha Washington. By some mischance the item had been omitted from the catalogue, but as the sale of it had been other-wise announced, it was decided to sell it, and a reserve price of seven hundred and fifty dollars was put upon it. The bidding opened with Bowden bidding seven hundred and fifty dollars, and as there were no other bidders the book was knocked down to him, much to the amusement of those present, whereupon he arose and made a speech. He said he was an Englishman, but he seemed to remember the name of Washington as that of a man who at one time had been prominent in the affairs of his country; he thought it remarkable that the booksellers present had left it to him, an English-man, to properly appreciate the value of a Washington family Bible, and he said that his price for the book was five thousand dollars! Before he left the auction room he was offered eighteen hundred dollars for his bargain, but he stuck to his original price—and got it from C. F. Gunther of Chicago.

I was very fond of Bowden, received many letters and bought a good many books from him. His judg-ment and integrity were unquestioned and unques-tionable. George D. Smith relied very largely on his knowledge at the time of the Hoe Sale, and he once tried to induce me to keep Bowden sober during the time of the sale, but I did not feel equal to the task. The last time I saw him was shortly before his death; we met in Fifth Avenue one afternoon and walked up the street together, he more or less under the influence of liquor—the picture of misery—and I not very. I never think of this fine old bookman without the recollection of a retort he once made to a very sancti-monious member of the trade, who told him that he

Dear Sir

I ask you many pardons for the trouble I gave you of yesterday. Upon more mature deliberation and the advice of a sensible friend I begin to think it indelicate in me to throw upon you the odium of confirming Mr. Colman's sentence. I therefore request you will send me play by my servant back, for having been apprised of having it acted at the other house, tho' I confess yours in every respect more to my wish, yet it would be folly in me to forego an advantage which lies in my power of appealing from Mr. Colman's opinion to the judgements of the town. I entreat if not too late, you will keep this affair a secret for some time. I am Dear Sir

your very humble servant
Oliver Goldsmith.

An interesting letter from Goldsmith to Garrick regarding the first production of "She Stoops to Conquer"

did not look like a bookseller or talk like a bookseller, he did not even smell like a bookseller. "Why, Blank," replied Bowden, "do you want to know why I'm a bookseller? It's on account of its Gawd-damned refinin' influence."

It is interesting to watch some one special item in its flight from one man's collection to another. Here is a fascinating letter from Goldsmith to Garrick relating to the first production of *She Stoops to Conquer*. I first noticed it in the famous Morrison Sale of autographs in London some years ago. From London it went to Paris, then back to London, then to New York, and at last it finds a resting place, for how long? in the library at "Oak Knoll."

It is not my intention to refer in any detail to the important book-auction sales held in this country prior to the Hoe Sale, although it might be interesting to linger over the John Allan Sale which was held in New York in the spring of 1864. Allan had supposed that his books would fetch about twelve thousand dollars; they brought actually a trifle less than thirty-eight thousand, although it was during the Civil War and the sale was several times interrupted by the passing of regiments of soldiers in the street to the accompaniment of drum and fife. One of the high spots of the sale was an Eliot Bible, for which a few years before Allan had unwisely squandered—as his friends thought—two hundred and ten dollars; it brought eight hundred and twenty-five, while his Kilmarnock Burns brought one hundred and six. The George Brinley Sale, held in March 1879, I remember hearing much spoken of at the time, as I was then working in the stationery department of Porter and Coates, not having, it was thought, sufficient intelligence to enter the book department. There were twenty-seven hundred items in this sale, and the total realized was just under fifty thousand dollars; it would be interesting to guess how many millions it would fetch to-day. The collection was largely Americana, and in no other line has there been such amazing appreciation.

But the record is held—and is likely to be held—by the Hoe Sale, which began at the Anderson Galleries on April 24, 1911. It was this sale which made Mr. Henry E. Huntington the premier book-collector of the world. George D. Smith was at the height of his fame, and Dr. Rosenbach's day had not yet come. In the front row of the crowded auction room sat George, with Mr. Huntington on one side of him, and frequently Bowden on the other; Harry Widener and I just behind them. Mr. Huntington once told me how he had bought huge blocks of real estate in a Western city, contiguous to a great railroad terminal he was building; when a "parcel" turned up, he bought it at whatever was the price—he never haggled. He bought books at the Hoe Sale in the same way, and some of us who were chiefly engaged in watching the proceedings wondered at the nonchalance with which G. D. S., representing him, took the star items, seemingly regardless of price. But what was the result? Mr. Huntington got the books he wanted, and at prices which now seem ridiculously low.

I have attended many auction sales both here and abroad, and I infinitely prefer the atmosphere of the New York auction room to that of London. An important sale, either at Anderson's or the American Art, is a social event; the sales are usually held after dinner and are attended by a good many men in evening dress, who are accompanied by ladies. The booksellers, numbering perhaps thirty or forty men, are seemingly on good terms with each other, but actually there is the keenest competition among them. Their *camaraderie* is purely superficial: they are there to buy books. In London, on the other hand, the auction room, like those who frequent it, seems to be very austere: no fellow feeling, making wondrous kind, is apparent, and yet a knock-out—which is a form of villainy practically unknown in this country—may be, and probably is, in operation. The knock-out cannot be explained too fully or too often; at country sales it functions, I should say, always; at important sales in London, not infrequently.

The knock-out operates in this way. A group of booksellers,—or it may be dealers in pictures, furniture, silver, or what not,—having attended sales together for many years and knowing each other well, go to a sale at which one man will buy all the items of a certain class, another man will buy in another class, and so on throughout the sale; there is not the slightest competition. After the public sale is over, there is another auction, this time a very exclusive affair, at which the books are resold, and the price they fetch above the price originally paid is divided up among those present according to some prearranged formula. It frequently happens that a man receives a very handsome sum of money merely for being among those present; he does not buy a single book. And if, by some mischance, a stranger enters the public sale, he is so severely disciplined by the trade that he is not allowed to have it except perhaps at a price which will make him hate himself and it forever.

Quite frequently, when one has sent one's bid abroad to some eminent house,—Quaritch, for example,—and subsequently reads in the paper that the book has been sold at or considerably below his bid, he is disappointed at not getting the item. The price given in the paper was a fictitious one; the book, having again been sold in the knock-out, may have brought a large advance on the ostensible price; the owner or the estate selling the book was cheated, it may be, out of half of the value of the library disposed of. It was to avoid the possible operation of the knock-out that the executors of the Hoe estate decided to sell the great library in New York rather than in London, where the dispersal of the library of "a rich American" might have been a slaughter, as was the Van Antwerp Sale, which took place at Sotheby's in 1907.

A priced copy of the Van Antwerp Sale catalogue is before me as I write, and while much water has gone over the dam since this small but lovely library was sold, it requires only a few moments' study to see that some sinister influence was at work. The same identical presentation copy of Keats's *Poems* which Mr. Arnold had bought for seventy-one dollars and sold for five hundred, six years before, brought only ninety pounds; and Milton's *Comus*, now appraised at twenty-five thousand dollars, brought less than eight hundred! One would suppose that some sense of honesty would operate to terminate the operations of the knock-out, but established customs die hard in England, and it will take legislation to kill it. And this may be coming. Only a few days ago Lord Darling, familiar to us for so many years as Mr. Justice Darling, introduced a bill to make illegal any agreement not to bid at an auction sale in competition with any other person, so that the property may be acquired afterwards by the person making the agreement. Anyone entering into such an agreement shall be liable, on conviction, to a fine not exceeding one hundred pounds or six months' imprisonment, or both. In the discussion that followed someone representing the Incorporated Society of Auctioneers said the knock-out was regularly resorted to by various classes of dealers, and that auctioneers were helpless against those combinations. While it would be difficult, he said, to stop private arrangements between two or more dealers, the proposed act would considerably reduce the activities of the ring. Of course, no one hates the knock-out more than the auctioneers themselves, as their profits depend upon the prices at which the merchandise is sold, be that merchandise what it may. The whole knock-out idea is a development of the old guild or trade-union spirit: a man who has not served his apprenticeship in the trade must keep out of it.

The romance of the auction room has never been written and it never can be; it would be too full of thrills for the human mind to stand; it would make the checkered career of "Nelly, the beautiful Cloak Model," commonplace. Priceless items go for nothing —not often, certainly, but sometimes. Not long ago at an important sale in London a batch of sheet music tied together with a string was bought by Joseph of the Charing Cross Road for three pounds, and he sold it to Thorpe of Guildford for twenty-five pounds. Did anyone surmise that the bundle contained a copy of the excessively rare Shelley item—*The Posthumous Fragments of Margaret Nicholson?* No, but it did, and after it had changed hands several times, Gabriel Wells sold it a few weeks later in New York for eight thousand dollars.

Was it possible that some dishonest employee of the auction house, knowing the value of the item, "planted" it in a lot of worthless sheet music, that someone in the know might buy it? I hope not, but the incident attracted so much attention that Messrs. Hodgson and Son of Chancery Lane felt impelled to write the *Bookman's Journal*, saying that this particular copy had not passed through their hands.

At auctions in this country there are three ways of procedure. One may bid one's self—this is fairly dangerous, for if the item is important the whole room is against you. One may entrust one's bid to the auctioneer—this may be folly. I recently heard of an example of this at a certain sale. There were four copies of the same identical book listed under four separate numbers in the catalogue. A friend of mine sent a bid to the auctioneer for, say, eight dollars for the third copy to be sold; the first copy sold brought three dollars, the second copy two and a half, the third copy eight dollars, and the fourth three dollars. Whereupon my friend addressed a letter to the auctioneer asking what had happened, and received a reply stating that "it was a coincidence that they could not explain." Naturally.

The third and best way is to place your bid with a reliable bookseller. This is not as simple as it sounds:

it requires intelligence and courage. One has to make up one's mind who is likely to have a commission for the coveted item; then he should go to the bookseller and say "Buy that item for me" up to the highest price he is willing to pay. At this point the negotiation becomes delicate: the bookseller may say, "That ought to bring it," or he may say, having already a higher bid or knowing of one, "You haven't a chance at that figure," or he may say, "Leave it to me," or he may say—anything or nothing. And anything may happen. Auctions are like the weather—uncertain. If Wall Street is booming, prices are certain to be high for good items; if Wall Street is depressed or in a panic,—and such things happen,—prices are almost certain to be low, except for items which must be bought now or never. The great thing is to make the right selection of your agent, and do not grudge him his ten-per-cent commission. By the selection of the wrong man to do the bidding I have frequently seen thousands of dollars thrown away; and in an effort to save ten thousand I saw a man at Anderson's lose the Gutenberg Bible that was there sold on February 15, 1926, "at about ten-thirty in the evening."

This was an historic occasion. It was at the end of the first night of the R. B. Adam Sale, and the room was packed; it was well known that a certain very rich man was prepared to pay a stiff price for the famous volume, and that it was his intention to give it to the Cathedral of St. John the Divine. The presentation had all but taken place. What happened? The last copy had been bought by a very astute collector for about sixty-five thousand dollars from Dr. Rosenbach—and it was a gift at the price. No one knew whether Dr. R. had or had not a commission for it, but I was perfectly certain that he would buy this copy, be the price what it would. The book was put up; a few words were said by Mr. Kennerley—not many were needed. The bidding began at fifty thousand dollars, all round the room. "Rosy" did not bid; it seemed to be a battle between Gabriel Wells and the Certain Rich Man—whom I shall designate by the initials C. R. M. Wells dropped out at seventy-five thousand dollars, and C. R. M. thought the book his at seventy-six, but he had still to reckon with Dr. R., who bid eighty, as who should say let's be done with this matter; whereupon C. R. M. bid eighty-five. And so the bidding went on, by one thousand and by five thousand, until at last C. R. M. bid one hundred and five thousand dollars, and Dr. R. one hundred and six thousand. That settled it. And C. R. M. had the same distinction that I had—that of not getting the book.

At the fall of the hammer there was a buzz all round the room. No book had ever brought such a price; was Dr. R. acting for himself or did he have a buyer? Guesses were numerous, but, as usual, wrong. A few days later President Angell made the announcement that Mrs. Harkness had permanently enriched the Library at Yale by the gift of a Gutenberg Bible. Dr. R. had acted with his usual shrewdness. He had no commission for the book; Mrs. Harkness was in California; but he had immediately communicated with her by telegraph, and before the smoke had cleared from the battlefield the book had been delivered and paid for. The chances are ten to one that, had not C. R. M. sought to save a ten-per-cent commission,—had he given his bid to Dr. R.,—that book would have been his at anywhere from seventy-five to eighty thousand dollars. It was the finest exhibition of how *not* to bid I have ever seen.

In recent years there has been much to-do over the autograph of Button Gwinnett, a signer of the Declaration of Independence. People collect "Signers" with a rigor unknown in any other game; men must have a Button Gwinnett to complete their collections. Gwinnett was an Englishman who came over here and settled in Georgia as a trader. In 1770 he bought a plantation and gave himself over to the life of a farmer. He always took an important part in the life of the colony, however, and was elected a member of the Legislature and sent as a delegate to the Continental Congress, where he signed the Declaration. While he was busy with the business of rebellion, the British seized his property and destroyed it. And in 1777 he met a tragic end. His great ambition was a commission of brigadier general; he was defeated for the post by a Captain McIntosh: from that moment McIntosh became his sworn enemy and he challenged him to a duel, and on the morning of May 15, 1777, it was fought. Both men were severely wounded; McIntosh recovered and Gwinnett died—at the age of forty-five.

Why are his signatures so scarce? That is one of the mysteries of Americana. Gwinnett lived in this country for more than twelve years; he was a merchant and must have signed many papers, receipts, and things of that sort, and he must have written letters, yet to-day only forty of his signatures are known to exist, and only one of these is attached to a letter. No one knows these facts better than Dr. R. I sat next to him at the famous Thomas Sale in Philadelphia, in November 1924, when he paid the then record price of fourteen thousand dollars for this elusive signature. When I congratulated him on his purchase, he said: "I have one in New York which I have been trying to sell for ten thousand dollars. Do you mind stepping to the telephone and saying that it is not to be sold at any price? I shall now ask twenty thousand for it." And he did, and got it, and within a year he paid twenty-two thousand, five hundred dollars for another, with Madigan as the underbidder. Ten years ago, when Colonel Manning paid forty-six hundred dollars for a Gwinnett, people called him a madman, but to-day the experts say that within five years fifty thousand will look cheap. People want to complete their collections of "Signers:" no one can complete his Shakespeare or many other things, but with the "Signers" in many cases it is only a Gwinnett that is lacking—hence the price. I have no more desire to complete my collection of—anything—than I have to complete my life. I have no collection that can be completed. I should be glad to have an "1865 *Alice*," but if I cannot get it I shall be content with my "1903 *Dynasts*," or with my Goldsmith letter or my *Treasure Island* map. For the omnivorous collector there are plenty of thrills left.

Immediately after any great auction sale the dealers in whatever it may be are very busy. Such an item fetched so much at the sale last night, they say. The woman who hesitates is lost; the man who deliberates loses.

This chapter was written several years ago and put aside; all the prices mentioned look silly to-day, as those of to-day will certainly look silly a few years hence. It is the functioning of the law of supply and demand: a constantly increasing demand and a decreasing supply. We had to wait only a year to see a Button Gwinnett bring fifty-one thousand dollars! And a few weeks ago when Dr. Rosenbach, in London, paid fifteen thousand four hundred pounds for the manuscript of *Alice*, there was at once a great hue and cry. "The manuscript ought not to leave England," they said; whereupon, Rosy offered it to the nation at cost and promised a subscription of a thousand pounds! Catch Rosy asleep! He is the greatest bookseller that the world has ever seen: I could prove it, but in Dr. Johnson's phrase, "I expect some statements to be accepted without proof." Naturally, his rivals will not agree.

In April 1925, George Barr McCutcheon sold his fine collection of Hardy, Kipling, and Stevenson. There has not been a good Hardy sale recently, and it is useless to speculate as to what good items would fetch now that the ashes of the Great Victorian have been placed in the Poet's Corner of Westminster Abbey, but there are two items which may be called the corner stone and the capstone, respectively, of any Hardy collection. The first is *Desperate Remedies*, Hardy's first book, which was published anonymously in 1871, in bright red cloth. Of this book John C. Eckel says:

"It is almost impossible to find in even fair condition. Usually copies are offered which have been under the book surgeon's care. Soiled covers, to say nothing of substituted end papers and restored and strengthened backs, are the attributes of the three volumes when they now appear. The first *Desperate Remedies* sold at auction, in this country, in many years

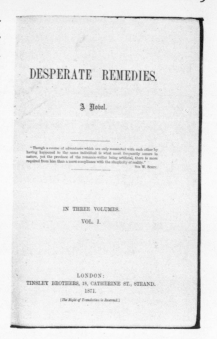

was the fine McCutcheon copy. One of the two letters 'tipped in' was written by the author concerning the book, in which he stated that the 'very first copies were in green cloth, issued about Easter, 1871. It was nearly snuffed out . . . I think that on its revival the volumes remaining in sheets were bound up in different colors.'" No copy in green cloth has ever reached the surface so far as known. The three volumes at the sale brought $2100. A Western dealer recently offered a copy for $2750, while Gannon, in New York, has just sold a very fine copy to Paul Hyde Bonner for a price said to be in excess of $4000. It is potentially a $10,000 book.

The capstone is *The Dynasts*. The accepted first edition of the first volume is dated 1904, but a few, a

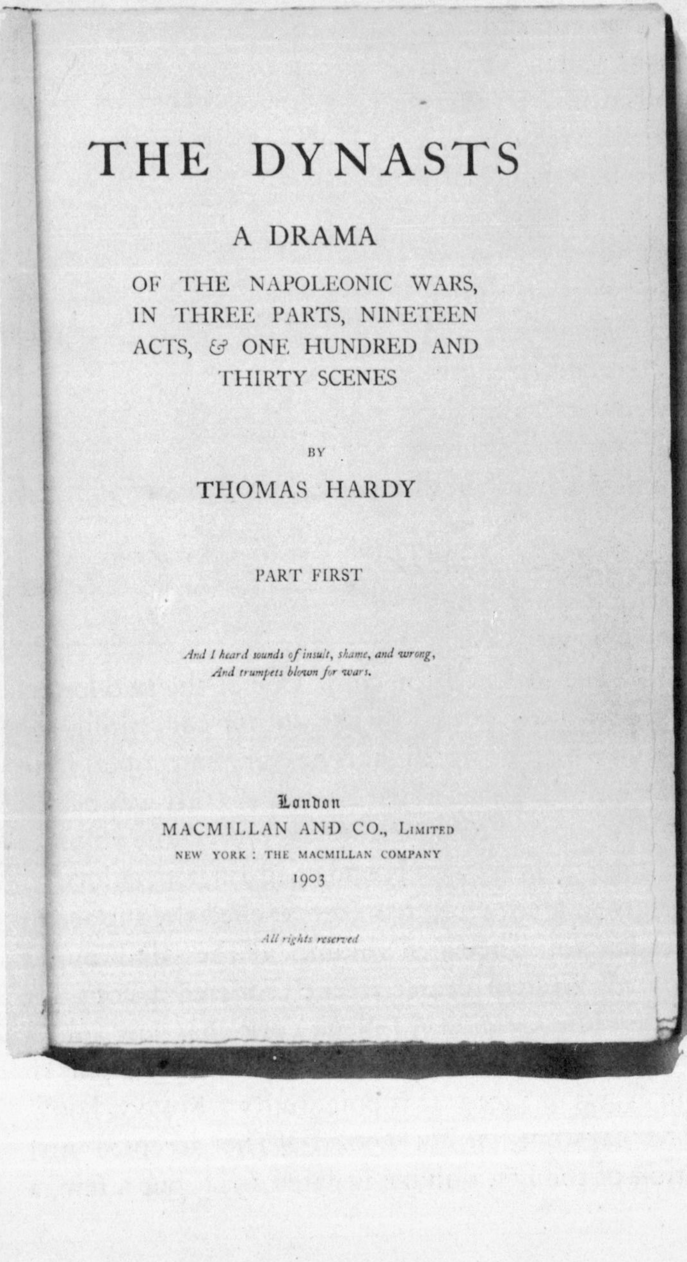

THE DYNASTS

A DRAMA

OF THE NAPOLEONIC WARS,
IN THREE PARTS, NINETEEN
ACTS, & ONE HUNDRED AND
THIRTY SCENES

BY

THOMAS HARDY

PART FIRST

And I heard sounds of insult, shame, and wrong,
And trumpets blown for wars.

London
MACMILLAN AND CO., Limited
NEW YORK : THE MACMILLAN COMPANY
1903

very few copies were published with the date 1903. The McCutcheon copy was the 1903 issue, and was presented "To Algernon C. Swinburne with the best wishes of Thomas Hardy." It brought twenty-one hundred dollars. A year ago a copy without an inscription fetched twenty-one hundred dollars, and was bought by Dr. Rosenbach for my friend and rival, Barton W. Currie. It may well be that a fine presentation copy, like the McCutcheon copy, would to-day bring ten thousand dollars.

I began collecting Hardy thirty years ago, when presentation copies could be had for ten or fifteen dollars! But this is very small compensation for being an old man.

In the case of Kipling, we are on safer ground, for as recently as January 16, 1928, there was a Kipling sale at the American Art Association in New York at which seemingly fantastic prices were paid—but prices have always been fantastic. No copy of *The Smith Administration* was in the sale, but a few weeks before a copy had been sold for fourteen thousand dollars, whereas a year before my friend Ellis Ames Ballard had paid only forty-six hundred for it. I have heard it said that the Ballard Collection is unsurpassed either in this country or in England.

It would seem, if one can judge the future by the past,—and how else can it be judged?—that it is always too soon to sell, at auction or in any other way. And *keep your "duplicates."* I made a mistake in selling some of mine: at the sale of "The Books of a Busted Bibliophile," in New York, a few years ago, good prices were realized, but I missed the books sadly. Indeed, it is not until a man can look upon at least two copies of his favorite book on his shelves that he can call himself a real collector. Heber, the great English bibliophile, insisted upon three, but I always thought that was a little extreme.

A famous novel in fine condition

VIII

CAVEAT EMPTOR

My first real awakening to the wisdom contained in the old Latin motto, *Caveat emptor* (Let the buyer beware), took place many years ago. In the estate of a deceased friend was a small but choice collection of bric-a-brac; under the terms of his will it was to be sold by an important auction house in New York, and in due course a man came over to Philadelphia, examined with great care the collection, and went into ecstasies over certain pieces, assuming stained-glass attitudes and exclaiming now and again: "A museum piece—nothing superior to it in the Metropolitan!" In due course the collection was carefully packed, sent to New York, catalogued, and put on sale. All was going well when, the day before the sale, a telegram was received requesting that an executor come at once to New York: an important discovery had been made. An executor went, and on his arrival was informed that most if not all of the finest pieces—the "museum pieces," so-called—were fakes.

What was to be done? To call off the sale was impossible; to announce that some of the most important items were of questionable value would cast doubt upon all. What, indeed, was to be done? A dealer of repute, an expert from whom many of the art objects had been purchased, was called in. He was, he said, prepared to stake his professional reputation on the genuineness of the items in question. The expert of the auction house said they were, at best, doubtful; he could not in common honesty recommend the purchase of any article the origin of which was questionable. The articles were what they were—interesting and beautiful. Two men—and seemingly the only two men in New York who knew—took opposite sides: it was a most distressing situation. The day of the sale came. The auctioneer spoke of the beauty of the objects to be disposed of; there was some question, he said, as to their genuineness—and "What am I bid?" A number of the important clients of the auction company bought what they wanted, and the rest were obtained for next to nothing by the expert, who shipped them to Paris, where they were disposed of for ten times what they cost.

The moral, as it seemed to me at the time, and still does, is never to buy anything of which only two men know the value, and always to be prepared for a clash of expert opinion. And from that day to this I have viewed a relic with skepticism, and in all my life I have acquired only one: a silver teapot once belonging to Dr. Johnson, with what seems to be an unimpeachable provenance. I came by it in the most curious manner. One day about a year ago, I bought from Gabriel Wells, under somewhat unusual circumstances, a first folio of Shakespeare and thereby hangs a tale quite foreign to the subject of this paper. I had long lusted after a "first folio:" meaning thereby, the first collected edition of Mr. William Shakespeare's Comedies, Histories & Tragedies, published in 1623. The "Oak Knoll" library already contained an excellent second folio, a superb third, and a good fourth, but a first was lacking. It was over a dinner table in Gabriel Wells' flat in London, in September, 1927, that the void was filled. Mr. Wells had as his guests, besides my wife and myself, Mr. William Roberts of *The London Times*, and we had reached that stage in our gastronomic proceedings when conversation had become more important than food: naturally, our talk was of books.

"Gabriel," I said, "have you acquired anything important since we combed the bookshops together last June?"

Our host paused for a moment and then said, "Only one item, but a very important one: I have just bought what is probably the finest copy of the First Folio obtainable. It is the famous Carysfort copy, clean, sound, unwashed, without the restoration of a single letter, perfect in every particular. It ranks number six in Sidney Lee's census; you had better buy it. You will then have first editions of all the most important books in English literature. You will never have another chance: take my advice and buy it."

"And the price?" I inquired.

He named a sum which, when I was a boy, I had set as the amount necessary for me to have and, having which, I intended to retire from active warfare (business).

"Where is the book?" I said.

"In the safe at Quaritch's."

"I'll take it," I said. "It will give my bank account a very severe purge, but I'll take it."

"What!" said my wife, "are you crazy?"

"But you haven't seen it," said Roberts.

"No," said I, "but I know very well what the book looks like, I know Sir Sidney Lee's census, and above all I know Gabriel: I'll take the book and that settles the matter."

But the next day I felt weak, as though I—as well as my bank account—had undergone a capital operation, and I vowed that I would not go into another bookshop for a long time; but subsequently—like Samuel Pepys —I repented me of my vow, and then remembered that there was no reason why I should not enter printshops

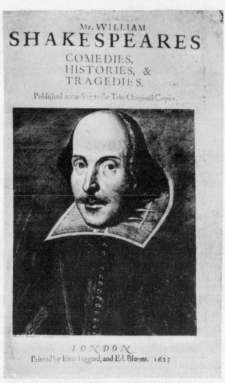

First Folio of Shakespeare

freely. In this mood I set out for Ackermann's in Bond Street. While there, a man came up to me and asked if I were Mr. Newton, the Johnsonian. I told him my name was certainly Newton, but in America, where I came from, there was only one man who deserved to be called "the Johnsonian," and that was R. B. Adam of Buffalo.

"Why do you ask?" I added.

"Because," said my friend, "I have a silver teapot which once belonged to Dr. Johnson, which I should like to show you."

"I never buy relics," I replied.

"But will you look at my teapot? I should like to know your opinion of it," the stranger persisted.

"I can give my opinion without looking at it: it is a fake," I said; and then, realizing that I had been rude as well as silly, I told him I should be glad to examine it, but that relics always left me cold. Whereupon I was told by the man who had addressed me that he was the manager of Ackermann's in Chicago; that he, being convinced of the genuineness of the relic, had bought it; that it was at his hotel—or somewhere—and that he would go and fetch it. I said I would return in an hour, and I did so. There was the teapot: of solid silver. It bore a long and tedious inscription upon one side, reciting the manner in which Sir John Hawkins disposed of Johnson's belongings, while Dr. Cruikshank, who performed an autopsy on the body of Dr. Johnson, was closing the incision in the next room. Careful readers of Hill's Boswell do not need to be reminded of what took place immediately upon Johnson's death, and the legend of how Sir John Hawkins, a "brutal fellow," enraged somewhat at Johnson's legacy to his black servant, Frank, sought to deprive him of the Doctor's watch. It found confirmation in the story engraved on the teapot that "while the surgeon explored the ruinated machinery of its dead master," Bray, the silversmith, was conveyed to Bolt Court in Sir John's carriage, thus hastily to buy the plate, and how this "unadorned vessel for its celebrated services was rescued," etc., etc.

The more carefully I studied the teapot and brought to mind the character of Hawkins,—"the unclubable knight," as Johnson called him,—the more interesting the object became. Everything about it testified to its genuineness, and I certainly should have become its owner but for the Shakespeare I had bought the day before—than which only few finer copies exist in the world. This transaction had "ruinated" me. I was in no mood to purchase anything; but in a moment of

My only relic, Dr. Johnson's teapot

hysteria I gave the owner of the teapot a letter, assuring him that but for the transaction with Gabriel Wells I should certainly have bought the teapot— whereupon I fled, and thought no more or very little more of the incident.

Time passed, as time has a habit of doing, and one day, several months later, I received a note from a charming woman, Mrs. Otis Skinner, telling me that she had seen at Ackermann's, in Chicago, a teapot which had once belonged to Dr. Johnson; that by all means I should own it and give her a cup of tea out of it on her next visit to "Oak Knoll." And there-upon I learned another lesson: namely, to "agree with thine adversary quickly, while thou art in the way with him." What was the use of my fleeing from temptation in London only to fall in Chicago? And I tell myself the woman tempted me,—that it was to oblige Mrs. Skinner that I bought the teapot,—and it is now an object of interest at "Oak Knoll."

But in general, as regards relics, I am very skeptical. People who loiter much in museums of natural history know that experts can reconstruct out of a few odd pieces of bone a very satisfactory skeleton of a pre-historic animal. In the same way, out of one genuine old chair they can make a dozen,—finely upholstered, in old velvet,—with a table thrown in for good measure. And in the matter of paintings there are, I suspect, more "old masters" in this country alone than all the old masters of Europe ever painted. And this, I fancy, is one of the ways we get them. An old gentleman, very hard up,—as many old gentlemen in Europe are these days,—picks up his newspaper of a morning and reads of some rich American having bought for an immense sum a portrait by—whom you will. As he reads, his eye lights upon a portrait of an ancestor, by that same master, and he says to himself: "If I could sell a couple of those old pictures for any substantial portion of the sum mentioned as having been paid by that damned American, I could pay my debts and live, at least for a time, in decency and comfort." Then, saying nothing to anybody, he goes up to London or to Paris, or any other important art centre, and seeks out a prominent dealer to whom he unfolds his scheme, which with minor variations is something like this. He asks that the dealer come to see him, and in the course of his visit he is to observe that several of his host's best pictures are going to ruin for want of proper care. If attended to now, the pictures can be saved; in a few years it will be too late. The lady of the house, proud as Lucifer, enters the discussion: she wants the pictures restored, but does not know where the money is to come from; they are devoured by taxes, etc. The art dealer talks much and learnedly: "You won't know the pictures after they have been rebacked," "It is an obligation which you owe to your family," etc. Finally it is decided to send them up to town; there they are skillfully copied. The copies are put into old frames, and, as originals, go back to the country house, and after a time the genuine paintings come to this country. Or, and more likely, the copies will be sold as the genuine paintings.

I doubt if one man out of a thousand buying pictures can tell a genuine painting from a good copy. Experts disagree, hence the name. An expert will swear to anything on a bunch of Bibles; especially, as we know, will they swear to the sanity or insanity of a client. All this is not news: in one form or another it has been going on since the world began. We know that the Romans tried to make their sculpture look like Greek, which was then most highly esteemed, and there is nothing under the sun that cannot be and is not faked. The sang-froid with which a collector buys gems and coins fills me with amazement. Even silver, with its hall mark, must be closely scrutinized, for an old morsel of silver in which is stamped a hall mark indicating a make and a date can be removed from one piece of silver and inserted in another.

I do not collect prints for several reasons; among them is the sufficient one that I do not understand "states." Occasionally I buy an eighteenth-century print for decorative purposes, but never in frames and under glass, except when they are admittedly restrikes. Once, when in Paris, in a very famous shop I bought five very fine prints; they were in faked old frames, as is not unusual, and came to a considerable sum. At the end of a cursory examination I made a small deposit and told the proprietor of the shop that I would call the next day with the amount necessary to pay for them. It was to be a cash transaction; I was to get the prints, but no bill or receipt, in order to avoid the luxury tax. The dealer, in the meantime, was to remove the prints from their frames, so that I might complete my examination in regard to margins, tears, and other possible defects, for the prints were supposed to be perfect: otherwise, they had no interest for me.

The next morning I presented myself with many

bundles of thousand-franc notes pinned together in lots of ten. As soon as I entered the shop I saw something was wrong; very frankly I was told—and it was hardly necessary, for I should have made the discovery for myself—that two of the prints were defective. One was remargined at the plate line,—exquisitely, to be sure,—but the restoration was quite obvious; the other had had a tear so perfectly concealed that only by examination with a magnifying glass could its presence be detected.

The danger of buying such things at auction is obvious. Defects are supposedly pointed out in the catalogues, but they are not always observed; and at an auction, too, you may give a discretionary bid to the very dealer whose property the print or other object is. I once bought at auction through a bookseller a lot of books and subsequently found that they had been the property of the man through whom I bought them! Not so good.

The pitfalls prepared for collectors are a thousand and one; that we should escape them all is impossible. I am now going to narrate a true story in which every name, except that of Francis Edwards, the hero, is fictitious, but every fact is true. One day last July I was in London and called on my friend Edwards, whose excellent bookshop is in the High Street, Marylebone, as everyone knows, and from him I had this story. A man had come into his shop a few days before, and, asking for the proprietor, introduced himself as Mr. Crawford of Melton Mowbray.

Said Crawford: "Mr. Edwards, I am a friend of the rector of our church in Melton Mowbray; he is a very old gentleman, a sporting parson, the last of his race, and is almost blind. He told me he was thinking of selling a small collection of books which he told me were very valuable. I know nothing about books myself; I never was a collector, but when my friend told me that he was going to send the lot to a bookseller in Leicester it occurred to me to suggest that he could do better by taking them up to London. But my friend would not hear of it; he told me that he had not been in London since the war and never expected to enter Sion House again; he thought he would do very well in Leicester. To make a long story short, I made my friend give me a list of some of the books he wanted to sell; not all, by any means, just a few; and I have the list here. It may be that the books are of no value; you will know better than I; I know nothing about books. I should only like to do my friend a good turn." Whereupon Mr. Crawford handed a list to Mr. Edwards for examination, he meanwhile looking at some sporting prints in which a man from Melton Mowbray might well be interested.

The list Mr. Edwards read contained at least a dozen items, to secure any one of which a bookseller would send a man across England. They were collectors' items, but the books would have to be examined with great care; if perfect, the little lot jotted down were worth several thousand pounds. Mr. Edwards had become interested. "How can the books be seen?" he inquired. Mr. Crawford thought there would be no difficulty about that: if Mr. Edwards would send him a wire the day before, he, Crawford, would meet him in his car at the railway station and

take him to the manse or rectory or vicarage, or
wherever the old collector lived. "You will see a
character," added Mr. Crawford. Mr. Edwards was
very anxious to meet an old clergyman of such fine
taste. Mr. Crawford then made it clear that he was
acting quite disinterestedly in the matter; he was to
receive no commission. Mr. Edwards was to give the
old man what in his judgment the books were worth;
he would have to attend to their shipment to London,
which he agreed to do. He was much obliged to Mr.
Crawford; he would wire him in a day or two; he
hoped he would find the books in good condition. Mr.
Crawford did not know; Mr. Edwards would have to
take care of himself. Whereupon the two men shook
hands and parted, and Crawford made his way to the
street.

Obviously this thing looked very good indeed to
Edwards, who, list in hand, was for a moment lost in
reverie. *Life of a Sportsman* in blue cloth, *Pickwick* in
parts—might be worth anything or nothing; *Vicar of
Wakefield*, first edition: the idea of taking an aeroplane
to Melton Mowbray did not seem so very absurd.
Someone touched Edwards on his arm. He came out
of his trance: Crawford again. "Another matter, Mr.
Edwards, " he said, "I quite forgot. In going over
some old papers that have been in my family since I
don't know when, I came across a drawing of an old
map which looks to me quite interesting: it seems to
be a plan of a battle of some kind. It is signed 'H.
Clinton, Major General,' and it is dated May 4, 1775,"
whereupon he handed Edwards a slightly torn and
somewhat discolored plan of the Battle of Bunker Hill!

By this time, with his mind still on the books, Edwards had his mind prepared for anything. Did Mr. Crawford wish to sell it? He did. And for how much? Mr. Crawford did not know. What would Mr. Edwards say to thirty guineas? Automatically Edwards's idea was twenty pounds—that would be quite satisfactory to Mr. Crawford. Mr. Edwards took from his pocket four five-pound notes—they would be better for Mr. Crawford's purpose than Mr. Edwards's check; he had a few small purchases to make—and Crawford departed.

Ten minutes later Mr. Edwards's manager came in and was shown the map. "What do you think of it?" said Edwards. "It looks too good to me; what did you pay for it?" "Twenty pounds." "Not enough—or too much." "That's what I think," said Edwards. "Put it away; it's a fake. Don't sell it: it's not worth a damn." And a few days later the whole story came out. The kind stranger, the friend of the old clergyman in Melton Mowbray, had a dozen such friends in different parts of England and in one day had disposed of a like number of such maps, all practically identical and all clumsy forgeries; but in order to work the ruse successfully the mind of the victim had to be carefully diverted from the fake map by the story of an old clergyman and his books. Mr. Edwards was the only bookseller I met who admitted being stung; all the others to whom I talked told me that one of their rivals had been the victim—the speaker, fortunately, had escaped by having his suspicions aroused. But Edwards told the story on himself, and gave me the map, which I here reproduce. And I venture to make

A fake map of the Battle of Bunker Hill

a prophecy: namely, that most of these maps will sooner or later make their appearance in the American market, where they will, of course, be detected, but not before much damage is done. Whether the plausible stranger forged the maps himself, or whether he worked with an accomplice, is not now known; but the swindler did an excellent day's work. And this now brings us to the subject of the perfectly proper restoration of books.

We do not need to be told at this late day that certain old books are worth, not their weight in gold, but their weight in bank notes. But many of these books are defective—some very; others lack merely a title-page or a last leaf. These may be supplied, perhaps, from other defective copies; most Shakespeare folios are made up in this way, or they may have the missing leaf supplied in facsimile. The unrivaled repairer of old books by pen or pencil was John Harris, who died in London in 1872. As a boy, he studied at the Royal Academy, and ultimately he came to devote his entire time to copying in facsimile not only title-pages and pages of text, but maps, portraits, and engravings—anything. Chiefly his method was lithography on old paper, and he became so adroit in the handling of his different mediums that experts admitted that they were unable to tell "a facsimile by Harris" from an original. In addition to his Shakespearean forgeries, if so they might be called, he made a superb title-page for the Great Bible of Henry VIII (1539) and the rare map in the Coverdale Bible (1535). So perfect did his work finally become that the trustees of the British Museum made an order that, to prevent the deception of future librarians, Harris should always identify his work with a note at the bottom of the page. One is not surprised to learn that the poor man's eyes gave out, and that he was at last compelled to abandon his trade, in which he had few equals and no superior.

I have a very rare edition of *Robinson Crusoe* which, I think, contains a page of Harris's work. Only one other copy is known, that in the British Museum. It has many defective leaves; mine is said to have but one. The leaf, seemingly, is printed on paper which is somewhat thinner than the rest of the book, but this may be due to the treatment it has undergone; I should not have known it, had it not been pointed out to me by the bookseller from whom I bought it.

I have no comment to make on the subject of forgeries of letters and inscriptions in books. We all meet them occasionally, and it is surprising that we do not meet them oftener. Certain "hands" lend themselves very readily to forgery—Byron's and Shelley's and Burns's, for example; of Boswell's or of Johnson's I do not remember to have seen any. It is amazing that persons with enough skill and intelligence to forge an inscription in a book will occasionally fall down in the matter of a date. To date an inscription or the signature of an author a year or two after his death reveals very crude work, and yet I have known it done.

Occasionally an entire book, or more frequently a pamphlet, is forged,—if that be the proper word for it,—and my friend Thomas J. Wise sent, a year or two ago, a letter to the *Bookman's Journal* on this subject. It reads in part as follows:—

May I be permitted, through the columns of the *Bookman's Journal*, to enter a warning against two impudent forgeries of rare books, of which a number of copies appear to have been planted upon the unwary, and which are certainly enjoying an unfortunate success? The two books in question are the first editions of Shelley's *Adonais*, printed in Pisa in 1821, and *Hellas*, printed in London in 1822. The forgeries now circulating have been prepared by taking copies of the very close reprints issued by the Shelley Society to its members in 1866, removing my own introductions, and then rubbing them in dust to impart an appearance of age. That the result is sufficiently misleading is testified by the fact that among the persons who have fallen victims to the fraud are two of the foremost and most widely experienced antiquarian booksellers in London, each of whom was misled by the apparently genuine appearance of the books. How many of the smaller dealers and private collectors have been likewise defrauded, and how many copies of the books have crossed the Atlantic, it is impossible to say. Both books are valuable (the *Adonais* in mint condition is now worth about £350), so the temptation to the fabricator to do his best—or worst—is a strong one.

Since the above was written, an *Adonais* has sold in this country for four thousand dollars, so the temptation increases.

Everything that art and ingenuity can do to a printed or written page, and more too, can be done to a binding; and much of this work is perfectly legitimate. A "shaken" cover can be strengthened; a badly stained book can be washed; a portrait supplied —the sophistications which a rare book may undergo are endless. It is important, if sometimes painful, to know what they are. In general, I try never to put a book upon my shelves for which I have to apologize either to myself or to my friends. Excessively rare books one must take as they come, or do without. No

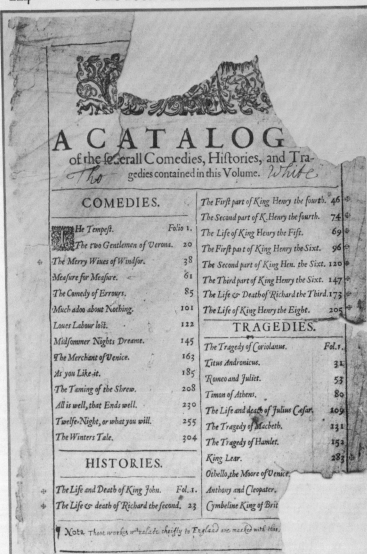

A page of a Shakespeare folio in need of "restoration"

A CATALOGVE

of the seuerall Comedies, Histories, and Tragedies contained in this Volume.

COMEDIES.

He Tempest. Folio 1.

The two Gentlemen of Verona. 20

The Merry Wiues of Windsor. 38

Measure for Measure. 61

The Comedy of Errours. 85

Much adoo about Nothing. 101

Loues Labour lost. 122

Midsommer Nights Dreame. 145

The Merchant of Venice. 163

As you Like it. 185

The Taming of the Shrew. 208

All is well, that Ends well. 230

Twelfe-Night, or what you will. 255

The Winters Tale. 304

HISTORIES.

The Life and Death of King John. Fol. 1.

The Life & death of Richard the second. 23

The First part of King Henry the fourth. 46

The Second part of K. Henry the fourth. 74

The Life of King Henry the Fift. 69

The First part of King Henry the Sixt. 96

The Second part of King Hen. the Sixt. 120

The Third part of King Henry the Sixt. 147

The Life & Death of Richard the Third. 173

The Life of King Henry the Eight. 205

TRAGEDIES.

The Tragedy of Coriolanus. Fol. 1.

Titus Andronicus. 31

Romeo and Juliet. 53

Timon of Athens. 80

The Life and death of Julius Cæsar. 109

The Tragedy of Macbeth. 131

The Tragedy of Hamlet. 152

King Lear. 283

Othello, the Moore of Venice. 310

Anthony and Cleopater. 346

Cymbeline King of Britaine. 369

The same page "restored"

one can hope to own a perfect Coverdale Bible, for example; the best that one can do is to get a Coverdale with a good provenance (mine is the Sir George Holford copy). But when I was last in London I lent myself quite willingly to a little deceit in the matter of a *Pamela*. I wanted a copy of this rare book: I just had to have it. For two years I looked in vain for one, and finally found one at Quaritch's. In conversation with E. H. Dring—who is in effect Quaritch—I was told that he had a *Pamela* the first two volumes of which, published in 1741, were in old calf; he had, at the time he bought these volumes, the two last published as a sequel to the story a year later, but in a different style of binding. In order to make the set match, he sent all four volumes to Zaehnsdorf with instructions to bind the last two exactly like the first two, but he would not sell me the set until I had seen it and was satisfied. I saw it, and was. Old leather had been secured and the greatest skill shown in its use; no one, unless his attention was called to it, could detect which pair were bound a hundred and fifty years ago and which yesterday.

Every detail of an old book must be studied with the greatest care, but with caution nothing very dreadful is likely to happen. And new books, which are likely to be perfect when we buy them, will turn to dust and ashes almost as soon as we shall. The paper out of which they are made is not made of linen or even cotton rags, but out of wood—wood decomposed in acid; in a few years the paper will become so fragile that one can hardly turn a leaf without breaking it; ultimately—not much after its author—it will

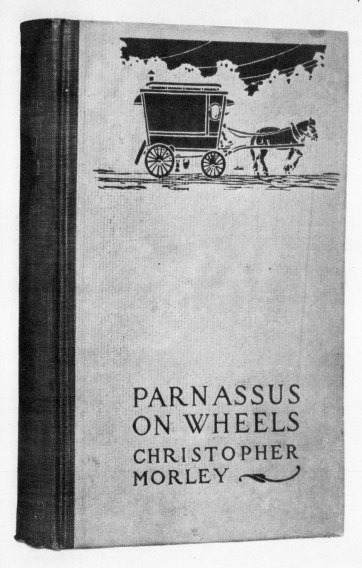

A first "Parnassus" "in mint state," now becoming very scarce

turn to dust. This melancholy thought occurred to me when, a few days ago, I paid forty dollars for Kit Morley's *Parnassus on Wheels*, to replace a presentation copy which had been borrowed by an appreciative friend. Luckily the manuscript had been carefully locked away, with other manuscripts from the same graceful pen.

to put them all in the store before Andrew saw them — except those from the Decameron Jones people, which sometimes held checks. Literary ~~folks~~ folks used to turn up now and then to interview Andrew, but generally I managed to head them off.

But Andrew got to be less and less of a farmer & more and more of a literary man. He bought a typewriter. He would hang over the pigpen noting down adjectives for the sunset instead of mending the weather vane on the barn which took a slew so that the north wind came from the southwest. He hardly ever looked at the Sears Roebuck catalogue any more, and after Mr Decameron came to visit us and suggested that Andrew write a book of country poems the man became simply unbearable.

A page from "Parnassus on Wheels"

Ballade of Librolarceny

When this ballade appears in print
    Someone will feel a guilty thrill,
So circulate it without stint
    And shout it loud on every hill.
    The bibliopilfering bibliophil
        Perhaps will ponder and repent
    To hear me cry with accent shrill
        Where are the books that I have lent?

Where are my Gissings gone, I hint?
    Whose bookcase do my Conrads fill?
And my Decameron? I squint
    Along my shelves and feel a chill:
    Lavengro gone! O imbecile
        To lend that book! Yes, I am shent.
    I'll put your conscience on the grill—
        Where are the books that I have lent?

My Daisy Ashford, my Peer Gynt,
    My Ocean Tramp — all gone! Until
Those books come back my heart is flint;
    My Trivia too — a bitter pill!
    Now, by the root of Yggdrasil
        I ask where my Max Beerbohms went?
    And so I roar, with metric skill,
        Where are the books that I have lent?

ENVOY

The bibliokleptomaniac will
Reply (of course) he truly meant
To bring them back last week .... but still
Where are the books that I have lent?

Christopher Morley

Dear Caliph — remembering yr
lamentation once, yr vanished
Parnassus I've copied this
out for you — it's not
new but you may
not had seen
it.
    Kit

Reproduction of manuscript of poem by Kit Morley

THE EIGHTH SIN

BY

C. D. MORLEY

"There is no greater Sin after the seven deadly than to flatter oneself into an idea of being a great Poet." *Letters of John Keats.*

OXFORD

B. H. BLACKWELL, BROAD STREET

LONDON

SIMPKIN, MARSHALL & CO. LIMITED

MCMXII

Handwritten inscription:

To A.E.N. with my love (April 1927)

Dear Caliph – I suddenly realize, seeing this pamphlet again, why it is that the author has no copy of his own primary indiscretion. He has no copy because he gave it to you. But unless there were testimony to that effect it might be supposed that you had obtained the pamphlet by sinister means. And so dear Caliph I rededicate to you this copy of a sheaf of peccadilloes which, when they were innocently committed, never dreamed of reaching a haven (or heaven) of edition, and bindings such as Oak Knoll & your very affectionate Kit Morley

Kit Morley's first and scarcest book

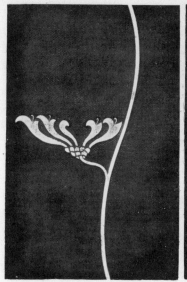
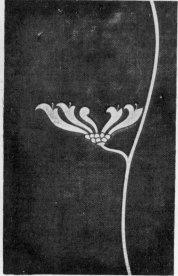

Correct cover stamp of first
edition of "Tess"

Cover stamp of second
edition of "Tess"

Since these pages were originally written, a very pretty piece of sophistication has come to the surface. First editions of Thomas Hardy are now in great demand: *Tess of the D'Urbervilles* is probably Hardy's most popular novel; it was published in 1891, and was bound in orange-brown cloth which soiled easily, and as most of the copies passed into the lending libraries, good, clean copies are scarce. A friend, seeing a copy advertised in an English catalogue as in "mint state" for sixty pounds, at once cabled for it, got it, and seeing that it appeared as represented, at once paid for it. Exultingly he showed it to John Eckel—just back from New York with a new "point" in his mind: he had it from James F. Drake. "The book is a good clean copy of the first edition, but the binding is the binding of the *second* edition," said John. "How do you make that out?" said my friend. "Look closely at the side stamp," said John. My friend looked and saw nothing out of the ordinary; then John pointed out a tiny difference. In the binding of the first edition, under the five-leaved flower are five tiny dots, under these are three dots, and under these the stem of the flower widened out at the top. In the binding of the second edition the widened portion of the stem is divided into three members, the centre member having a small dot on either side. Some enterprising bookseller had secured a copy of the first edition, good inside but in a soiled binding: this cover had been replaced with a clean binding of the second edition! Only the most careful scrutiny, such as few give their books, would reveal the deception practised, but once one's attention was called to it, it was quite obvious. I had the right first and the wrong first photographed side by side that he who runs may read—if he be very expert in reading. I understand that the Maggs Brothers in London were the first to discover this "point," which confirms a statement once made to me by Thomas J. Wise, that no book could be reproduced, except by photography, in which sooner or later some variation would not be discovered. Reader, somewhere deep down in my memory I have hundreds of these "points," and I verily believe that Mr. Wise has tens of thousands of them. If I could make one-half of Mr. Wise's "points" my own, I, too, would be famous.

IX

"ABUSES STRIPT AND WHIPT"

UNDER this caption, which was first employed as a title for a volume of verses by George Wither, I shall deal briefly with two gentlemen whose names have attached themselves to two vices, both, luckily, now disappearing, but which for a century or more exerted enormous influence over the game we play with such enthusiasm. I shall first strip Dr. Bowdler and then proceed to whip Dr. Grainger.

Tom Bowdler was born near Bath in 1754, and it is his distinction to have discovered that Shakespeare used many words and phrases which were not suited to the polite society of his (Bowdler's) day; he therefore proceeded, in 1818,—when he was old enough to know better,—to produce what he called *The Family Shakespeare*, in which he modestly says that, while he has added nothing to the original text, "he has deleted from it all those words and expressions which cannot with propriety be read aloud in a family." The work had a large sale and exerted an enormous influence; indeed, we are only now fully escaped from it.

It was Tom's belief that any word or expression unfit for chaste ears, or eyes even, ought not to be spoken or written or printed, and, if printed, should be erased. This would make hash of most classics, including the Bible, which indeed he says "calls imperiously for erasement;" and no doubt, had he been "spared," he would have answered the call, but the last years of his life were devoted to "purifying Gibbon."

ABVSES

STRIPT,

AND

WHIPT:

OR

SATYRICAL ESSAYES.

By GEORGE WITHER.

Diuided into two Bookes.

Πολλακὶ τοὶ κὶ μωρὸς ανὴρ κατακαίρεον ἔιπε.

Despise not this, what-ere I seeme in show :
A foole to purpose speakes sometime, you know.

LONDON,
Printed by *Humfrey Lownes*, for *Francis Bur-*
ton: and are to be sold at his Shop in Paules
Church-yard, at the signe of the Greene
Dragon. 1615.

In a Gibbon's *Rome*, designed for the use of families and young persons, he reprinted from the original text, "but with the careful omission of all passages of an irreligious or immoral tendency." In the preface he was complacent enough to assert that he felt sure that Gibbon himself would have approved his plan and that his version would be adopted by all future publishers. His nephew, who saw the book through the press, added a note in which he says that it was his uncle's peculiar happiness to have purified both Shakespeare and Gibbon, "that they might no longer raise a blush upon the cheek of modest innocence nor plant a pang in the heart of the devout Christian."

Had Bowdler lived long enough, he doubtless, after having worked his way through literature, would have taken on the arts and painted over offending pictures and clothed the legs of statues in pantalettes. But let us not laugh too loudly at him: we have only recently lost our own peerless one, William Jennings Bryan, who was a man of the same stripe.

It is really amazing in how many different ways men get their thrills or "kick" out of life. There is, I take it, no reason why a man should not amuse himself by "bowdlerizing" a classic for his own amusement; the harm arises from the publication of a text which purports to come from the pen of an author as he wrote it and which bears upon its title-page no suggestion that it has been "purified" to meet the whim of an old woman—of either sex.

Bowdler's influence lasted for a hundred years, and thousands of books have been expurgated to meet the views of his followers. In the early editions of Pepys's

Diary, whole pages of naïve naughtinesses were omitted; so it was with the letters of James Boswell of Auchinleck, Esquire, until they were taken in hand by Professor Tinker. But to-day it is regarded as an editor's first duty to secure and publish a corrupt text, if such be the text as the author left it. (If this is a pun, as I suspect it is, let the reader make the most of it.)

The question arises: should certain diaries and letters—John Keats's letters to Fanny Brawne, say—be given to the world? That is another matter; but, if published, they should not be expurgated without letting the reader know, at least by asterisks, where certain words or paragraphs have foundered—"marking the spots by buoys," as someone has said, that one may, if necessary, return and dredge for them. Gibbon when squeamish, which was not often, veiled himself in the obscurity of a learned language; this is unkind to the reader who has not Latin at his command. I know nothing more tantalizing than, right in the middle of a spicy story, to have it terminate in a dead end, as it were.

A collateral question also arises. Some time ago a gentleman by the name of Tinker (not my friend, the Professor, but another) went to the Morgan Library in New York to see some manuscripts of Lafcadio Hearn, and was informed by Miss Belle Greene that they had been destroyed several years ago. Mr. Tinker expressed his horror that such an act of vandalism should have been committed, whereupon the librarian explained that the manuscripts were indelicate, and casually stated that in that very room she herself had burned a number of Washington letters. (The reader will, no doubt, remember that Lord Byron's journals and some of his letters were in the same way, and for the same reason, destroyed by John Murray, his publisher, in the library of his house in Albemarle Street.) But to return to the Washington letters: they were smutty, too, the librarian said, and, "as we did not want them to become public and smudge the reputation of the Father of his Country, we destroyed them."

"Could you afford to pay the price and then destroy your investment?"

"We could and did," promptly replied Miss Greene. Whereupon Mr. Tinker vented his indignation upon the suppression of "historical data" and declared that all of us have, to a greater or lesser degree, an inherent interest in the "slightly salacious." There you have it: to what extent shall salacious curiosity be satisfied? So far as the Washington letters are concerned, it may well be that when Mr. Morgan bought them he bought them with the idea of preventing their getting into print, but I think, had I been in his place, I should have kept the letters and made them accessible only to scholars, as similar letters of Franklin are. We all know that great men have their weaknesses, their vices, perhaps; and when, owing to the general nobility of their character, as in the case of Washington, or to their wisdom and general usefulness, as in the case of Franklin, they have been placed by posterity upon a pedestal, I would not have them toppled therefrom that the "salacious curiosity" of the public be satisfied. In a historic sentence Commodore Vanderbilt tersely expressed my opinion of the public.

Graingerizing is the second abuse to which I should like to call attention. It has been called an art, but I should prefer to call it a crime, in that it consists, too frequently, in the destruction of many books for the production of one, which when completed is likely to prove a white elephant upon one's hands.

The Graingerized book takes its name from Dr. James Grainger, an eighteenth-century print-collector and bibliographer, who obtained a vicarage and "early retired to independence, obscurity, and content." This suggests a man of wisdom. Politically, he was a Whig, and Dr. Johnson, speaking of him, said, "The dog is a whig: I do not like much to see a whig in any dress, but I hate to see one in a parson's gown." Grainger is, with his followers, responsible for at least the partial destruction of thousands of books; his fame rests upon a *Biographical History of England*, a book I think I have never seen, although it passed through several editions. It was designed by its author to be a sort of thread upon which he could string an endless series of engraved portraits. Up to the appearance of his *History* in 1769, five shillings, it is said, was regarded as a good price for a fine engraved portrait. Immediately upon publication there was a rush to illustrate the book, and libraries were ransacked and priceless volumes mutilated; a sharp knife, better still a wet thread, and lo! some book was stripped of a portrait and replaced upon the shelves. The destruction was enormous; to this very day it is almost impossible to find books of a certain class unmutilated by some follower of the well-meaning clergyman. One contemporary who kept his head during this South

Sea Bubble of the printroom said, "If this *goût* for prints continues, let private owners and public libraries look well to their books, for there will not remain a single unmutilated volume in the kingdom." Engraved portraits rose to many times their original price. Dr. Johnson said of the *History:* "It is full of curious anecdotes, but might have been better done" (the author was a Whig, it will be remembered). Boswell wrote to the lexicographer: "I have, since I saw you, read every word of Grainger's *Biographical History;* it has entertained me exceedingly." And it was, of course, a book after Dibdin's own heart—Thomas Frognall of that ilk.

It was impossible that so virulent a craze should stop with the *History*, where it began; it extended to other books: nothing escaped. It may be of interest to refer to some of the great books which have been Graingerized into a sort of infamous immortality. Dibdin, the librarian of Earl Spencer, tells of a Shakespeare that took sixteen years to complete. A Bible which extended to forty-five volumes, valued at three thousand guineas, brought, when sold at auction, four hundred and five pounds. A copy of *Clarendon's Rebellion* cost ten thousand pounds to illustrate, and a copy of Voltaire was extended to ninety volumes—twelve thousand engravings were inserted in it.

It is only within our own time that the craze has subsided, having been kept alive by many of the London and New York booksellers who have found it profitable. Biographies, especially Boswell's *Life of Johnson, The Memoirs of Count Gramont*, with his stories of the unblushing beauties of the Court of Charles II, topographical books, and books on the stage, lend themselves especially to this treatment, and years may be pleasantly and profitably spent in assembling material for the illustration of one's favorite volume; but the sport should end there unless one is prepared to see a heavy shrinkage, should one for any reason decide to dispose of one's material. I have never seen an extra-illustrated book bring much over ten per cent of its cost. My first impulse when I acquire such a book—and I occasionally do at auction, they go so cheaply—is to resolve it into its component parts, to break it up. But that seems a pity and I never do.

My advice to anyone seeking to extra-illustrate a volume is Mr. Punch's advice to one about to get married: DON'T. But if you must, then carefully index your material and keep it in a cabinet. The moment the work is complete and bound, it has lost its interest and its value *unless* it is your intention to give the work to some public institution; in any case, I insist upon an index. In my time I have owned several extra-illustrated Boswells; I still own one. Originally it was given, in boards, "To James Boswell Esquire Jr. from his affectionate Father, the Authour." At the sale of his effects it passed into the library of the great Heber, who put his stamp therein, and at his sale it was bought by a Mr. Rodd, and from him purchased on January 13, 1835, by John Murray (Byron's Murray) for two pounds, ten shillings, as his signature and a note record. Murray had it extra-illustrated; the two volumes were extended to four, and a printed index made, which occupies a fifth volume. Here, now, is an extra-illustrated volume with a provenance, not the article of commerce such as Goodspeed, of Boston, produces—a volume of which the most fastidious collector need not be ashamed. Originally it was a part of the "Sentimental Library" of Harry B. Smith. What a collection of books was that assembled by that enlightened collector! The Rosenbachs bought the library *en bloc*, and first offered it for sale, as ill luck would have it, on the day the Lusitania was sunk by the cowardly act of a German submarine; incidentally, securities sank as suddenly; war seemed imminent, but I felt that such another opportunity would not again occur, and I bought all that I could afford—I think five times the prices I then paid would not now be high. In the case of the manuscript of Charles Lamb's *Dream Children*, ten times would not be regarded as excessive.

To return to Dr. Grainger. He was a poet as well as a preacher, his most famous production being a blank verse effort called *The Sugar-Cane*. It was read aloud from the manuscript one evening at Sir Joshua Reynolds's, in spite of Dr. Johnson's protests. "Who could make a poem on a sugar-cane?" the sage inquired; "one might as well write a poem on a parsley-bed or a cabbage-patch." However, the reading went on, until the poet began a verse with the line:—

"Now, Muse, Let's Sing of *Rats*."

This occasioned much merriment, and "rats" in the printed version was changed to "whisker'd vermin." It's hard to kill a good idea!

Grainger died early, in his fifty-third year, insane as some think. Just before his death he preached a sermon before the Archbishop of Canterbury, which he subsequently printed with this dedication to his congregation: "To the inhabitants of the parish of Ship-lake, who neglect the services of the church and spend the Sabbath in the worst kind of idleness, this plain sermon which they never heard, and probably will never read, is inscribed by their sincere well-wisher and faithful minister, J. G." The right to print is inalienable.

I had just finished writing the above when a letter arrived, which I venture to give practically in its entirety, first ascertaining that its writer is, like myself, a happy man—for I have never found anyone who would dispute Dr. Johnson's saying that "the happiest life is that of a man of business with some literary pursuit for his amusement." My unknown correspondent, Frank C. Deering, of Saco, Maine, is a man of affairs, bank president, philanthropist, scientist, collector, and an extra-illustrator—obviously, my superior. I had never heard of him until his letter arrived, but I look forward to making his acquaintance. I have recently bought a new motor car and, wishing to exercise it, I shall accept his invitation. My excuse for publishing his letter is because it gives the other side of the extra-illustrating game, and gives it so succinctly that it cannot but prove interesting and valuable to the reader. And Mr. Deering's letter proves another thing: namely, that I argue, not for victory, but with an honest desire to enlighten and inform, however mistaken I may be in my judgments. Here is the letter:—

"Some years ago my daughter presented me with your volume, *The Amenities of Book-Collecting*. On page fifty-seven I found a gentle slam at extra-illustrating. I have always felt a little bit sore about that criticism, but in reading your article in the *Atlantic Monthly*, published last December, I found a remark that gave me courage, and soothed my wounded feelings: 'If I were to begin again, I would collect Americana.' You may be sure of this: if you had devoted yourself to collecting Americana you could not write as delightfully as you do. The dry atmosphere of early American History is not conducive to brilliant literary production." This will make that brilliant librarian, Randy Adams, laugh, but what of that?

Just a word about extra-illustrating. I have had many gentle reproofs for pursuing what is, to me, a real pleasure, mainly because those who have chided me have not understood what I have tried to do. It always seemed to me to be a mistake to crowd a volume and make it a museum rather than what it is intended to be; so from odd places, here, there, and everywhere, I gather historical articles, carefully split them, and put them together to make a continuous volume.

Now and then I have found an obscure pamphlet, such as one picked up in Nova Scotia some years ago which had a very clear account of the Acadians. There were some two hundred pages, each six inches long by two and one-half inches wide. This, you see, was a very awkward shape to make into a book, so I carefully split each leaf, mounted it, then inserted some nice wood engravings, each mounted with an India-paper background. Completed, the book numbered about two hundred and fifty pages, size seven inches by ten, bound in full Levant with modest tooling. It had no particular history and never had belonged to any celebrated literary character. I made it myself, so it seemed pardonable to dress it in a nice suit of clothes, because I certainly do love to handle crushed Levant.

An old fellow, whose eccentricities I knew and appreciated, wrote and published in the local newspaper some years ago the History of Fryeburg, Maine. I am sure most of those newspapers must have long since perished. I split each column of the article carefully, mounted it, inserted a few prints, including one of the old gentleman, and again indulged in full Levant.

You will note by the enclosed newspaper clipping that five hundred volumes are the product of my industry. A large portion of them have been along the same lines I have described. I am sure you will let these pass without condemning them too severely. Of course I have done Napoleon and Gramont, also others of like nature. I am sure I have never sacrificed good books for the sake of prints, and I have rescued hundreds of the latter from actual loss.

Will you pardon too frequent use of the pronoun I? I have always felt grieved over your reference to extra-illustrating, and more than once have been tempted to write a word in explanation of the way the work can be done—instead of being destructive, prove the reverse.

Your remarks about keeping rare volumes in their original binding are absolutely right. I never mar the simplicity of my early Americana with either print or autograph. They are kept in either slip or Solander cases, and absolutely as the early New Englander handled them.

I have no reply to make to Mr. Deering's letter. Shall I have a reader who does not envy me its receipt?

X

WHAT TO COLLECT—AND WHY

I HOLD that book-collecting is the best of indoor sports, and I think I can prove it; at any rate, I shall try. It may be admitted at the outset that we book-collectors do not make the splash that the picture-collector does: we don't spend so much money and we don't get stuck so often, and we like to think we improve our minds more. But it is not my intention to run down the other man's hobby; I only hope he gets as much fun out of it as I do out of mine. I wonder whether you, reader, remember a best-seller of many years ago—*David Harum*. It was an excellent story: David was a sort of New York Yankee, full of wise sayings, one of which was "A reasonable amount of fleas is good for a dog; they keep him from broodin' on bein' a dog." In the same way a hobby is a good thing for a man: it takes his mind off his business—

and we hear somewhat too much of business, big and little, in this country to-day. The fact is, we can do pretty much everything as well as the other fellow— except live; and if you'll stop to think for a moment you will see that life is most important: we are always going to live, but never do. Out of the window, across the lawn, I see a sundial, and the motto on it reads:—

> I'll live tomorrow
> You delaying cry—
> In what far country
> Does tomorrow lie?

Or put it another way, as my friend Dr. Johnson did—and he was a very wise man, almost as wise as his great contemporary, Benjamin Franklin. Dr. Johnson used to say, "Sir" (he almost always began a remark that way), "to seize the good that is within our reach is the great art of life;" and we, in our terse way, say, DO IT NOW—and then don't do it.

I wish that someone would give a course in how to live. It can't be taught in colleges: that's perfectly obvious, for college professors don't know any better than the rest of us—sometimes I think they know less. "All work and no play makes Jack a dull boy." Very true, but I am not strong for games. They are all right for boys—a boy should be able to stand any sort of racket; but after a man has turned forty and settled down nicely to his job of making a living and raising a family, games become pretty strenuous. And when we play them we play them to excess, as we are prone to do everything.

The other day, going up in an elevator in one of our large office buildings, I heard one man say to another,

"What did you do yesterday, Charlie? Played golf, I suppose." "Yes," replied Charlie, "thirty-eight holes, and when I got through I was all in, believe me." Instantly I thought of a friend of whose death I had read in the paper not long before. My friend was a captain of industry: big, rich, powerful, and busy— very busy. A few months before he had, in England, played thirty-eight holes; then he had an attack of something, and Lord Dawson, the King's physician, was sent for and looked him over carefully, inquiring, "What have you been doing? Playing golf? It's too strenuous for a man of your age and habit." My friend admitted that he had. "Well, don't do any more of it; I fear you have permanently weakened your heart." A few months later my friend was dead "from indigestion" (this is a word physicians have agreed shall cover up a certain proportion of our many deaths from heart disease).

Now I maintain that a man who lives on a battlefield—and to a certain extent a man's office is a battlefield—I maintain, I say, that a certain amount of quiet relaxation is what he needs of an evening. Some get it with a pack of cards: they mess up the cards and fix them this way and that, and call it solitaire, and if anyone calls and wants to talk they resent it. We book-collectors, on the other hand, mess around with our books: we fix them this way and that; we catalogue them and compare prices and what we call "condition," and if anyone calls and wants to talk about them we are delighted.

As I have said before, I sometimes think that the best part of book-collecting is the delightful acquaintances one makes, and when acquaintances become friends, and visits and letters and experiences are exchanged, one feels the joy of life. And more: if we play the book-collecting game with any skill, we come to know a good deal about some one thing and something about a good many things, and this goes to make what is usually called an educated man—and we have none too many of them. Anything which enlarges one's horizon is good, and reading does—there is good authority for it. And at last the game is called; the curtain falls upon the play, and our toys, our books, are put away or sent to the auctioneer to be sold, and our friends will say, "I had no idea Blank's library was so valuable. I remember when he paid seventy dollars for that copy of Keats's *Poems;* I thought him a fool. Did you see what it brought at the auction? Thirty-three hundred dollars! Think of it!" And a certain, if limited, immortality is conferred upon the book-collector in that years after his death, if a book that has once been his and has his bookplate in it comes upon the market or is otherwise discovered, he is remembered as having been, in his time, a man of some importance. And of course, if one plays the game with the skill of a Huntington or a Morgan, one's name will be remembered as long as our civilization holds.

Have I made good my claim that book-collecting is the best of indoor sports? Have I told you *why*?

No.

Let me try again: let me mount my hobby and put my animal through its paces. It can be ridden in all weathers, indoors and out, fast and furious, disregarding all obstacles—or sedately, as befits one no longer in the first flush of youth. You can stop when you like, and the expense stops too. This is not true of keeping a string of horses, or a kennel or a yacht; it is not even true of a motor, for there is a depreciation charge running all the time—with books it is the other way about.

Mind you, I do not say that books are a good investment; for the average man over a term of years there is nothing as good as a share or, better still, several shares of stock in a good railway company like Atchison or United States Steel or General Motors—I mention these because I haven't any of them. If I had bought a lot of any of these years ago, I should be a rich man to-day—but then, look at the fun I'd have missed. When a bookseller tells you that such and such a book is a good investment, laugh at him and tell him that when you are in an investing mood you will seek a banker, that when you come to him you are about to be extravagant. Sometimes extravagance and wise investing go together, but not as often as your bookseller would have you believe; you hear of a man paying fifty dollars for a book and selling it for five hundred, but not of his experiences the other way. A man boasts of his gains, but he does not speak so freely of his losses; he thinks it is a reflection on his judgment. Be satisfied when the game is called to get your money back; if you collect with any skill you may certainly expect to do that.

In this paper I shall try to tell you how you may eat your own cake and have it, and I shall assume that you have a sort of fondness for reading, especially for history and for biography—which is, after all, only history in miniature; and that you can read, with pleasure, a good sound novel—I don't mean the trash that pours in a continuous stream from the press; and that somewhere in your inner consciousness a fine poem such as—never mind what, there are thousands of them—makes appeal. If you are a man of middle age with a substantial bank account—good! If you are a boy with very little money to spare— so much the better: the best collectors I know began young.

And now I am going to throw reticences to the winds and write just as I should talk if you were sitting in my library—for writing, as Laurence Sterne says, when properly managed, is only a different word for conversation.

Not long ago I found on my library table a large substantial volume of over two hundred pages. It was the ninth and final volume of the catalogue of the library of a friend, Thomas James Wise of London, who is, without doubt, the most learned book-collector we have to-day. He is not a college man; that is to say, he did not study at a college; but as the University of Oxford has honored him with a degree, it will be admitted that he is a scholar. Mr. Wise is, or was, a business man,—or, as they say in London, a City man,—and, judged by our present-day standards, he is not and has never been a very rich man; yet this is what he has accomplished: He has formed what is, by common consent, the finest library of its kind in the world. He takes the year 1640 for his starting point. For the quartos of Shakespeare—those little slender volumes each containing a single play—he early decided that he was born too late or too poor. Had he been born a

Thomas James Wise

generation earlier, he would have had them, for they were then available for a few pounds apiece; to-day they run up into the thousands—of pounds, mind you, not dollars—and, if you want exceptionally fine or scarce copies, into the tens of thousands. Mr. Wise then, knowing that the quartos could never be his, decided that, within certain limits, everything else should be. Perhaps he did not consciously arrive at this conclusion, but he reached it all the same, and to-day his library is the admiration and despair of the entire English-speaking world. Fiction is a thing of comparatively recent birth; poetry is an older and men say a greater art; at any rate it is an art in which the English surpass the whole world, and this is the field which Mr. Wise has made peculiarly his own.

Each volume of this great catalogue has an introduction written by some friend or scholar, in which the writer seeks to do justice to Mr. Wise's skill and knowledge as a book-collector. In one volume I tried my prentice hand at singing his praises, but in the volume before me the writer points out several facts that I knew but had forgotten: namely, that the owner of this great library had collected every book without the assistance of agents or advisors; that he had collated—that is, examined minutely—every page of every book; and that he had written every word of the catalogue with his own hand. To accomplish this, two things were essential; colossal industry and a marvelous memory. He carries, indeed, in his head every bibliographical detail of every book that has passed the severe test of admission into his library, for only the best need apply; a poor copy of a book, unless it is known to be unique, can by no means enter. Indeed I may say that until I saw, and saw repeatedly, Mr. Wise's books I had no idea that it was possible to secure so many volumes in such faultless condition. Incidentally, let me say here that "condition" is always more important than "price" in buying a book. A superb copy of any desired book is always cheap at any price; a poor copy is generally dear.

If I have lingered unduly over Mr. Wise's books, it is only to point out that what man has done man can do—with a difference, certainly, for never again can such a library as Mr. Wise's be created. But because one cannot form a library like Mr. Wise's, or Mr. Huntington's, or Mr. Morgan's, shall one not do what he can? Half a loaf is better than no bread, and perchance with a slice one must be, perforce, content.

But the reader may say, and with truth, that Mr. Wise sat at the gate; nothing passed either in or out of London but that he had a look at it; every bookseller, proud of having Mr. Wise as a client, favored him. Very true—but what shall be said of another friend, Paul Lemperly of Cleveland, Ohio? Cleveland is by way of being a gateway to the Great Lakes, if you will, but by no chance—although it is the home of a group of book-lovers who founded the Rowfant Club—could you call it a bibliographical centre. And Mr. Lemperly has always been, comparatively, a poor man; but within his limits—and they are modest—he has a collection of books which, were they to knock at Mr. Wise's door, he would bid welcome. If the locale and the learning and the pounds, shillings, and pence of Mr. Wise are superior to Mr. Lemperly's, the enthusiasm which led him many years ago to buy books with caution and cunning is identical with that of Mr. Wise. Take an illustration. There is a small volume of poems much in demand with collectors to-day, called *A Shropshire Lad*, by A. E. Housman. It was published in London in 1896 for a few shillings; a copy sold last week in New York for three hundred and fifty dollars. When this book came out Lemperly saw that it had merit and, before either the book or the author was generally known, bought a copy for one dollar and seventy-five cents. When the second edition came out, several years later, Lemperly wrote the author and asked if it contained anything new. Housman answered as follows:—

DEAR SIR:

The second edition of *A Shropshire Lad* contains nothing new except a few misprints. I have not published any other book.

I am much obliged by your letter and bookplate. I think yours is the only letter containing no nonsense that I have ever received from a stranger, and certainly it is the only letter containing an English stamp that I have ever received from an American. Your countrymen generally enclose the stamps of your great and free republic.

I am yours faithfully   A. E. HOUSMAN

This is what I call playing the game with skill: it is akin to landing a very large trout with a very small fly.

Take another instance. There are two very scarce books which collectors of modern authors go to great lengths to secure. In both cases the much-sought-for volumes are identical with the first editions of the same book; the only difference is the matter of the date, and a date on a book is quite as important as a signature on a check. The books in question are Lewis Carroll's *Alice in Wonderland*, 1865 (Lewis Carroll is a nom de plume: his right name was Dodgson and he was a lecturer on mathematics at Oxford) and Thomas Hardy's *Dynasts* (1903). By some chance—no one now knows just how—a few copies of each of these books with these dates got into circulation, whereas the generally accepted first editions bear the date of the year following. Both books are now worth ("worth" is the right word, if a thing is worth what it will bring) about twenty-five hundred dollars. Paul Lemperly's copy of *The Dynasts* cost him under twenty dollars! And I haven't the least doubt it has the "dust wrapper" on it.

Now this is what I call intelligent book-collecting. To be able to draw one's check for a large sum for a small book is very nice, but it is much nicer to use one's mind than one's money, for the more the mind is used, the better it is, whereas—but no doubt you get me. Good collecting depends on two things—money and intelligence; with either you may go far; with both you are irresistible. And now I must enlarge somewhat upon what collectors call "condition;" I have used the word before. In former days all one wanted was the book,—the text, so to speak,—but that is not the case now. The fastidious collector has declared for "old binding" or "in parts" or "in cloth" or "in boards;" in other words, the condition in which the book originally appeared. The moment a book has been tampered with, "rebound" or "washed," or improved by the insertion of a leaf from another copy to complete it, it must be looked upon with suspicion. And here we must differentiate. If one is speaking of an excessively rare book, of which only a few copies are known and these in public libraries, and another copy turns up at auction,—some Shakespearean quarto, say, or a masque like Milton's *Comus*,—the wise collector will buy that book if it be in his line and within his reach financially, and subsequently will do, or have his binder do, what he can to improve it; but if it is a book which he may reasonably hope to get "right," as the saying is, he will wait until a good copy comes along—and it usually does.

All things considered, it is surprising how many fine books there are. It would seem, indeed, as though someone, on the occasion of the first issue of a book by an unknown author, had immediately secured a copy and, locking it in a chest, had thrown away the key. George Grasberger showed me, not long since, a copy of Longfellow's *Evangeline*. It is a scarce book in any condition, but this copy, in the original lemon-color pasteboard covers, was as fresh and crisp as the day it was published over seventy-five years ago. It was in what collectors very properly call "mint state," borrowing the term from the coin-collector.

A large book is a self-protective book; it is the small books that disappear, especially if they are published in two volumes. How frequently does one come across the second volume of a book like Dr. Johnson's *Rasselas*, or the first volume of Stevenson's *New Arabian Nights*, the mate to which has disappeared, and forever, because someone "took it into the other room" and never brought it back. Then, too, certain books like Walton's *Angler* and Bunyan's *Pilgrim's Progress* instantly became so popular that the first editions were literally read to pieces; and when it comes to children's books like Goldsmith's *Goody Twoshoes*, these were, as someone has said, literally loved to shreds.

It usually develops that the first edition of any book which comes to be collected has an eccentricity of some sort by which it comes to be distinguished from subsequent issues. It is a bibliographer's job to discover and record these points, and battles are won or lost over a single word or even a misplaced letter or comma. Some books have one point on which the whole structure hangs; others have many. Let me illustrate. A scholarly pamphlet comes to my writing table from Professor Robert Metcalf Smith of Lehigh University; its title is *The Variant Issues of the Second Folio of Shakespeare*. From a glance at this piece of bibliographical work it would appear that there are *nine* variations of the title-page. Every collector having a copy of this book—and most of us have; it is by no means rare—will wish to ascertain whether his copy is one of the scarcer issues, and why. We have long known that there are six or seven different title-pages to the first edition of *Paradise Lost;* and now we are told that Milton's famous Epitaph on Shakespeare, his first published utterance, "What neede my Shakespeare for his honor'd bones," exists in at least three different forms. All of which is of importance—or not—depending upon how one is constituted.

Take another famous book, Walton's *Compleat Angler*, one of the loveliest books in our literature, and excessively rare in good condition. Most copies have been rebound, and in the binding the long line on page 245,

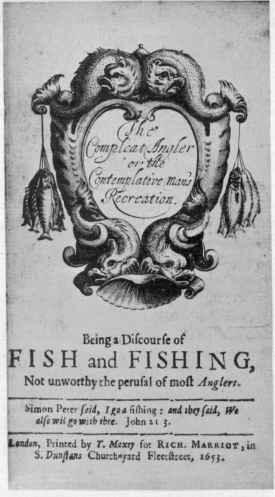

The Compleat Angler or the Contemplative mans Recreation.

Being a Difcourfe of

FISH and FISHING,

Not unworthy the perufal of moft *Anglers.*

Simon Peter *faid, I go a* fifhing : *and they faid, We alfo wil go with thee.* John 21. 3.

London, Printed by *T. Maxey* for RICH. MARRIOT, in S. *Dunftans* Churcheyard Fleetftreet, 1653.

Title-page of the first edition of Walton's "Angler"

ending with the word "loves," followed by a comma, is usually cut into by the binder's knife. A discriminating collector will want the entire word "loves" intact, and the comma too, if possible. This makes for "condition;" but there is still another matter. On the same page there should be the word "contention;" the sense requires "contentment," but "contention" is the "point" of the first issue. To be contented with "contentment" when one can have "contention" is like taking a widow when one can have a maid.

> The Complete Angler.   245
> Could I be more then any man that lives,
> Great, fair, rich, wise in all Superlatives;
> Yet I more freely would these gifts resign,
> Then ever fortune would have made them mine
> And hold one minute of this holy leasure,
> Beyond the riches of this empty pleasure.
>
> Welcom pure thoughts, welcome ye silent groves,
> These guests, these Courts, my soul most dearly loves,
> Now the wing'd people of the Skie shall sing
> My chereful Anthems to the gladsome Spring;
> A Pray'r book now shall be my looking glasse,
> In which I will adore sweet vertues face.
> Here dwell no hateful looks, no Pallace cares,
> No broken vows dwell here, nor pale fac'd fears,
> Then here I'l sit and sigh my hot loves folly,
> And learn t'affect an holy melancholy.
> And if contention be a stranger, then
> I'l nere look for it, but in heaven again.
>
> Viat. Wel Master, these be Ver-
> ses that be worthy to keep a room in
> every mans memory. I thank you
> for them, and I thank you for your
> many instructions, which I will not
> forget

The key page to a first "Angler"

Robinson Crusoe is so full of points that Henry Clinton Hutchins has written a large and handsome volume, published by the Columbia University Press, called *Robinson Crusoe and Its Printing*, to which I contributed a foreword which I am afraid Mr. Hutchins thought rather flippant, for in it I said: "How amazed Defoe would be if he could take up this Bibliography and follow the fortunes, not of Crusoe and his man Friday, but a mere word through several pages: the word 'apyly' or 'pilate,' for instance. Finally a matter of life and death seems to hang upon a colon—not that unpleasant thing we carry about in our insides, but a mark of punctuation; a stop, our English friends call it, or even half a colon."

Take another: *Humphrey Clinker*, in three volumes. The first volume must have an error in the date, 1671 being printed for 1771. If you wish to become involved in a pretty bibliographical puzzle, consult Edgar H. Wells, 41 East 47th Street, New York; after an interview with him, you will wrap a cold, wet towel about your head.

Take *Pickwick Papers*. My friend John C. Eckel, the Dickens bibliographer, has spent years in running down its thousand and one points—points which make one copy look cheap at fifteen thousand dollars and another dear at five hundred. All of which will soon be made clear in a book, *Prime Pickwicks in Parts*, in a format worthy of its subject, for *Pickwick* is one of the world's great books.

In the first edition of *Ben Hur*, the dedication reads: "To the Wife of my Youth." Upon the author being asked how many wives he had, he added to the dedication the phrase "who still abides with me."

Coming right down to date, there is Mrs. Edith

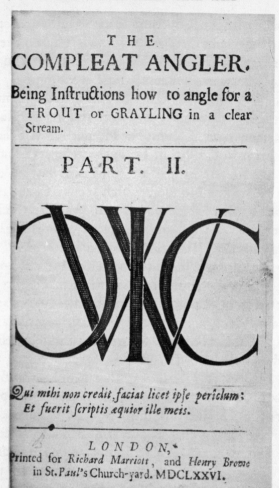

Wharton's excellent story, *The Age of Innocence*. In the early issues the author made an amusing slip on page 186. In a wedding scene the clergyman begins: "Forasmuch as it hath pleased Almighty God." It sounded so nice and pat that the writer, her several proof-readers, and thousands of others, did not realize that these words constitute the opening lines of the *burial* service, until an indignant clergyman wrote a letter to the publisher asking whether Mrs. Wharton did not know the difference between a funeral and a wedding.

Even *The Amenities of Book-Collecting* has its amusing "point." By some mischance I referred on page 268 to the Carlton Hotel's being in Piccadilly; as everyone knows, it is in Pall Mall. I caught the mistake in time to correct it, but instead of doing so I put an errata slip opposite the blunder, which reads: "The Author has made a slip of the pen in locating the Carlton Hotel in Piccadilly and not on the corner of Pall Mall and the Haymarket. His attention has been called to it, but he preferred to leave the blunder as it was—and is —as a sort of lightning rod for critics, to divert their attention from — possibly — probably — more serious blunders." Now anyone desiring an *Amenities* as first issued should make sure that it has this blemish and also the errata slip. It certainly never occurred to me when I baited this little trap that people would be so enthusiastic over my blunder as to pay forty or fifty dollars for a book containing it. The moral is: never destroy anything that is a part of a book; it does no harm and it may become important. This includes advertisements, dust wrappers; in a word, anything.

It is no fun to collect what nobody wants: to get a real "thrill" out of the collecting game, one must search for and occasionally find something that one's fellow collectors are especially keen about. The desire to collect things is as old as Egypt; one can hardly imagine anything in the line of personal property that is not, or has not been, by someone collected. Within the limits of my means I have sounded the entire gamut,—stamps, coins, pipes, canes, prints, and I have heard of those who collect buttonholes,—but, in my opinion, one can collect books with greater safety and profit than anything else. It is, however, of no use to tell the average man of the thrill that comes from the purchase or possession of a first folio of Shakespeare. Fifty thousand dollars—or whatever the price is—is a good deal of money; so is a thousand dollars; so is a hundred. Every important book I ever bought was followed by a moment of acute suffering—when I came to pay for it —akin to the drawing of a tooth, but its possession was a comfort comparable to the next day's feeling of sore but satisfied—it's over.

One usually begins by collecting the books he personally likes; then the author he likes; then the books of a certain period or class, and almost before he knows it he comes to think of himself as a collector. A man's joy in collecting depends not so much on the size of his bank account as on his emotional sense. One does not have to be a Huntington to get joy out of one's possessions. We, Mr. Huntington and I, were once talking of our books, and I asked him what was the most important Franklin item he had. Promptly he replied, "The manuscript of the *Autobiography;* what have you?" "The first edition of *Cato Major* in a fine old binding," I replied. Proportioned to our means, we each had just what we should have had. And it was so with our investments, too; in answer to my question, he once told me that his holdings in a certain property were about twenty million dollars, and I replied that mine were a few thousand, which, he remarked, was a very

pretty block and he hoped its possession would be a
source of pleasure and profit to me. It has. A pint pot
certainly does not hold as much as a barrel, nor a barrel
as much as a hogshead, but if it be full to overflowing
it makes a very pretty receptacle just the same. And
when one once makes a start, there is no telling how
far he may go. Great libraries, like great enterprises,
have small beginnings. Had a man told me when I
bought my first copy of that lovely book, White's
Natural History of Selborne, for fifteen cents, at Leary's
old bookshop, that the time would come when I should
pay several hundred dollars for Horace Walpole's copy
of the first edition, or that the greatest bookseller in
the world and I would some day be knocking about
London together and that I should see him give a
monarch's ransom for the original manuscript of this
great book—I should have thought him dreaming.

Leary's! How many readers and book-collectors
that famous old shop—Nine South Ninth Street,
Philadelphia—has made! Alas! it has disappeared, and
a newer and finer establishment has taken its place,
but it will not have the old aroma for fifty years—and
then where shall I be? (Reader, it is for my Maker, and
not you, to answer this question: I put it to you
merely as a matter of courtesy.) I am glad that I
secured a photograph of Leary's before the march of
improvement swept it away. Its proprietor became the
mayor of Philadelphia and the governor of the state,
and everyone loved and respected him and called him
Ned Stuart; even I did—and for me to love and respect
a mayor and a governor is something very unusual—
almost as unusual as for us to have governors and

to such, ... *from it's situation.* ... *in the district:* ...

In the [cent] of the village, & near the church is a square piece of ground, surrounded by houses; ... & vulgarly called the Plestor; in the midst of this spot stood in old times a vast Oak with a short squat body & huge horizontal arms extending almost to the extremity of the area. This venerable tree, surrounded with stone-steps, & seats above them, was the [delight] of old & young, & a place of much resort in summer-evenings; where the former sate in grave debate, *while* the latter frolicked & danced before them. Long might it have stood, had not the amazing tempest in the year 1703 overturned it at once, to the infinite regret of the inhabitants, & the vicar, ... who bestowed several pounds in setting it in it's place again: but all his care could not avail; the tree withered & dyed. This oak I mention to shew to what a bulk planted oaks *also* may arrive: & planted this tree must certainly have been, as will appear from what will be said farther concerning this area, when we enter on the antiquities of Selborne.

On the Blackmoor estate, *called Losils* there is a small wood of a few acres that was lately furnished with a set of oaks of a peculiar growth & *great* value: they were tall & taper like firs, but *standing* near together had very small heads, only a little brush *without* any large limbs. About 20 years ago the ... bridge at the Toy near Hampton-court *being* much decayed, some trees were wanted for the repairs that were 50 feet long with out a bough, & would measure 12 inches diameter at the little end. Twenty such trees did a purveyor find in *this* wood; with this advantage, that many of them answered the description ... at 60 feet. These trees were sold for

Reproduction of a page of the manuscript of one of the most popular books in English literature, White's "Selborne." Dr. R's property mayors worthy of respect. I met a senator a few days ago,—but never mind. It was at Leary's, too, that I bought my first volume of the *Essays of Elia*. I have my *Elia* and my *Selborne* among my rare books; they are, in effect, first editions to me.

Gilbert White discovered the formula for complete happiness, but he died before making the announcement, leaving it for me to do so. It is to be very busy with the unimportant. The author of *The Natural History of Selborne* became so interested in the birds and bats, the frogs and fishes, even the vermin of his parish, for he was a clergyman by trade, that he entirely forgot everything that was going on in the world—he even forgot to get married. I love an absent-minded man: like Charles Lamb's friend, George Dyer, who once walked right into a river; or like the old German college professor that my friend and eminent scholar, Morris Jastrow, used to tell about, who became so absorbed in his Chinese studies that during the Franco-Prussian War he inquired of a correspondent in China whether he had heard any of the details of the siege of Paris! Gilbert White was the specialist par excellence, and it is important for a man to know what he wants to become, and then go to it. In the collecting game a man must decide whether he will become a specialist or whether he will, like myself, buy in any or all directions just as his fancy takes him. All that I ask of a book is that I can read it, and my aim, so far as I have one, is to secure as many of the great books as I can pay for. I want the "landmarks," the "milestones," the books which mark the development of, to me, the most glorious thing in the world—English

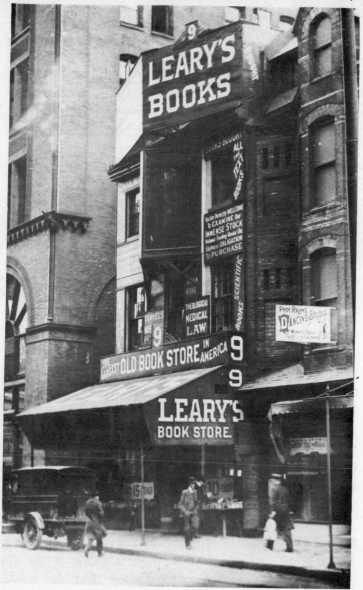

"Leary's," an old landmark—now disappeared

literature. I have no more wish to complete my collection of any one author than I have to complete my life.

I never allow myself to get into such a jam that I must have any particular item, for just then some rich collector, some man with soft hands and a hard face,— as Roosevelt, our master phrase-maker has it,—is sure to come along and snatch the coveted morsel away. If I can't get one thing, I can get another. I should very much like to have a *Gammer Gurtons Nedle*. It is the earliest of the so-called university plays, but Carl Pforzheimer bought the only available copy, so I contented myself with a copy of *Thersites*, (1560), which is even rarer. There is no copy either in the British Museum or the Bodleian.

If I have any reputation at all, it is as a Johnson collector; yet my Blakes have cost me more than my Johnsons. I have not yet bought Johnson's first book, which is commonly called *Lobo's Voyage to Abyssinia*, a translation from the French, which appeared anonymously in 1735. It is not a scarce book. When I first began to collect Johnson, over forty years ago, it was worth only a few shillings, but it never interested me; and if I boast a copy of Husband's *Miscellany* (1731), which contains Johnson's first printed composition, it is only because my friend Colonel Ralph Isham, taking pity upon my poverty, found and sent me a copy.

I think if I were asked what book had most profoundly influenced my life I should say Charles Reade's *The Cloister and the Hearth*. This requires a bit of explanation. It may be remembered that the hero, Gerard, when in Rome, goes skylarking one day on

A new Enterlude called Therſytes

¶ Thys Enterlude Folowynge
Dothe Declare howe that the
greateſt boeſters are not
the greateſt
doers.

¶ The names of the players

Therſites	A boſter.
Mulciber	A ſmyth.
Mater	A mother.
Miles	A knyght.
Telemachus	A chylde.

the Tiber, in company with a lot of libertines, each of
them bringing with him his mistress; Gerard—not
having a mistress—dressed up his servant lad, Andrea,
in woman's clothes and introduced him to the com-

pany as his ladylove, Marcia. But Marcia's shape and beauty excited the envy and curiosity of the women of the town, one of whom, becoming suspicious, asked the girl (in appearance) if she cared for almonds, and, upon receiving a reply in the affirmative, threw a handful of them into her lap; whereupon Andrea brought his knees together, as a male instinctively would do,—whereas a woman would have parted hers to make with her skirt a larger "lap," a larger receptacle,—and thus gave himself away, to the confusion of Gerard and the delight of the company.

Being struck with this story, I mentioned it to my friend, who said, "Yes, I remember the incident: Reade got it from *The Autobiography of Benvenuto Cellini*, and Mark Twain went to the same source for the story and put it in *Huckleberry Finn*. There's a book you ought to read, *The Autobiography of Benvenuto Cellini;* it is one of the great books of the world." Shortly afterwards my attention was again directed towards the book by an essay, "A Rogue's Memoirs," in a charming little volume, *Obiter Dicta*, by Augustine Birrell—the "Rogue" being, of course, Cellini. The *Autobiography* reads like a romance,—indeed, Cellini might have stepped out of the pages of Dumas,—but its effect on me was to stimulate my curiosity to know more of Francis I of France and Charles V and Henry VIII, and almost before I knew it I was deep in Prescott, Motley, and other historians. I read history and biography interchangeably; they go well together, for biography is only history in miniature.

A few years ago, being in Florence in company with Dr. Rosenbach, we called on Dr. Guido Biagi, the

Reproduction, much reduced, of a page of the manuscript of "The Autobiography of Benvenuto Cellini," in the Laurentian Library in Florence distinguished scholar and custodian of the Laurentian Library, and in conversation I told him of my interest in Benvenuto Cellini; whereupon he asked me if I had seen the manuscript of the *Autobiography*, and upon my replying no he sent for it, and I, with reverence and wonder, turned its pages. I suppose the most dramatic incident in the book is the story of the casting of the Perseus. Murder—of which there is enough—is commonplace compared with it, and I asked Dr. Guido Biagi if he could not have made for me a photograph of the page on which this incident is described. "Nothing easier," he replied; and that is how, and quite by chance, I am able to show my readers how a page of this famous *Autobiography* looks in manuscript.

A man may well consider, after he has accumulated a lot of books and spent a lot of money in so doing, what he expects will happen to them after his death. The chances are ten to one that no one in a man's family cares to accept the responsibility of caring for a large and valuable library. The responsibility is real: there is the constant danger from fire, water, theft, and neglect of servants. If it is a miscellaneous collection, it should undoubtedly be sold: it represents nothing except the momentary whim of the collector. If, on the other hand, it is the collection of a specialist, it should never be "disseverated," to use Gabriel Wells's word—it should always be kept together as a monument to the industry and patience of its creator. The final destination of the first editions of the great masterpieces of literature is a public library or museum. I have met scholars who have little sympathy with collectors of these editions. "All I want," they say, "is a good and readable text." They seem to forget that the most important books in all the great libraries of the world were once the cherished possessions of private individuals, who, it may be, sacrificed much to obtain them.

It is usual to decry the present price of books. Books have always been too high—and they have always gone higher. A few years ago a man writing an article in a magazine on book-collecting said, "I *anticipate* a slump in Dickens." He meant to say "expect"—but let that pass. A *Pickwick Papers* has just sold for forty-five hundred dollars! Such a price he considered "fantastic." It has since brought almost four times as much. Great authors are not born every day: the Hardys and the Kiplings are few; and personally I have a very high opinion of George Bernard Shaw. Keep on the highway, avoid detours, and you are safe. Pay the highest price ever heard of for a great book, and then go about your business and let your heirs, executors, and assigns worry. They won't; it is much more likely that they will rise up and call you blessed.

XI

AMERICAN LITERATURE

By this rather self-sufficient phrase we distinguish what we have accomplished in the last two hundred years in the way of belles-lettres. Much has not been expected of us, and much has not been produced. A century ago Sydney Smith wrote: "In four quarters of the globe, who reads an American book or goes to an American play, or looks at an American picture or statue?" And since this complacent statement was written England has produced very few artists and no sculptor or architect—judged by world standards—worth mentioning. England's modern architecture, when it is not pathetic, is ridiculous; Sydney Smith might well have contented himself with stressing England's superiority in the matter of literature.

Whether because we have had to subdue a continent, rich in practically every form of potential wealth, or for some other reason, our literary accomplishments have been meagre. The coterie of New England authors, so much esteemed fifty years ago, has now taken its proper place in the world's perspective—and it is not high. We respect Emerson, we esteem Hawthorne, we occasionally quote Lowell, but Longfellow we now know was hardly a poet. Holmes was a physician as well as the "Autocrat," and Whittier is a mere legend. Edgar Allan Poe has an assured place in the world, and James Fenimore Cooper still has his admirers; they are not numerous, but their number will increase. There remain Walt Whitman and Mark Twain: these I venture to believe will survive the flood which submerges all except the greatest. I cannot read Walt Whitman,

but the fault, I freely admit, is mine. There are a few
lesser names: Washington Irving, William Cullen Bryant, Bret Harte; I am getting to the end of the list,
having kept what may be the greatest name for the last
—Herman Melville. *Moby Dick* is America's supreme
contribution to world literature. For years we have
been looking for the great American novel, not knowing or not remembering that it appeared in 1851. On
this subject more anon. The list is not impressive, and
if I have to answer the question, "Why are not American authors collected in the sense that English authors
are?" I should say not only because they are not absolutely of first rank, but because they are not interesting.
Literature reflects life: we are a most uninteresting
people; industrious, well-meaning, philanthropic, educated—up to a point—generous, but tiresome; and, by
the same token, present-day English authors are little
if any better, and we are collecting them with too much
enthusiasm, I fear: it is not necessary to name names.
Democracy—which, in other words, means knocking
off the peaks to fill up the valleys—is responsible in
both countries. Tennyson has said: "The individual
lessens and the world is more and more." If you do
not care to put the blame where it belongs—on Democracy—blame it on the weather. Virginia is too hot,
and Massachusetts is too cold; in Pennsylvania do we
not boast our Charles Brockden Brown? Boast! He is
hardly more than a name to most of us. But as certainly
as we are now filling our houses with early American
furniture (much of it is, I suspect, spurious), putting
pine tables and settles and chairs in our drawing-rooms,
and paying absurd prices for glass bottles and Currier

Walt Whitman

Mark Twain—Doesn't look much like a humorist, does he?

and Ives lithographs, so surely will the time come when American authors will be collected. The desire to collect something is natural as soon as a man has provided himself with food, clothes, and shelter; and if we cannot collect one thing, we will another. The supreme books of the world—the *Paradise Losts*, the *Robinson Crusoes*, the *Vicars*, the *Elegies*, these and others like them—will continue to advance in price, but I should be wary of paying very high prices for books which Father Time has not yet permanently placed upon his shelves.

We have books of extreme interest printed in America, but they take rank as Americana rather than as literature. There is the *Bay Psalm Book*, undoubtedly the most valuable and interesting book printed in America; Mrs. Cornelius Vanderbilt owns the only copy now in private hands, her husband having paid twelve hundred dollars for it many years ago at the Brinley Sale. It will be interesting to see what becomes of it, for the final resting place of any excessively rare book is sooner or later a public institution. There is *Spiritual Milk for Boston Babes in either England, Drawn out of the Breasts of Both Testaments for their Souls' Nourishment:* Dr. Rosenbach owns a unique copy in his amazing collection of American Children's Books, now on exhibition in the superb Free Library of Philadelphia—for after years of delay, under the capable direction of its distinguished librarian, John Ashhurst, Philadelphia is now able to boast of one of the finest public libraries in the country. There is that amazing book of verse, *The Day of Doom*, elsewhere referred to, of which no early copy exists—it verges upon literature; and there is Poe's *Tamerlane*. No conceivable price is too high to pay for the first book of so great a genius as Edgar Allan Poe. After these—and a few more—the declension is rapid. Hawthorne's *Fanshawe*, written when the author was a student at Bowdoin College, whose rarity is due to the fact that Hawthorne himself destroyed the greater part of the edition; Lowell's *Commemoration Ode;* a few volumes of Thoreau—and the roll is called. Thoreau's first book, *A Week on the Concord and Merrimac Rivers*, is a desirable item, but my own choice is for *Walden;* perhaps because more than forty years ago, in company with a charming Boston girl, I made a pilgrimage to Walden Pond and to Concord and met there an old man—his name, I think, was Bartlett—who took us to all the places of interest in that lovely village and regaled us with stories of the great and near-great men who had once lived there. I remember thinking that he seemed to have been more than a little sweet on Louisa Alcott, and had read for her the proof sheets of that classic story, *Little Women*.

The most important collection of American authors recently made was that of the late Stephen H. Wakeman of New York, whose collection was dispersed at auction in April 1924, at the American Art Association. Mr. Wakeman, a business man, started out twenty-five years ago to collect his favorite authors—Bryant, Emerson, Hawthorne, Holmes, Poe, Longfellow, Thoreau, Lowell, and Whittier. He collected the finest obtainable examples, securing, where it was possible to do so, presentation copies. These showed, as was quite natural, a sort of mutual admiration

society at work. Poe presented to Hawthorne, as did
Lowell; Longfellow presented to Bryant, as did
Thoreau; Emerson presented to Thoreau—and so on.
There was no *Tamerlane*, and the highest price of the
sale was the dedication copy of *The Raven and Other
Poems*, "To Miss Elizabeth Barrett with the Respects
of Edgar A. Poe:" it brought four thousand two
hundred dollars, and would bring ten thousand to-day.
Bryant's *The Fountain*, with the inscription, "Charles
Dickens Esquire from his friend and admirer, William
Cullen Bryant," brought only four hundred dollars.
Bryant wrote what is, in my judgment, the finest
poem written by an American: I refer, of course, to
Thanatopsis, written when he was only nineteen years
of age. I don't know much about poetry, but if there is a
finer—something—to be aimed at than that contained
in the last nine lines of this poem, I am not aware of
it. To return: Bryant's first book, *The Embargo*, by a
youth of thirteen,—uncut and stitched as issued,—
brought five hundred dollars. Hawthorne's first book,
Fanshawe, brought ten hundred and twenty-five dollars;
while a copy of *Twice-told Tales* with an inscription,
"Miss Sophia A. Peabody" (whom he afterwards married) "with the affectionate regards of her friend Nath.
Hawthorne," brought a thousand. *The Scarlet Letter*,
to the same lady (she was now Sophia A. Hawthorne),
brought four hundred dollars; and a presentation copy
to his sister brought three hundred and fifty.

Of the Lowell items—and Lowell is an author not
sufficiently read to-day—the most important was the
Commemoration Ode: this brought eight hundred dollars.
A Year's Life, with an inscription in Lowell's hand,

"To Alfred Tennyson from the Author, Boston, U. S.," brought three hundred and twenty-five dollars. Holmes's *Memoir of Emerson*, presented to Whittier (the last book sold by George D. Smith to Mr. Wakeman just before G. D. S.'s sudden passing), brought seven hundred dollars.

But of course the Poes and the Hawthornes brought the high prices of the sale, although to-day they look cheap enough. *Al Aaraaf, Tamerlane, and Minor Poems*, the copy used by him in preparing the 1831 edition of his *Poems* and given by him to his cousin Elizabeth, brought twenty-nine hundred dollars; we are able to follow this copy to the Pierce Sale in 1902, when it brought eighteen hundred dollars, and to the Moore Sale, ten years earlier, when it brought only seventy-five. In the Foote Sale of 1894, which was the first important sale of American literature as opposed to Americana, several of these items appeared for the first time. In that sale a copy of *Tales of the Grotesque and Arabesque*, in which had been inserted five lines of writing in Poe's hand, brought seventy-two dollars; with the writing was a prospectus of a magazine which he proposed to publish. The five-line manuscript and the prospectus at the Wakeman Sale brought a thousand dollars, and the *Tales* alone three hundred. A copy of the *Tales*, revised in Poe's autograph for a new edition, brought thirty-four hundred dollars; while an inscribed copy of *The Raven and Other Poems*, to Sarah Helen Whitman, brought twenty-six hundred, and another copy of *The Raven*, with an autographed copy of the last verse laid in, brought twenty-nine hundred. Poe's own copy of *Eureka*, with many corrections, brought two thousand; this had been Griswold's, his literary executor's copy, and in the Hurst Sale in 1905 had brought five hundred and thirty dollars.

From these prices it will be seen that Poe commands to-day higher prices than any other American author, and it may be said that he and Whitman are our only two authors that are greatly esteemed out of their own country. This is not the place, nor am I competent, to make any estimate of Poe's genius, but it may be said without fear of contradiction that his *Tales* are unequalled in subtle and well-sustained horror, and his *Poems* are as faultless in rhythm and finish as they are impossible to explain. His life was sombre, and his death in his thirty-eighth year was tragic. He has all the elements which go, inevitably, to make a "collected" author—but where will you find the books? My own collection of the Americans is not much to boast of: I have a presentation *Raven and Other Poems*, with the inscription, "Miss Sarah Virginia Durant from her very sincere friend the author," and the last lines of an attack upon Henry B. Hirst (Poe was always either attacking or being attacked), who had accused the poet of plagiarism. This was formerly in the collection of Edmund Clarence Stedman, at whose sale I also secured a painting of Poe, in oils, by Gabriel Harrison.

Unfortunate in his life, Poe was also unfortunate in the selection of his literary executor, Rufus Wilmot Griswold; he was a Baptist minister, a profession which he deserted for literature. Temperamentally he was the last man either to understand or to sympathize with Poe's genius, but his book, *Prose Writers of America*,

by Mr Hirst, published in the last January
number of "Graham's Magazine":

"
  Mine the tongue that wrought this evil — mine
      { the false and slanderous tongue

  That done to death the Lady Gwineth — O, my
                  { soul is sadly wrung)!
  'Demon! devil!' groaned the warrior — 'devil
                  { of the evil eye!
  Look upon the awful horror wrought by thy
                  atrocious lie!'"

Now my objection, in this case, is not
to the larceny per se. I have always told
Mr Hirst that, provided he stole my
poetry in a reputable manner, he might
steal just as much of it as he thought
proper — and, so far, he has behaved
very well, in largely availing himself
of the privilege. But what I do object to,
is the being robbed in bad grammar.
It is not that Mr Hirst did this thing —
but that he has went and done did it.

Fragment of manuscript of Edgar Allan Poe

"Uncle Tom's Cabin," first edition, in the usual cloth binding

published in 1846 and enormously popular for many years, is a volume which no intelligent collector of American authors can afford to neglect.

No paper, however casual, on the subject in hand but must make reference to Harriet Beecher Stowe's *Uncle Tom's Cabin*. I shall, I think, never read it again, and I doubt whether I could sit through a performance of it; but who that has seen it as a boy, as I have, from the front row of the gallery of a crowded theatre, can forget it? The pathos of Uncle Tom, the pathos of little Eva, Eliza's escape over the ice from the bloodhounds, the humor of Topsy, the ferocity of Simon Legree, the death of— but no, I cannot bring myself to think of that child's passing. There was not a dry eye—not a dry handkerchief—in the house. It was written as a piece of "propaganda" (but I doubt if Mrs. Stowe had ever heard that now overworked word), and it swept over the country like a prairie fire. Published in Boston by John P. Jewett Company, in 1852, three thousand copies were sold the first day, and within the year no less than three hundred thousand. Eight power presses were kept working day and night to supply the demand; and its success in England was no less instant and enormous. In this country the book appeared on March 20; in England it was *reviewed* in the *Athenæum* two months later—pretty quick work. Cassel brought out a fine edition, illustrated by Cruikshank (a copy recently sold for sixteen pounds, ten shillings), and within the year twelve—perhaps more —different editions were being offered for sale at prices varying from half-a-crown to sixpence.

"Uncle Tom's Cabin," first edition, especially bound for presentation, very scarce

Never before and never since has there been any success like it: authorities say that in England and her colonies its circulation exceeded a million and a half copies. Further than this, it was translated into many European languages; there were eight different translations into French—and anyone wishing to enjoy a good laugh will have it upon turning to a French *illustrated* copy. I have seen a picture of Uncle Tom bedecked in the epaulettes and gold braid of an officer of high rank in the navy, sitting on a coil of rope on the deck of a channel steamer talking to a dangerous-looking soubrette,—who is, of course, Eva,—and this was supposed to depict life on the Mississippi River in the early sixties. The net result of all this was fame and fortune for the author, and it probably kept England out of war on the side of the South, for in spite of the sufferings our Civil War caused them the common people of England were, with the Queen, always on the side of the North.

Eugene Field is, I suppose, not much read to-day, but every book-lover and collector should have him and should get some of him by heart, as I have. We have historians and scholars; none certainly of the rank of Gibbon, but Gibbons are not common even in England. Our lack—and it is a grievous one—is in works of imagination in poetry and in fiction; having said which, let us remember *Moby Dick* and be calm. "The greatest thing written in English since *Paradise Lost*," is the way one foreign critic speaks of it; and Tomlinson inquires whether, outside of St. Paul's Epistles, there is a better sermon than that preached in the little chapel in New Bedford; he ranks Melville's epic among the first half-dozen books of modern literature, classing it with *Don Quixote* and *Gulliver*. *The Eugene Field I Knew*, by my old friend Francis Wilson (while writing these lines a letter from him was handed me—what a coincidence!), tells what manner of man he was: poet and wit and bibliophile *par excellence*—may his name ever be held in affectionate remembrance. And is there a sweeter story than "Hop" Smith's *Colonel Carter of Cartersville?* If there is, tell me about it. I once had the pleasure of telling the creator of Colonel Carter what I thought of his book and that I owned a copy which, years before, he had given to Augustine Daly. Our world lost a charming and distinguished gentleman when Hopkinson Smith died.

Do we write poetry to-day? I wonder: I do not know. Verse by the ream falls from the press, I am aware, but poetry is a different matter. What is it that "The Simple Cobbler of Agawam" says?

> Poetry's a gift wherein but few excel;
> He doth very ill, that doth not passing well.

Do you know Nathaniel Ward? "The Simple Cobbler of Agawam," he called himself; his verses were printed in Old England in 1647 and in New England in 1713. It is a scarce book. I haven't one, and may misquote, but the idea is there. Personally I agree with that fine critic, the elder Weller, when he said to his son, "Sammy, never let yourself down to poetry, it's unnat'ral"; and moreover, like M. Jourdain, I affect prose. But I buy and buy in the hope that some fine day, fifty years from now, someone will find in my library an immaculate copy, uncut and unopened, of some rare volume of poems, and that it will fetch three or four thousand dollars, as a copy of *The Rubaiyat* did at auction not long ago.

I am led to speak of a short and famous story, *Ethan Frome*, by Edith Wharton. Two copies are before me: the first edition, from the press of Charles Scribner (1911), for which I recently paid fifteen dollars—it is an immaculate copy; and another, one of an edition of two thousand copies designed by Bruce Rogers, for which I paid six. No reprint of a book, however fine, is as desirable as a first edition. It may well be that

Mrs. Wharton has written one of the finest—I should say the finest short story that has been written in this country for fifty years; if *Ethan Frome* is not literature, I am much mistaken. But I never met an Englishman who had heard of it; indeed, their ignorance of all that we have done and are doing would be amazing, had it not always been so. What they take from us is invariably our worst—the tone of our newspapers, our plays, and our movies. When we do a fine thing—such as, for example, *The Education of Henry Adams*—they pass it by. The only Englishman I ever met who knew this brilliant and fascinating autobiography was Sir Esme Howard, the British Ambassador. We, on the other hand,—and very properly,—devour a book like Strachey's *Life of Queen Victoria*, and ask for more from the same pen. Strachey has revolutionized the writing of biography, but whether for good or evil remains to be seen.

I had just written these lines, and stopped to turn the leaves of an English magazine before "calling it a day," when quite by accident my eye fell upon an article on Austin Dobson, whose verses and essays I always admired, and whose funeral I attended in company with my friend, the late Clement Shorter. In the course of the article I came upon a letter written to Dobson by Thomas Bailey Aldrich, in 1878, in which he said:—

It is fortunate for New England authors that they are not obliged to depend on English criticism for appreciation. With very few exceptions, it is only our fourth-rate writers who make popular successes in England—Artemus Ward, Joaquin Miller, etc. Can you explain it?—men who are not successes in their own land. In point of critical penetration I think America sets England an example. We take none but England's best. Of course there is a market in this country for those litters of blind novels of which England seems so prolific; but the English authors who rank highest in Boston and New York are the men and women who rank highest in London and Edinburgh.

Of course, Austin Dobson could not explain it, but I can. It is based on the deep-rooted dislike which Englishmen in the mass have for Americans in the mass—a dislike which was disguised during the war, but which is now functioning with ever-increasing vigor.

Wise men are constantly endeavoring to bring about a better understanding between ourselves and the English, but all the good accomplished by exchange professorships, Rhodes scholarships, English-Speaking Unions, Pilgrim Dinners, and the like, is nullified by the sneer of Sir Owen Seaman, the editor of *Punch*, for we very well know that *Punch* represents English opinion as perhaps no other journalistic enterprise does.

It is unusual for an American business man to admit being outmanœuvred by a British tradesman, but I sometimes think that the bookseller of the British Isles can and does put rings around our own. Having already sold us, at ever-increasing prices, practically all their desired books,—all the time complaining of the rich Americans who have denuded most of their important private libraries,—they now stimulate the collecting of second- or third-rate English moderns to the almost entire neglect of our own first-class authors. Take Agnes Repplier, for example. For the price of half a theatre ticket one can buy a volume of her essays, compounded of wit, wisdom, humor, irony, and ex-

quisite learning, the like of which one would look for
in vain in England to-day. The reader will not wish
to laugh loud, certainly not, but a persistent chuckle
should not displease him, and Miss Repplier's best
volume, *A Happy Half-Century*, will certainly produce
it. I was present once when she was introduced by a
man, at a Bluestocking Club, as America's most distinguished *female* essayist. I felt that her introducer
was in for his bad quarter of an hour, and I was not
mistaken. Candor compels me to say that the lady has
one grave fault: "first editions" leave her cold, very
cold. Some people are like that.

What shall we say of a man collecting Peacock and
neglecting Cooper; or appraising *A Shropshire Lad* (1896)
at four hundred dollars and William Cullen Bryant's
Poems (1821), at sixty?
The price of Bryant's
Poems is no indication
of its scarcity. G. A.
Baker & Company had
a copy in one of their
catalogues a year ago: I
sped over to New York
to get it. "Sold; could
have sold it half a dozen
times," Mr. Harzof told
me. Thereafter I searched
everywhere, and in vain.
And I should be without
the book to this hour
had not that canny
book-hunter, Paul Hyde

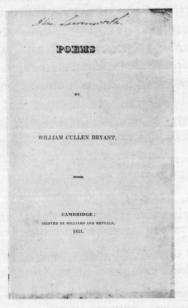

Bryant's "Poems"

Bonner, put me in the way of getting a copy. Here is the first book of an important American author published over a hundred years ago, a book which contains some of the best poetry written in this country, including "Thanatopsis"—which has found its way into every anthology—and we, collectors, appraise it at,—well, say seventy-five dollars as a top figure. If I were a younger man I should expect to see this slender volume bring ten times this figure.

Think of a man in his senses buying flippant English moderns and neglecting our own Donald G. Mitchell. I saw a copy of *Reveries of a Bachelor* in one of James F. Drake's catalogues only yesterday, priced at twelve dollars and a half. I bought the Frank Maier copy, autographed by the author, for five!

We make the market for English books in this country; let us turn our attention to our own too-long-neglected authors. Hawthorne is, at last, becoming collected; some of his earlier and little-known books, like *Grandfather's Chair*, *Famous Old People*, and *Liberty Tree*, are delightful—and scarce, but still obtainable: buy them now. And above all things do not neglect Whitman. I am on record, somewhere, as saying that *Leaves of Grass* will some day outrank any book published in the nineteenth century except *Pickwick*, and I am still of this opinion. Democracy is its theme, and, while I detest it, the whole world is moving in that direction. *Leaves of Grass* is what one of our late Presidents would have described as "a forward-looking book." It is to be judged by its best rather than by its worst, of which there is plenty; but that is the way we judge Wordsworth—and indeed all the poets. Whitman labored over his copy, as the most casual glance at any of his manuscripts will show, and when he was not catalog-

The history of this famous book is remarkable. Written in various places and at different times, from 1771 to 1789, it was first translated into French—by whom, nobody knows—and published in Paris in 1791. The original manuscript having disappeared, it was translated back into English by two different and unknown hands, and published by two rival firms in London in 1793. William Temple Franklin (Franklin's grandson) having located the manuscript, published it in 1818, with such alterations as he saw fit to make. The first and only edition which pretends to accuracy is John Bigelow's published by Lippincott in 1868. The original manuscript is in the Huntington Library

ing the universe he usually—ultimately—found the right word. His merit, however, is the merit of the prophet rather than the merit of the poet. His prose has not yet been sufficiently considered, but my advice to the collector is, secure every scrap of Whitman in manuscript and in first editions while it is available.

And of Mark Twain I would say the same thing. As Whitman is valuable for his prophetic quality, so Mark Twain will be valued for his pictures of an era which has already passed away; his *Life on the Mississippi* is a great book, and *Huckleberry Finn* and *Tom Sawyer* take high rank as novels—of a sort. Galsworthy ranks *Huckleberry Finn* among the world's twelve best works of fiction. Unfortunately, Clemens's books are distressingly ugly in format, and were published in enormous editions, but they were so immensely popular that to find copies in reasonably good condition to-day is difficult, which is all the more reason why the collecting of them should not begin (their collection began years ago), but continue with unabated zeal. And it was one of Clemens's griefs that, having attained world-wide fame as a humorist, no one would take him seriously: that was the penalty he paid for his popularity. His *Personal Recollections of Joan of Arc* is the work of a scholar, but few people would have it so. He was a professed wit, and, as Gilbert says, "when a professed wit says 'pass the mustard' the table roars."

Before leaving the subject of American books, let me ask a question. Can anyone tell me why *Franklin's Autobiography* is not "collected?" It is one of the world's great books: its history is a romance and a puzzle. "What is the first authentic edition?" Authorities differ. Perhaps this is the reason.

XII

CONVERSATION IN THE LIBRARY
AT "OAK KNOLL"

Guest. This is a nice room. I have heard that you have some fine books. Let's talk about them.

Host. Are you a collector?

Guest. Not in the least, but I am fond of reading. Why do you ask?

Host. Because, when a collector begins to talk books with one who is not, he is in a fair way to become a bore. I am willing to talk either to a collector or to a reader, but I like to know which one I am talking to before I begin.

Guest. Cannot one be both?

Host. Certainly—I am both, myself.

Guest. You write, too, I have heard.

Host. Yes, occasionally; not too much, I hope.

Guest. Have you ever written anything about George Moore?

Host. I don't think I ever have. It is always dangerous for a man to write about a living author: the writer is usually unimportant and seeks by his writing to make the acquaintance of the author. It's a great mistake.

Guest. What's your opinion of George Moore? I see you have a lot of first editions here.

Host. Yes, and over there is another lot, all presentation copies. I have been collecting him for thirty years. He is, in my judgment, capable of writing finer English than any man now living. A little studied, perhaps, but a great artist—we have had few greater. I wish I could admire the man as I do his work.

GUEST. What's wrong with the man?

HOST. Oh, I don't know. I never heard a man in London speak well of him.

GUEST. And a woman?

HOST. I never heard a woman speak of him at all, personally. They say that he kisses and tells.

GUEST. That's rotten, of course. Who do you mean by "they?"

HOST. The men I have talked to about him.

GUEST. What do you think of his poetry?

HOST. I don't think much of it—nor does he, I believe. I read somewhere the other day that when he discovered that his poetry was bad he was very disconcerted and gave up writing and went to Paris to study art; then he saw that his pictures were worse than his poetry and he gave them up and turned to prose, which is undoubtedly his proper *métier*.

GUEST. What did you pay for *Flowers of Passion?*

HOST. I don't remember; I bought it years ago. Here is a nice *Pagan Poems*. It has the errata slip; and look at the title-page: "To Oscar Wilde with the author's compliments. G. M."

GUEST. Not bad!

HOST. I should say not. Speaking of poetry, Moore says somewhere that George Meredith was no novelist, but will be remembered by his verse. It may be that Meredith's novels will be forgotten and that his verse will live, but I don't think so.

GUEST. What was the first novel of Moore's that you read?

HOST. *Evelyn Innes*, which Jim Huneker says is the

best musical novel ever written; I know what he means, of course, but I wonder whether that is the way to describe a novel? The question is, is it a good novel? I read *Evelyn* when it first came out, and greatly enjoyed it; it may not be in the same class with *A Mummer's Wife* or *Esther Waters*, which are indeed first rate, but the English circulating libraries would not allow either of them on their shelves, which was silly, for unpleasant as they undoubtedly are, they are not vicious. It would be just as reasonable to condemn a hospital because diseases are studied there —and relieved—as it is to object to a book because it is unpleasant. If these books have a "tendency," it is a good one.

GUEST. He was much attacked once.

HOST. Yes, and he fought back and won; he's a born fighter—like all Irishmen—and neither gives nor asks for quarter. The trouble really began with *A Modern Lover*, a three-volume novel published by "old Tinsley" in 1883. It met with the approval of the reviews like the *Athenæum* and the *Spectator;* but an old lady wrote to William Mudie of the "lending library" in Oxford Street and protested against his circulating the book. People then did not buy novels— they got them from the "libraries"; and these, becoming rich and powerful, finally came to dictate as to what should and should not be published. They had no objection to sin; on the contrary, they rather liked it; but the sinner had to be a lady. George Moore's sinners were common people, as Zola's were, and he had to be suppressed. It is difficult to suppress an Irishman, and Zola—the prototype of all that was dreadful in English eyes—lived in Paris beyond reach of the English law. But his publisher could be arrested, and was.

GUEST. You don't say?

HOST. Yes, a vigilant society was formed to guard the morals of the public, and Henry Vizetelly, an old man of seventy-three, was arrested. It was with difficulty that he got a lawyer to defend him; finally he was tried, convicted, and cast into Holloway Gaol, the establishment patronized by Oscar Wilde. And to add to the absurdity, shortly after the prosecution of Vizetelly by the Attorney-General of one administration, Zola, whose disciple George Moore was, came to England and was publicly welcomed by the Attorney-General of another administration, at a dinner attended by the most distinguished literary men of the time; meantime, old Vizetelly died of a broken heart.

GUEST. Well, I'll be—

HOST. Sure you will. It is often said that nature disregards the individual, that nature is cruel, and the like, but society is equally cruel—and ridiculous, which nature never is. Here was an old man done to death by the British public in what Macaulay called one of its periodic fits of morality. Nowadays we let authors run amuck and content ourselves with attacking clergymen who use their minds.

GUEST. The crowd is always ridiculous.

HOST. Always. Moore—"the English Zola," as he was called—was in the thick of the fight. The other day, in one of James F. Drake's catalogues, I saw a book priced at seventy-five dollars that I bought when it came out, in 1888, for ten shillings. Here it is. It

Oscar Wilde, from a caricature by Max Beerbohm, now first published

consists of extracts from all the great English classics, showing that the legal suppression of Zola's novels would logically involve the bowdlerizing of some of the greatest works in English literature. The letter to the Solicitor of the Treasury, although it is signed by Vizetelly, is generally supposed to have been written by G. M.

GUEST. Who selected the extracts?

HOST. It was always said that G. M. did. He would know how.

GUEST. I never saw it before.

HOST. This is the only copy I have seen in years. The letter to the Solicitor is not a part of the book, but when you buy the book you want the letter. "What do I think of Moore's later books?" Well, since the *Memoirs of My Dead Life*,—which is beautifully written, but is as inflammable as guncotton in the unexpurgated edition,—I have only read three: *The Brook Kerith* and *Avowals* and *A Storyteller's Holiday*. By the way, did you ever hear the story of the publication, by Appleton, of the American edition of the *Memoirs of My Dead Life*?

GUEST. I never have.

HOST. A set of the English sheets came in the post one day and Mr. Appleton handed them to his secretary, a very demure young lady,—there were such twenty years ago,—saying, "Take this home and read it, and let me know what you think: I've agreed to take it." A day or two later the girl came back, and when asked for her opinion gave it briefly. "I think if you publish it you'll go to jail," she replied. "As bad as that, eh?" said Mr. Appleton, who valued his liberty more than George Moore's good opinion; so the edition he published was very rigidly expurgated.

GUEST. I suppose that is why the first English edition is worth thirty dollars, and the first New York edition thirty cents.

HOST. That holds good of any American reprint of an English book. It is always best to pay a dollar or two more in the first place and get a first English edition. A woman—it was probably a woman—who dropped into Dutton's, in the autumn of 1924, and got a first English edition of *When We Were Very Young*, by Milne, was handsomely rewarded.

GUEST. How is that?

HOST. It's worth about forty dollars to-day; the reprint, published by Dutton, is worthless from a collector's point of view. But we were talking about George Moore.

GUEST. What do you think of *The Brook Kerith?*

HOST. It is a marvelous book: a dignified treatment of the Life of Christ. At first it seems a little strange, but that is not due to any flippancy on the part of the author, but to the fact that we are chiefly used to the story of Christ in one setting only. It shows great power and could only have been written after an immense amount of study. It is a *tour de force* in style; it is almost impossible to believe that from one and the same pen came books so different as the *Memoirs of My Dead Life* and *The Brook Kerith*. Now if Thomas Hardy had had the inspiration to write a book about the life of Christ, rather than Moore, we should have had the greatest piece of pessimism in any language.

GUEST. You rank Hardy above Moore?

HOST. Yes. They will hardly plant George Moore in the Abbey, or Shaw either. We have only three great writers left to-day: Kipling, Moore, and Shaw. Shaw gives me the most pleasure. But Kipling is as sure of the Abbey as any living man can be: he is the real poet laureate of the British Empire. But how he hates Americans!

GUEST. Why, do you suppose?

HOST. Well, we are a bumptious people, for one reason; and the other is that we shall never again play second fiddle to the English. No Englishman can be expected to forgive us that.

GUEST. What do you think of Galsworthy?

HOST. I had forgotten Galsworthy for the moment: he is a sort of cross between Thackeray and Trollope. I think the *Forsyte Saga*, beginning with *The Man of Property*, the most important novel or series of novels that has appeared since Hardy wrote his last novel, *Jude the Obscure*. Perhaps I should include some novel by Conrad, but he is an author I never could read.

GUEST. Not *Lord Jim* or *The Nigger?*

HOST. No, none of them.

GUEST. You must be deficient. Have you read *Ave?*

HOST. No, I haven't read *Ave* or *Salve* or *Vale*. I tried to, and couldn't,—with pleasure,—so I quit. *Avowals* is another matter: every admirer of Moore will wish to own it, but I resent its format. I don't think it quite fair for an author to throw over his public and his publisher and bring out books privately at a price that many of his lifelong admirers cannot afford to pay.

GUEST. Why did he do it?

HOST. To make money, of course. The British author is about the most mercenary male animal existing; the best defense is an attack. To conceal this trait in himself, and having the ear of the public, he accuses us of being a nation of dollar-chasers, and we sit patiently under the accusation.

GUEST. You don't seem to.

HOST. I know that it is not true. We are the only people that have any disinterested ideals: look at our treatment of Cuba. The English always look out for Number One.

GUEST. You know I'm English.

HOST. Yes, and you know how true what I'm saying is. But we were talking of George Moore, who is Irish. When he was asked why he published in the manner he now does, he said: "I know that by publishing as I do I have cut myself off from many readers, but no publisher would take the risk of printing what I write, and the alternative is to stop writing." That is sheer nonsense. He publishes as he does because he wants both the author's and the publisher's profit. He is always fussing with his books, and it is quite likely that after he has exploited the fifteen-dollar market he will finally "yield to pressure" and bring out his books in a cheap edition. He smashed the expensive novel once, and he may do it again. He had the intelligence and courage and persistence to smash the old "three-decker," and, now he is secure of his public, he tumbles out clumsy, expensive books, obviously written for money, while "corrected proof sheets" and "suppressed chapters" and "galley proofs" are to be found on every dealer's shelves. It looks like sucker-bait, if you ask me. I leave those ugly George Moore books to others.

GUEST. But you have *Avowals*.

HOST. Yes, and I've read it, but it is badly printed on heavy, stiff paper; it is hard to hold, and, owing to the nature of the book and the absence of quotation marks, is difficult to read. Listen to his dialogue between Moore and Edmund Gosse:—

> GOSSE. Have you read *The Scarlet Letter?*
> MOORE. No, and I never shall; the subject is too painful.

Surely the creator of Kate Lennox ought not to balk at Hester Prynne. But it is interesting to learn his opinions, and of course he is quite right when he says that the genius of the English people expresses itself in poetry, as Germany expresses herself in music, and France and Italy in plastic arts. It is, however, disconcerting to a man who knows but one literature, and is not very strong on poetry, to be told that his favorite writers cannot write prose. To be sure, Moore excepts the essayists, for which I am indeed thankful, as I am to find that "Defoe was inspired," at least during the first half of *Robinson Crusoe;* but there is, I fancy, a great deal of truth in his remark that, in the parlance of the racing stable, "English fiction is hackney; French and Russian narrative shows more breeding."

GUEST. What do you think of the Russians?

HOST. They are only names to me. Their novels are interminably long and very gloomy. Here is an excellent little volume called *Aspects of the Novel;* it is a series of lectures—or talks, rather—given by a Fellow of Trinity College, Cambridge. Listen to what he says: "No English novelist has explored man's soul as deeply as Dostoevsky. And no novelist anywhere has analyzed the modern consciousness as successfully as Marcel Proust. Before these triumphs we must pause. English poetry fears no one—excels in quality as well as quantity. But English fiction is less triumphant: it does not contain the best stuff yet written; and if we deny this we become guilty of provincialism."

GUEST. Not very encouraging.

HOST. Not very, but English fiction is good enough for me. I don't want to explore the soul of a man—or a woman—whose name I can't pronounce. I read for pleasure, not to become involved in "the modern consciousness," whatever that may mean. Let's get back to George Moore.

GUEST. I liked *Avowals*.

HOST. So did I—enormously. One would have to go far to find more delicious prose than Moore's in this same volume. His description of his visit to Paris, seeking in vain for the warmth and movement and color of the life there in the seventies and eighties, is exquisite. If he is right in saying that "language is a piano on which Thackeray performs with the grace and skill of the trained artist and on which Dickens plays so brilliantly, if somewhat boisterously, by ear, striking now and then a false note which we forgive on account of his genius," with equal truth may it not be said that George Moore uses it like the violin and that his technique is almost faultless?

GUEST. What do you think of his essays?

HOST. Excellent. The man has great knowledge, the

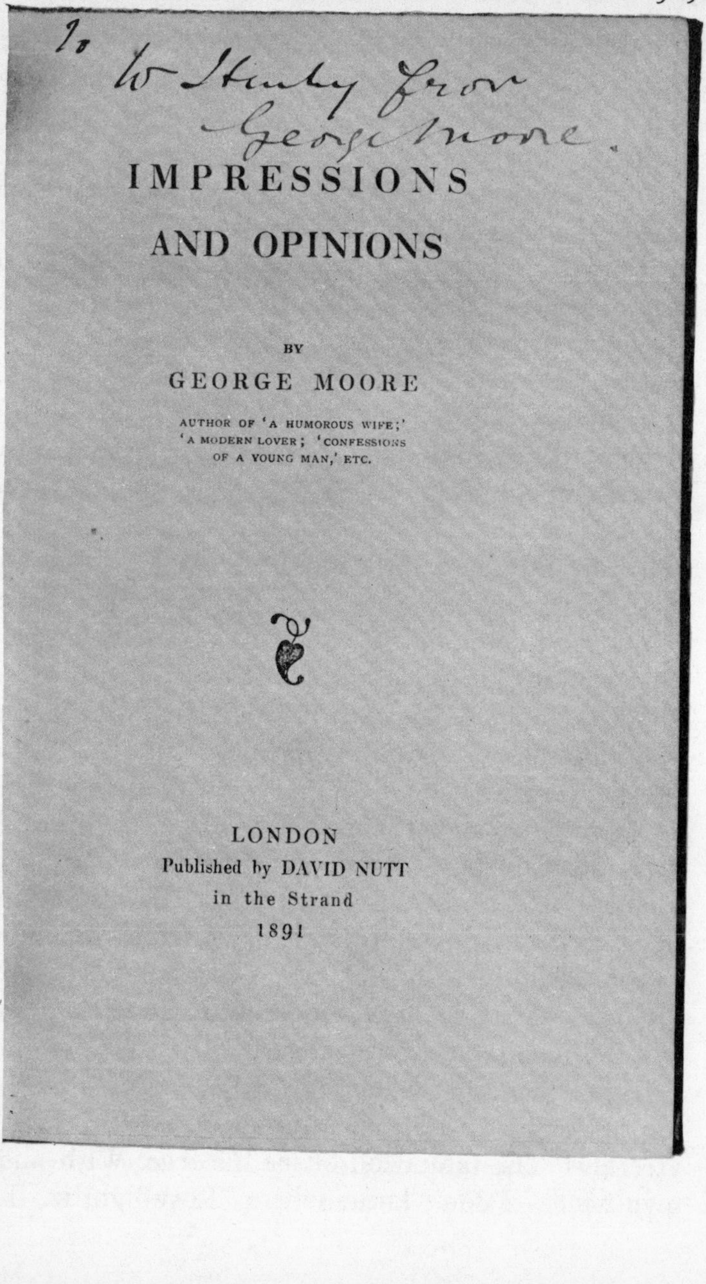

To Henley from
George Moore.

IMPRESSIONS

AND OPINIONS

BY

GEORGE MOORE

AUTHOR OF 'A HUMOROUS WIFE;'
'A MODERN LOVER; 'CONFESSIONS
OF A YOUNG MAN,' ETC.

LONDON
Published by DAVID NUTT
in the Strand
1891

gift of a fine style which he has improved, and the greater gift of humor. One of his papers is so amusing that I never tire of it.

GUEST. What is it?

HOST. "Royalty in Art," in the volume called *Modern Painting*. Don't you know it? It is a sheer delight; I have read it aloud twenty times. Here is a curious volume. Look at the title-page.

GUEST. I see: it is presented to Henley.

HOST. Yes, but the title-page reads, *Impressions and Opinions* by George Moore, author of *A Humorous Wife* —instead of *A Mummer's Wife*. I think it is a copy rushed through the press and hastily bound, and sent to Henley to review.

GUEST. Why hastily bound?

HOST. Because on the spine is merely the word *Essays;* it should, of course, be *Impressions and Opinions*.

GUEST. Are there many copies like this?

HOST. No one knows how many. I should have said that it is unique, but in my experience, the moment a man thinks he has a unique book, another copy turns up—sometimes several copies.

GUEST. Isn't that a picture of him?

HOST. Yes, "Rosy" gave it to me. And just alongside of it is a superb photograph of Whitman, of whom I should be glad to have Moore's opinion.

GUEST. What is "The Moore Literary Circle," to whom this picture was presented?

HOST. I haven't the least idea; all I know is that the inscription reads: "To the Moore Literary Circle with greetings. The salutation of me, George. With mine own hand." I don't know where "Rosy" got it.

George Moore, from a photograph

GUEST. How old is he?

HOST. I have been told that he is seventy-five. His age is not given in *Who's Who*. He conceals it as carefully as a prima donna.

GUEST. Isn't it given in that book about him by John Freeman?

HOST. I don't know: I have never read it, and never shall. One can discover all one wants to know about George Moore in his books, where, as Dr. Johnson says, the best part of every author is to be found.

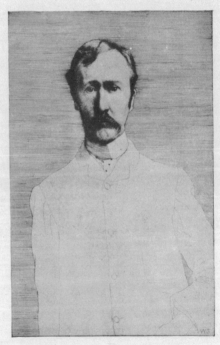

George Moore, forty years ago

XIII

HUMOR AND PATHOS OF
DR. JOHNSON'S DICTIONARY

WE are apt to think of this great book as the work of a pious, not overclean old scholar, much given to talk and tea, and somewhat too fond of abusing people. It will come, therefore, as a surprise to some to learn that the Dictionary was the work of "an obscure young man" (I am quoting Dr. Burney, Fanny's father), who, "single-handed" and alone, began it when he was little more than thirty-six years of age; that he had completed it before he had received any degree from any university; that he kept back the title-page until the authorities at Oxford had time to confer upon him a small degree, that of Master of Arts; that it was many years later that finally and forever he became "Dr. Johnson."

It was Robert Dodsley, the publisher, who first made the suggestion that Johnson should undertake the work, but Johnson told Boswell that he had long thought of it himself; and it was another publisher, Andrew Millar, who, associated with Dodsley and others, carried on the negotiations which led to Johnson's receiving fifteen hundred and seventy-five pounds for the complete work, out of which he was to pay the expenses of his six amanuenses while the book was in progress. It was not much, but Johnson never complained: he said he hated a complainer, and years later, when Boswell remarked that he was sorry he had not received more for his work, his reply was, "I am sorry, too, but it was very well; the booksellers are generous, liberal-minded men; they are the true patrons of literature."

Johnson, when he made his bargain with the book-sellers, expected that he would be able to complete the work in about three years, and, when a friend pointed out that it took the French Academy, which consisted of forty members, forty years to compile its Dictionary, replied, "This, then, is the proportion: forty times forty is sixteen hundred; as three is to sixteen hundred, so is the proportion of an Englishman to a French-man." But it took him, in fact, seven years: when he first began his labors he was living in Holborn, but he soon took a large house (still standing) at 17 Gough Square, just off Fleet Street, in the garret of which, fitted up like a rude counting-house, he carried to completion his work.

William Strahan, the printer of the Dictionary, had his printing establishment not far off, and it was to be near him that Johnson indulged himself with the most commodious residence he ever had; and, moreover, had he not just been promised fifteen hundred and seventy-five pounds?—which he may have thought a magnificent sum. Poor fellow! He little thought that after the completion of his great undertaking he would be arrested for a debt of five pounds, eighteen shillings, which amount he was to borrow from Samuel Richardson, the author of *Pamela*, and thus free himself from the bailiffs. I have always thought it curious that Samuel Johnson never met Benjamin Franklin: both were living in London at the same time, and both were intimate friends of Strahan's, to whom, it may be remembered, Franklin addressed one of his cleverest letters. One is permitted to wonder what would have happened at a meeting of the wisest and wittiest American that ever lived with the wisest and wittiest Englishman of his time. I believe it has not yet been decided what takes place when an irresistible force meets an immovable body.

It is rather curious too that, although Johnson affected to dislike Scotchmen, practically all who were concerned with the Dictionary were Scotch: five out of six of his amanuenses were, as were also Millar, his publisher-in-chief, and Strahan. Millar must have been sorely tried by Johnson's lack of punctuality, for we are told that when the work was finally done, and the last sheet brought to him, he exclaimed, "Thank God I have done with him." Johnson, on being told this, replied with a smile, "I am glad that he thanks God for anything."

Eight years before the Dictionary was published, Johnson had printed what he called *The Plan of a Dictionary*, addressed to the Earl of Chesterfield. It was an elaborate outline of what he hoped to accomplish by his work, but the noble lord paid no attention to it until, on the eve of publication, Dodsley informed him that, after many years of toil, the book was about to make its appearance, and no doubt reminded him that the Plan had been addressed to him, and perhaps suggested that if he expected the work to be dedicated to him it was time for him to make some sign of his approval. Chesterfield took the hint and wrote two letters to the *World*, which were fulsome in their flattery. In one he said, "In times of confusion we must chuse a Dictator. . . . I give my vote for Mr. Johnson . . . and I hereby declare that I make a total surrender of all my rights and privileges in the English language as a free born British subject, to the said Mr. Johnson during the term of his dictatorship. Nay, more, I will not only obey him, like an old Roman, as my Dictator, but like a modern Roman, I will implicitly believe in him as my Pope, and hold him to be infallible."

This, it will be admitted, was very handsomely said, but in between the time when the Plan was published and the Dictionary completed, something had happened: Chesterfield had totally neglected the Lexicographer, who was, indeed, the proudest man in England. "Ay, sir," said Johnson, when Boswell taxed him with it, "but mine was defensive pride." "And," continued Johnson, "after making great professions he had, for many years, taken no notice of me, but when my Dictionary was coming out he fell to scribbling in the *World* about it." But Johnson—although he defined himself as a lexicographer, and a lexicographer as a "harmless drudge"—was not to be beguiled, and, seizing his pen, he wrote what is probably the most smashing letter in all literature:—

Seven years, my Lord, have now passed since I waited in your outward room or was repulsed from your door, during which time I have been pushing on my work through difficulties of which it is useless to complain, without one act of assistance, one word of encouragement, or one smile of favour. . . . The notice which you have been pleased to take of my labors had it been early, had been kind, but it has been delayed till I am indifferent and cannot enjoy it; till I am solitary and cannot impart it; till I am known and do not want it.

It is a great letter—too long to quote in its entirety —and it must have crushed, utterly, a man less vain and complacent than the man to whom it was ad-

dressed. Carlyle called it a "blast of doom, proclaim-
ing into the ears of Lord Chesterfield, and through
him to the listening world, that patronage should be
no more." It was indeed a Declaration of Independence.

The book appeared in two large folio volumes, on
February 20, 1755. It was a time of profound depression
for Johnson: he had, as he said, "devoted the labor of
years, to the honor of my country that we may no
longer yield the palm of philology without a contest
to the nations of the continent," but, as he also said,
"I have protracted my work till most of those whom
I wished to please have sunk into the grave, and
success and miscarriage are empty sounds: I therefore
dismiss the book with frigid tranquillity—having
little to fear or hope from censure or from praise."

In this brief paper I shall not attempt to conceal the
fact that I regard the present great esteem which the
world—our world, that is—has for Dr. Johnson, his
Life, and his works, with some amusement. It may be
that I am to some extent responsible for it: at any rate,
if you enter any good bookshop in England and ask
for any book by Dr. Johnson in first edition you will
almost certainly be met with a sad shake of the head
and the remark that Johnson, in first editions, is
almost impossible except at prohibitive prices, and
that this advance is due to the American demand. And
then you may be told—as I have been, more than
once—that "a man in Philadelphia is largely responsible for Johnson's being collected; before he began to
write about him, Boswell's Life, a big ugly book in
two volumes, was hard to sell at three guineas; there
was no more demand for Johnson's Dictionary than

there was for—Fox's *Martyrs*, and now you can't get them fast enough."

Forty years ago my friends used to say, by way of disconcerting me, "Eddie, tell us something about Dr. Johnson," and usually I did so, for I had just fallen under the spell of Boswell and was by way—as far as a man with a treacherous memory could be—of knowing him by heart. It is a happy possession and affords one an apt quotation in every conceivable discussion and upon every possible occasion. Have you a difficult business matter to discuss? Discuss it after a good dinner and not before: remember what Dr. Johnson says: "Sir, a good dinner lubricates business."

Since then I have met many Johnsonians, and have come to believe that all Johnsonians are good fellows,—"clubable" men, as Dr. Johnson would say,—and as the years passed and I came to know wiser and better Johnsonians than myself this suspicion became conviction. Finally came the desire to own, and in some measure to know, the books of the Great Lexicographer himself.

But I remember that my copy of the first edition of Boswell's Life was purchased for twenty dollars,—a good copy cannot now be had for less than three hundred,—and the first *Rasselas* I ever bought cost me but ten, and the last, two hundred. And as for the Dictionary—well, Mrs. Thrale-Piozzi's copy, probably given her by Johnson, with her inscription and a fine holograph letter from the Lexicographer, cost me only sixty dollars; and a fine copy in boards, uncut, thirty-five! Taking a census of the Johnson Dictionaries now in my library, I find I have in all six copies of the

*Reading from top to bottom, Charles Dickens's copy, Mrs. Thrale's copy,
Mrs. Vesey's copy, a common or garden copy, and a copy in boards uncut*

first edition, besides a copy which was once Charles Dickens's, with his notes therein, and an excellent—shall I say common or garden copy?—a reprint from the author's last folio edition, in one volume, for ready reference, which was once E. Coppee Mitchell's.

Why so many?

Let me explain. One copy I bought to show people to whom one copy is as good as another: this saves wear and tear on the copies I highly value. Two came in this way: On the fifteenth of February, 1926, my great friend and fellow Johnsonian, Mr. R. B. Adam of Buffalo, had a sale at the Anderson Galleries in New York of a portion of his library—not of his wonderful Johnson collection, but of books of which he had tired or which did not fit into the period which he has made peculiarly his own. With the idea of paying him homage, I gave a little dinner in New York, the first night of the sale, to a small group of friends and booksellers (friends also). It was a speedy affair: including speeches, we were at the table just one hour and fifteen minutes, and it may be remembered by those present that Mr. Owen D. Young—that accomplished gentleman who, in company with General Dawes, brought order out of chaos in Germany—signally failed to secure a hearing at our little dinner party; whereupon the meeting adjourned to the auction room.

The sale had just begun, and as we took our seats my wife joined my friend Mr. William Jay Turner, who had been one of my party, and I took a seat in the back part of the room next to Walter Hill, the Chicago bookseller, and immediately bought a book I didn't want just to prevent him from getting it. (He didn't want it either.) We were in just the form that brings joy to the heart of an auctioneer. The books were fine and the sale went merrily.

After a time a copy of the Dictionary, first edition, two volumes, old calf, was put up, and I saw at once that it was not Adam's best copy: it was what might be called "a spare." The bidding started at fifty dollars, went to one hundred and fifty,—the then proper price for the book,—then more slowly to three hundred; and finally it was knocked down at three hundred and twenty dollars to—of all people in the world—my wife, who wanted it as a souvenir of a pleasant evening. Whereupon, discovering that my friend Turner was the runner-up,—he wanted the book for the same reason my wife did, and would have paid any amount had he not discovered that he was in competition with Mrs. Newton,—I rose and assured all present that there was, obviously, no knock-out in the room—and the sale went on.

Subsequently, in talking over the events of the evening, which is one of the delights of a good auction, Mr. Turner asked me to watch my chance and pick up for him a good copy of the Dictionary, which I promised to do. Several months later, in the catalogue of an English bookseller, I noticed a copy—Mrs. Vesey's copy—priced at forty pounds, and I at once cabled for it. Mr. Vesey was a member of "the Club" founded by Dr. Johnson, was elected through the influence of Edmund Burke; and it was Mrs. Vesey who gave the famous bluestocking parties. She didn't wear blue stockings herself—a man by the name of

*R. B. Adam, of Buffalo, whose collection of Johnson
is unsurpassed and unsurpassable—and his son*

Stillingfleet wore them; Mrs. Vesey's were—what they were; certainly not the skin-colored kind so much in evidence to-day. Her copy of the Dictionary, then, was one which Dr. Johnson might have seen in the library in her house in Clarges Street, and, conceivably, the not too Reverend Laurence Sterne might have referred to it to settle some disputed point in conversation—for, it will be remembered, he was much with Mrs. Vesey, on whom he was very sweet, as he was on every other pretty and attractive woman he met.

Here, then, was a copy of the Dictionary with a "provenance" of which anyone might be proud, and I certainly hoped to get it; but in due course I received a letter from the bookseller saying that he was sorry he could not send me the desired item, as an hour before my cable arrived he had received a cable from Mr. Adam of Buffalo, to whom the volume must be dispatched. "That settles that," said I.

But not so. A month later a bulky package arrived at my office; opening it, I found Mrs. Vesey's copy of the Dictionary, and a wonderful letter from Adam telling me that he had immediately made up his mind not to take my wife's money for his copy of the Dictionary (she had paid for it out of the household account, and we had been living on short rations); that this was a better copy; that it had once belonged to a famous lady and had her signature and bookplate; that it was bound in three volumes, with a separate title-page for the third volume, to be easier for reference; and, finally, that I was to take the copy which had once been his, and upon some suitable occasion to present it with his compliments to the Shakespeare Society of Philadelphia, over which my friend Dr. Furness presides with such distinction. Here, then, was a very pretty "amenity,"—which Johnson defines as "an agreeableness of situation,"—and such are not of infrequent occurrence among those who play at this book-collecting game.

It is a wonderful book, is Dr. Johnson's Dictionary; and think of the circumstances under which it was composed: "with," as its author says, "little assistance of the learned; without any patronage of the great; not in the soft obscurities of retirement, or under academic bowers, but amidst inconvenience and distraction, in sickness and in sorrow." "What do you read, my lord?" "Words, words, words," replies Hamlet. Buckle read it through to enlarge his vocabulary; so did Browning; and no other dictionary can be read with such pleasure and profit, for in it Johnson gave—and for the first time—quotations from esteemed authors illustrating the use of words he defined. He fitted himself for this mighty task by diligent reading, underscoring with a pencil the selections which were subsequently copied out on slips of paper by his amanuenses: his marvelous memory, of course, stood him in good stead, while the range of his reading was boundless. And yet he always spoke and thought of himself as lazy. One day, entering Mrs. Thrale's drawing-room and seeing her dog asleep before the fire, he remarked, "Presto, you are, if possible, a lazier dog than I am."

Every reader of Boswell will remember the kindly interest that Johnson took in Fanny Burney: how he called her his "Little Burney," and extolled her first—and only good—novel to the skies; saying it was superior to the work of Fielding and equal to that of Richardson. I have always thought this excessive eulogy was by way of return for the interest her father had shown him at the time the Dictionary was published. Charles Burney, not yet the distinguished Doctor of Music which he subsequently became, was then living in Norfolk. He does not appear to have known Johnson personally, but to have made his acquaintance through his *Ramblers*. When the Dictionary was announced in the newspapers, he wrote Johnson a kindly letter and offered to subscribe for six copies for himself and his friends. I have an autograph letter in Johnson's hand, in which he says, "I was bred a bookseller and have not forgotten my trade," but he was not soliciting orders for his book, and asked that Mr. Burney direct his inquiries to Mr. Dodsley, "because it was by his recommendation that he was employed in the work." But note the modesty of the great man: "When you have looked into my Dictionary, if you find faults I shall endeavour to mend them; if you find none I shall think you blinded by kind partiality."

Then followed further letters on the subject, and seemingly Mr. Burney was insistent that he be sent a prospectus, order forms, and the like—what we would to-day call "literature" on the subject. A letter has recently come into my hands, from which I must quote, as it shows only too clearly Johnson's habit of procrastination and at least one reason for his depression. This letter is addressed from Gough Square to Mr. Burney, and reads, in part:—

Sir,

That I may shew myself sensible of your favours, and not commit the same fault a second time I make haste to answer the letter which I received this morning. The truth is, the other likewise was received, and I wrote an answer, but being desirous to transmit you some proposals and receipts, I waited till I could find a convenient conveyance, and day was passed after day, till other things drove it from my thoughts, yet not so, but that I remember with great pleasure your commendation of my dictionary. Your praise was welcome not only because I believe it was sincere, but because praise has been very scarce. A man of your candour will be surprised when I tell you that among all my acquaintance there were only two who upon the publication of my book did not endeavour to depress me with threats of censure from the publick, or with objections learned from those who had learned them from my own preface. Yours is the only letter of goodwill that I have yet received, though indeed I am promised something of that sort from Sweden.

Can we wonder at the great man's depression? Years of work rewarded by poverty and neglect, and one letter of goodwill and a promise of something from Sweden. The day of the patron was past, and the day of the logroller had not yet come.

Slowly, and by degrees, Johnson's Dictionary became a best seller, and a best seller it remained for almost a century. "What I like about your Dictionary, Mr. Johnson," said one old lady to him, "is that it has no naughty words in it." "Madam, I hope you have not been looking for them," replied the Lexicographer. And to another, who remarked that for steady reading it changes the subject pretty often, Johnson admitted that it had that fault in common with most dictionaries. Again, to someone who said that the word "ocean" was omitted, he replied,

"Madam, you will look for it in vain if you spell it *O-S-H-U-N*." Garrick, his old friend and former pupil, broke into verse about it, and so marvelous an actor was the little man that his cleverness as a poet of occasional verse has never been fully recognized. Let me quote his lines:—

> Talk of war with a Briton, he'll boldly advance,
> That one English soldier will beat ten of France;
> Would we alter the boast from the sword to the pen,
> Our odds are still greater, still greater our men:
> In the deep mines of science tho' Frenchmen may toil,
> Can their strength be compar'd to Locke, Newton, and Boyle?
> Let them rally their heroes, send forth all their pow'rs,
> Their verse-men, and prose-men; then match them with ours!
> First Shakespeare and Milton, like gods in the fight,
> Have put their whole drama and epic to flight;
> In satires, epistles, and odes would they cope,
> Their numbers retreat before Dryden and Pope;
> And Johnson, well arm'd, like a hero of yore,
> Has beat forty French, and will beat forty more.

Some of Johnson's definitions have given the world amusement since the day of publication. Let me give a few examples.

A *blister* sounds worse than it is: he defines it as "a pustule formed by raising the cuticle from the cutis, and filled with serous blood."

Buxom, now understood to mean "plump and comely," was defined thus: "It originally signified *obedient*. Before the reformation the bride in the marriage service promised to be obedient and buxom in bed and at board." Alas! the word has gone, and "obey" is going, we are told. I am against change in any form and would put 'em both back.

Johnson's opportunity of studying wild animals at close range was slight, even had his eyesight been good. A *camelopard* "is an Abyssinian animal taller than an elephant but not so thick. He is so named because he has a neck and head like a camel; he is spotted like a pard" (a pard is a leopard) "but his spots are white upon a red ground. The Italians call him a giaraffa."

Cant was particularly offensive to Johnson, and he was frequently heard to say, when in heated argument with a friend, "Clear your mind of cant"—which was "a whining pretension to goodness, in formal and affected terms."

A *chicken* was, among other things, "a term for a young girl." You have seen a chicken flap its wings: hence "flapper," the word of to-day; and I have observed as I get older that flappers get better-looking and wear fewer clothes.

Much danger lurks in a *cough:* it is "a convulsion of the lungs, vellicated by some sharp serosity." Mrs. William Lowell Putnam of Boston has written a priceless poem—and a poem is "sense enriched by sound"—which I wish Dr. Johnson could have known:—

> To cough and sneeze
> Will spread disease.
> So does spit;
> Take care of it.

Perhaps because Johnson was himself an essayist, he does not rate that form of composition highly. An *essay* he calls "a loose sally of the mind; an irregular indigested piece; not a regular and orderly composition."

The thought of death in any form was at all times abhorrent to him; hence we are not surprised to learn that *death's-door* "is now a low phrase."

The definition of *excise* is one of the Doctor's most

famous: "A hateful tax levied upon commodities, and adjudged, not by the common judges of property, but wretches hired by those to whom excise is paid." This definition roused to fury the Commissioners of Excise, who sought the opinion of the Attorney-General, afterward Lord Mansfield, whether or not it was libelous. He thought that it was, but wisely suggested that the author be allowed an opportunity of altering his definition; it was not changed.

One definition of *favourite* is "a mean wretch whose whole business is by any means to please."

Grubstreet: "Originally the name of a street in Moorfields in London, much inhabited by writers of small histories, dictionaries, and temporary poems." The street still exists, but it is now Milton Street—not named after the poet, as is generally supposed, but after a builder of that name.

Leeward and *windward*, though of opposite meaning, are both described as "towards the wind."

A *lexicographer* is "a writer of dictionaries; a harmless drudge, that busies himself in tracing the original, and detailing the significance of words." Johnson was not above making fun of himself as well as others.

Network has indeed a portentous definition: it is "anything reticulated, or decussated, at equal distances, with interstices between the intersections."

Oats is equally famous: "A grain, which in England is generally given to horses, but in Scotland supports the people." "Very true," was the retort of Lord Elibank, "and where will you find such men and such horses?"

Pastern is defined as "the knee of a horse." It led a

lady to question him how this slip was made. Johnson's reply is historic: "Ignorance, madam, pure ignorance."

And his definition of *patriotism*—that is to say, "reform"—is not in the Dictionary, but it should be worn as a sort of badge by every would-be reformer: "The last refuge of a scoundrel."

A *pension* is "an allowance made to anyone without an equivalent. In England it is generally understood to mean pay given to a state hireling for treason to his country." When, subsequently, Johnson accepted a pension from the King, this definition was brought up against him, but it moved him not an iota. "I wish," he said, with a laugh, "that my pension had been twice as large, that they could make twice as much fun of it."

A *poetess* is a "she poet." I am afraid this is not a very gallant definition. Perhaps Johnson had in mind Anna Seward, alias "the Swan of Lichfield," as she loved to hear herself called.

A *stockjobber* is "a low wretch who gets money by buying and selling shares in the funds." We should now say "stockbroker," and it will occur to some that the definition is not obsolete.

Tory "is a cant term derived" (Johnson supposes) "from an Irish word signifying a savage," but he indulges himself in one of his rolling periods by adding: "One who adheres to the ancient constitution of the state, and the apostolical hierarchy of the Church of England." No one doubts that Johnson was a Tory.

Whig is defined as "the name of a faction"; and in

conversation he did not hesitate to say that "the first Whig was the Devil."

But it was in the "Grammar of the English Tongue" that Johnson made his most risible slip—where he says: "*H* seldom, perhaps never, begins any but the first syllable." Wilkes, the scamp, pounced on this instantly with the sarcastic remark: "The author of this observation must be a man of quick appre-hension, and of a most compre-hensive genius." Johnson, no doubt, felt the shaft, but malignancy, if it is to be kept in the air, must, like the shuttlecock, be struck from both sides: Johnson let it pass and the sneer was forgotten. It was not until the fourth edition that he paid his compliments to Wilkes in this sentence: "It sometimes begins middle or final syllables in words compounded, as in block-head." Johnson would never permit anyone to "get his goat," as we should now say.

The list might be longer, but to what end? Only, as Johnson said, that the "few wild blunders might for a time furnish folly with laughter." So much for his definitions. Scholars say that his etymologies are defective; Macaulay calls them wretched, and it may be that they are. I hate to quote Carlyle, that dyspeptic prophet, but, after all, no one had a juster appreciation of Johnson than he. Listen to him: "Had Johnson left nothing but his Dictionary, one might have traced there a great intellect, a genuine man. Looking to its clearness of definition, its genuine solidity, honesty, insight, and successful method, it may be called the best of all Dictionaries. There is in it a kind of archi-tectural nobleness: it stands like a great solid square-built edifice, finished: symmetrically complete; you judge that a true Builder did it."

Johnson's Dictionary was based on a work compiled and published in 1721 by Nathaniel Bailey. Bailey's dictionary is a mere list of words. Johnson had an interleaved copy of it made, and worked therefrom. This book was exhibited at Stationers' Hall in London so recently as 1912. Who has it now? Johnson's own copy of the last edition of his Dictionary to be published in his lifetime is now one of the treasures of the John Rylands Library in Manchester. I wonder whether this is the copy that at the sale of Johnson's library after his death, in "Mr. Christie's Great Room in Pall Mall," brought the magnificent sum of thirteen shillings! But then, it was disfigured by his notes, and we must remember, too, that his first folio of Shakespeare, similarly disfigured, brought only twenty-two. And consider the price of the smallest scrap of Johnsoniana to-day!

Let us allow our imagination to play for a moment and fancy that the tools of Johnson's trade—his library—could be reassembled and resold in New York City to-morrow, at Mitchell Kennerley's Great Room. What competition there would be, with "Dr. R." and "Brick Row" and "Dunster House," to say nothing of the "Wells of English undefiled," and Drake, and Beyer, and Walter Hill—all of the talent, with unlimited bids from Adam and Isham and Young and Clark and Pforzheimer and Hearst, and all the lesser fry of Johnsonians who are numbered as the sands of the sea. I should have at such a sale just as much chance as a canary at a cats' congress; and yet, Doctor, if I did not set your ball a-rolling, I certainly gave it acceleration. They tell me that there are Johnson collectors in England; are there forsooth? And they put a price of five pounds on your Life by Boswell; we, of "the Plantations," put it at fifty, and it is worth a hundred. It is the greatest biography in the world, and the best part of it, a taste of its quality, was published the year after your death, and is known as *A Tour to the Hebrides:* it is the quintessence of Boswell.

Why is all the world "Johnsonianissimus" to-day? Johnson had, according to Taine, "the manners of a beadle and the inclinations of a constable." Every Johnsonian will have a different answer, and they will all be right. This is Austin Dobson's opinion:—

> Turn now to his Writings. I grant, in his tales,
> That he made little fishes talk vastly like whales;
> I grant that his language was rather emphatic,
> Nay, even—to put the thing plainly—dogmatic;
> But read him for style—and dismiss from your thoughts,
> The crowd of compilers who copied his faults,—
> Say, where is their English so full and so clear,
> So weighty, so dignified, manly, sincere?
> So strong in expression, conviction, persuasion?
> So prompt to take colour from place and occasion?
> So widely remov'd from the doubtful, the tentative;
> So truly—and in the best sense—argumentative?
> You may talk of your Burkes and your Gibbons so clever,
> But I hark back to him with a 'Johnson forever!'
> And I feel as I muse on his ponderous figure,
> Tho' he's great in this age, in the next he'll grow bigger.

A happy coincidence enables me to display to my friends an important manuscript of which not every Johnsonian knows the existence.

In 1772, Johnson, then being in his sixty-third year, wrote in Latin a long ode addressed to himself, with a Greek title which translates, "Know Thyself."

In it he compares himself—and to his disadvantage—
with the great French scholar, Scaliger, and says that
indolence and a penury of mind coöperate to prevent
him from taking on another task, if indeed he has the
requisite knowledge. Instead of which he confesses
that he seeks

> At midnight clubs, where wit with noise conspires,
> Where Comus revels and where wine inspires

(I am quoting from a translation), relief from the dull
melancholy which at all times dogs his steps. The
poem closes:—

> What then remains? Must I in slow decline
> To mute inglorious ease old age resign?
> Or, bold ambition kindling in my breast,
> Attempt some arduous task? Or, were it best,
> Brooding o'er Lexicons to pass the day,
> And in that labor drudge my life away?

How he answered the self-imposed question is beyond
the scope of this paper.

Finally,—and I seem to hear the sigh of relief which
is occasionally audible in church at the end of a long
sermon,—I wish to dip my flag to the latest descendant
of Dr. Johnson's genius, the *Concise Oxford Dictionary*.
I own that colossal monument of wordy learning, the
New English Dictionary, now finally completed, but its
possession is a species of swank.

Doctor Johnson once called a certain man good and
pious because, although he had not entered a church
for many years, he never passed one without pulling off
his hat. And if the Doctor continued in the same gracious manner, were he to enter my library, he might
think kindly of me (although he would at once detect
that I am not a scholar) because I have a copy of the

New English Dictionary on my shelves. I never pass the book—and I pass it more frequently than I enter it—without raising my hat.

Unless one has made a book, one has no idea how much toil enters into the feeblest publication, and I am, I think, within bounds when I say that for sheer labor, learning and scholarship, the *New English Dictionary* is the greatest literary achievement that the world has ever seen. No one should attempt to undertake a serious piece of literary work without it. It is, in brief, an immense series of essays, alphabetically arranged, upon what we call the English language.

Several people sought to prepare themselves for a life of authorship by reading Dr. Johnson's Dictionary through from cover to cover, and no doubt they were rewarded for so doing, but what shall be said of a man who, knowing how to spell it, looks up the simple word RUN in this great book? He will never run again: he may walk, loiter, crawl, creep, strut, march, parade; he may, in short, do anything that expresses motion on earth, but never run. *Festina lente* will thereafter be his motto: he will feel that to run is to set in motion forces that will never stop. This is only another way of saying that the essays on this simple little word cover many large pages, three columns to a page, of fine print.

Few individuals, except scholars, really require the *New English Dictionary*: but every school of the higher grade, every club, college, university; in brief, every place where men and women congregate and use language,—not merely crudely to express their thoughts and their wants, but as an instrument on which they perform with what skill they may,—should be possessed of a copy.

Looking at this great book—it is a book in many large volumes—one wonders who would dare attempt its condensation into a single small volume (the Concise Oxford), yet it has been done; and again into one still smaller, and into another especially adapted for us Americans, but the N. E. D. remains what it was when more than fifty years ago its building was begun—not for profit but for glory—a tribute to the scholarship of the English people of the world, but chiefly, of course, to the learning of the great Oxford scholars who have dedicated their lives to its perfection.

But the Concise is ever at hand. It is a masterpiece of reference and condensation. Derivations do not much interest me, but I like to have some idea of the meaning of the words I am using, and, as I dictate more than I write, I have forgotten—if indeed I ever knew—how to spell. Every foreign word that has worked its way into our language is given in it, and one small joke, for which I love it. I can imagine several learned old gentlemen, sitting and sipping their port after a dinner at the "high table" in some Oxford college, debating whether the joke might be permitted: wisely they agreed that it might. Turn to the word "wing": it is defined, "One of the limbs or organs by which the flight of a bird, bat, insect, *angel*, &c., is effected." How do we know that angels fly? Who ever saw one? But this is no place for skepticism: the authority of the greatest of universities is not to be challenged by an insect.

THE FORMAT OF THE ENGLISH NOVEL

THE novel undoubtedly had its beginning in the Garden of Eden, when Adam, his resistance lowered from the effects of a minor operation, found Eva making eyes at him. And a notoriously wise person—was it Solomon?—once observed that the way of a man with a maid was too much for him. How, then, shall we who are not wise be expected to solve the greater problem—that of a maid with a man? We cannot; nevertheless, with this fascinating proposition we shall attempt to divert ourselves for an hour.

The novel is the last and most popular of the great forms of literature, and scholars have long debated where the English novel begins; but I, not having a heavy intellectual background, after making honorable mention of *Robinson Crusoe*, shall arbitrarily begin with Samuel Richardson. I should like to begin with Defoe,—for I have a great fondness for old Dan; and I am not weak in first editions of him,—but, after all, his masterpiece does not exactly meet the requirements of a novel. Defoe told stories, to be sure, but he left out one important thing: he left out sentiment—which for the purposes of this paper may be called love. It is not easy to say exactly what the requirements of the novel are, but they appear to be first met by Samuel Richardson in his *Pamela*, which appeared, according to the title-page, in 1741, actually in November 1740, and was immediately and enormously successful. No book just like *Pamela* had ever appeared before, and it would have greatly amazed the middle-aged tradesman if he had been told that he had set rolling a ball which has been rolling with constantly increasing acceleration ever since.

And this ball in its rolling took various forms. First, it was several small volumes bound in leather: for convenience I shall refer to this as the Age of Calf. Second, it was two, usually three, somewhat larger volumes bound in Boards: that is to say, in the flimsiest of pasted boards with a paper label, bearing the title on its spine. This was followed by the Age of Parts. These parts came out monthly; usually there were twenty of them, actually nineteen, the last being a double number. Illustrations had by now become an important feature, and the price per part was a shilling. Then came the Victorian novel: three volumes, well printed on good paper, substantially bound in cloth: the "three-decker," it has been called. And finally, there is the cheap and nasty novel of to-day— I am speaking of the format, mind you—in one volume; the novel of commerce; written on a type-writer, printed and bound by machinery, sold by hundreds of thousands, and forgotten as soon as read.

Now let us return to *Pamela*. As not everyone has read *Pamela*, let me try to tell very briefly what this story is about. A lady dies leaving an unmarried son and an indeterminate number of servants, amongst whom was Pamela, a virtuous and beautiful young woman of amazing talents. The son, taken with the girl's beauty, seeks her as his mistress; she resists, and finally, there being no other way to possess her, he offers marriage; she accepts, and they live happily ever after. That is the whole story, and Pamela tells it to her father and mother in an interminable series

"Pamela" in a characteristic binding

of letters, to which she receives occasional replies from her father telling her to guard her chief possession, her virtue, at any cost; she assures him that she will. Now, as Dr. Johnson once remarked, anyone who reads Richardson merely for the story will hang himself: its merit is that *Pamela* was sentimental, emotional, reflective—it was no mere narration of incident.

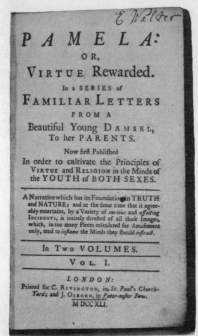

When Richardson's stories first appeared, —as Dr. Cross tells us in his admirable little book on the English novel,—it was usual for someone to read them aloud in the family circle. When pathetic passages were reached, the members of the family would retire to separate apartments to weep (we are in the age of tears as well as calf), and after composing themselves they would return to the fireside and the reading would proceed. I reread *Pamela* only a few months ago: I found it interesting, which its author intended it should be, and very amusing, which its author would have been greatly shocked to hear. We who read *Pamela* to-day are pretty sophisticated and we ask ourselves, Did the chaste, handsome, and intelligent servant girl, carrying her eggs—her virtue, that is—to the best market, have her eye on the main chance? That question has been asked for one hundred and seventy-five years: there is no answer. Whatever her intention, she succeeded in marrying a rich, handsome, and infatuated youth—and what more does any girl want?

Mr. B., Pamela's would-be betrayer, her lover, and

finally her husband,—always referred to as Mr. B.,—
certainly never for a moment supposed that Pamela had
any idea that if she resisted his disgraceful and sometimes cruel overtures he would at last lead her to the
altar; but we cannot but ask ourselves the question,
as we read letter after letter in which Pamela tells
over and over again of the horrible traps that are laid
for her and of her fixed determination to keep her virtue
though the heavens fall. She talked to her fellow servants about it: the head gardener bade her cultivate it;
the head coachman urged her to let it ride. She came
within an ace of losing her most cherished possession
more than once. Telling her parents not to worry, she
kept them constantly on the rack.

After some horrible experience—in which Mr. B.,
folding her in his arms and kissing her repeatedly, tells
her how lovely she is—she escapes from him, and returning to her closet she writes one, two, five, ten long
letters to her father telling him that she is bitterly
beset, but she will die rather than yield to Mr. B. She
was not familiar with that fine old blurb in Bartley
Campbell's *The White Slave* in which the heroine
rushes down to the footlights and declares that "rrags
are rroyal rraiment when worn for virtue's sake" (it
takes a telephone operator to roll the *r*'s properly),
and she could have escaped a hundred times and one
from her master, but she was prevented by her desire
to do her duty by him, to finish embroidering a waist-
coat or some other fool thing; all the time, I fancy,
making eyes at her lover until he finally becomes so
enamored of her and so exhausted by the chase that he
offers to marry her.

Immediately upon receiving the blessing of the clergyman, Mr. B.'s faults are forgotten and he becomes the most admirable of men; this forgiving nature argues well for his continued happiness. Pamela's lover and husband is a great gentleman: it would be disgraceful to mention his name, but finally Henry Fielding announced that he had discovered the carefully guarded secret—Mr. B.'s name, he said, was BOOBY!

It is not easy for us to-day, surrounded by every form of novel, to realize the immense vogue of *Pamela*. Servant girls—who could read—read it; so did duchesses; so did men about town and men who could only spell out the story with difficulty. Four editions—something unheard of for a book of the kind—were published within six months. It was translated and dramatized and it was sung and it was burlesqued by Fielding, in a small and very rare little volume called *Shamela*, and finally in a full-length novel, *Joseph Andrews*. Joseph is Pamela's brother, and he resists the lewd advances of his mistress very much in the manner in which his virtuous sister re-

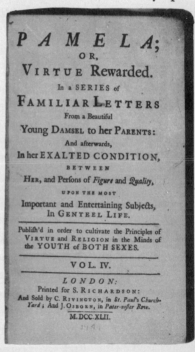

The last of Pamela

"Tom Jones" in old calf

sisted Mr. B. This made Richardson very angry, but he recovered his temper and was unable to withstand the temptation of adding to the original two volumes two more in which Pamela's conduct as an affection-ate wife, a faithful friend, a polite neighbor, and an indulgent mother are recounted at such endless length that one finally tosses the volume aside and takes up something else.

In due course *Pamela* was followed by *Tom Jones*, which is, all things considered, the greatest of English novels. The story goes that the manuscript was offered by Fielding, who was hard pressed for money, to a second-rate publisher for a nominal sum, but it was refused. By the advice of Thomson the poet, Fielding then went to Andrew Millar, the great publisher of the day, who—as was his habit with works of light reading—handed the manuscript to his wife, who advised him by no means to let it slip through his fingers. Millar then invited Fielding and Thomson to "meet and drink" at a coffeehouse in the Strand, where after dinner the bookseller with some hesitation offered Fielding six hundred pounds. The novelist was amazed at the largeness of the offer. "My good sir," he cried, "the book is yours; give me your hand—and, waiter, bring us a couple of bottles of your best port." Before Millar died he had cleared eighteen thousand pounds by his bargain, out of which he is said to have made Fielding various presents to the amount of two thousand pounds; and when he died he bequeathed a handsome legacy to each of the author's sons.

"Evelina"

An early "three-decker;" one has only to read this book, extravagantly praised by Dr. Johnson, to see how far the technique of the novel has progressed since his day

Well may Dr. Johnson, who was a great friend of the publisher, have said, "Sir, Andrew Millar is the Mæcenas of the age." When Johnson undertook to butter a man he buttered him good, and when he hated a man he hated him the same way: he once said he loved a good hater. Gibbon, too, knew how to turn a phrase—no one better. Never, I suppose, has a novel been praised so magnificently and immortally as when, in his *Autobiography*, he refers to *Tom Jones* as "that exquisite picture of human manners which will outlive the palace of the Escurial and the imperial eagle of the house of Austria:" a prophecy one-half of which has already come true. *Tom Jones* was published on the twenty-eighth of February, 1749, and note, if you please, its publisher's announcement in a newspaper of that date. Following the title of the book is this: "It being impossible to get Sets bound fast enough to answer the Demand for them, such Gentlemen and Ladies as please may have them sewed in blue paper and boards at the price of sixteen shillings a set." And a few years ago when one of these unbound copies turned up in Sessler's Book Shop in Philadelphia it brought exactly the price which Fielding received for the manuscript: namely, six hundred pounds, and my friend Jerome Kern bought it—beating me to it for the reason that he had the money and I hadn't. I saw it first.

Between 1749, the year of *Tom Jones*, and 1816, when a perfect novel, *Emma*, appeared, no advance had been made in telling a story. I have called *Emma* a "perfect" novel: I think it is. Jane Austen used a small palette, but her colors were faultless. Lord Rosebery ranks *Emma* as the second-best novel in the English language, placing *Tom Jones* first. Listen to what Kipling says of the author of *Emma*.

Jane lies in Winchester—blessed be her shade!
Praise the Lord for making her, and her for all she made!
And while the stones of Winchester, or Milsom Street, remain,
Glory, love and honor unto England's Jane.

There was a serious blemish in *Tom Jones*, and the same kind of blemish appears in *Nicholas Nickleby* (1839). The progress of both narratives is interrupted by the recital of one or more long stories which have nothing whatever to do with the main theme: they do nothing but interrupt it. In 1859 another novel, *Adam Bede*, was published: again a woman produced a faultless novel. No author's name appeared on the title-page of *Emma*, and on the title-page of *Adam Bede* was the once misleading name of George Eliot. Both novels were, as we now know, written by women; fiction is the one art in which women rank equally with men.

We now believe that every incident in a story should have some bearing on the characters in that story, and that the characters should develop logically out of the situations in which they find themselves. In support of my position let me quote two paragraphs from *The Upton Letters*, that now almost forgotten volume of essays in which its author says: "What I want" (in a novel) "is to step as simply as possible into the presence of an emotion, the white heat of a situation. With Henry James" (Benson was speaking of Henry

"Rasselas," old calf

James), "I do not feel certain what the situation is." Who does? I would inquire.

Let me digress to quote the wag who remarked that Henry James's work fell naturally into three periods: "James First, James Second, and James the Old Pretender." I wish I had said that—but it is something to repeat it. Returning again to *The Upton Letters*, the writer says: "I want to get at what there is without a mental agility which is unnecessarily fatiguing. A novel ought to be like a walk; George Meredith makes it into an obstacle race." There's a fine bit of criticism! That Meredith is caviar to the general may be admitted —but so much the worse for the general.

And now as to the format of all these celebrated novels. "Format" is a French word which has been Anglicised, and which is defined in the *Concise Oxford Dictionary* as "the shape and size of a book"—to which definition I, for the purposes of this paper, would add the word "style." *Pamela* was first published in two small volumes of about four hundred pages each, the size of the page being six and one-quarter inches by three and three-quarters. Each

"Rasselas" in boards

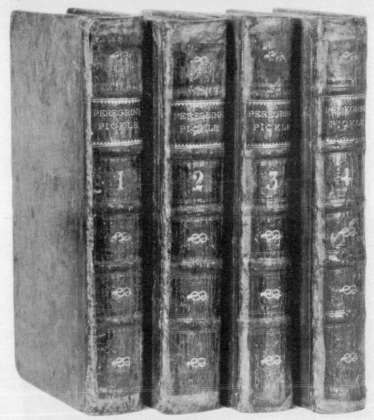

"Peregrine Pickle"

volume was bound in calf. I do not mean to suggest
that it was not possible to obtain the volumes in wrappers, unopened—that is to say, stitched merely in a
blue-gray paper without any indication whatever of
the title thereon. It probably was; but, speaking generally,—and I shall so speak throughout this paper,—the
book was strongly sewed and trimmed with a binder's
knife and bound in calf; it probably had its title in
gold letters upon a little leather label, or perhaps it

had nothing whatever on the back except the number of the volume, and even this was occasionally omitted. But in any event, we are in the Age of Calf.

Dr. Johnson, in 1759, writing to his friend Strahan in regard to *Rasselas*, says, "The story will make two volumes like little *Pompadour*, that is about one middling volume." *Pompadour* was a rather naughty little book which had appeared the year before, but it shows that the thought of the world had turned towards small books; and Johnson's further observation was that "a small book which could be held easily in the hand and carried to the fire side was the most useful after all," to which I am sure we all agree. In brief, in the middle of the eighteenth century, when the novel came in,

"Cranford." No gentler, sweeter story was ever written

the fashion was for small books, well printed, on good paper, and bound in calf. And these are the books so much in demand to-day. *Pamela* has always been a scarce book, and, while it is still possible to procure a copy, you will be lucky if you stumble upon one within a year, in an old binding and at twenty-five hundred dollars, perhaps twice as much: it is indeed, potentially a ten-thousand dollar book!

Leather—calf—was indeed the obvious binding: it was leather or nothing. In the eighteenth century the reading habit was not general and books were bought only by people of means and cultivation. Occasionally these old books were bound in paper boards with a calf back, or in a blue-gray paper, and as this was looked upon as a merely temporary binding, there was usually no lettering of either title or volume number on the spine. And this is the condition in which the fastidious collector will endeavor to secure his books if he can: "in boards uncut." "Uncut," of course, does not mean unopened; it merely means not cut with a binder's knife, which necessarily reduces the size of the volume. In a rare book, "size" is a matter of the utmost importance. Life, to be worth living, must have an occasional thrill: to see a book advertised as of especial value because of its wide margins, and then to discover that your own copy is a quarter of an inch taller or wider, is a joy to the collector—and an innocent one.

All of Richardson's novels were published in small volumes, as were also Fielding's, Smollett's, and Sterne's. Smollett, in my opinion, does not rank with Fielding or with Sterne, but *Peregrine Pickle* is a good story, though *Humphrey Clinker*—written when its author was a dying man—is a better. But there are three other famous books which must never be overlooked in any consideration of eighteenth-century novels, each one characteristic not only of its author, but of a class: there is *Rasselas* (which dear Miss Jenkyns in *Cranford* preferred to *Pickwick*), *The Vicar of Wakefield*, and *Evelina*.

All of these famous books were bound in calf, and it

THE
HISTORY
OF
THE VALOROVS
AND WITTIE
KNIGHT-ERRANT,

DON-QVIXOTE
Of the *Mancha.*

Tranſlated out of the Spaniſh.

LONDON
Printed by *William Stansby,* for *Ed. Blount* and
W. Barret. 1612.

Title page of the first English edition of the
world's greatest novel

may fairly be presumed that, if and when they were acquired in sheets, after being read they were usually sent to the binder and put in leather covers. My copy of Sterne's *Sentimental Journey*, however, remains in its original condition, "sewed in blue paper," and my *Tristram Shandy* is in "boards"—but I shall deal with "boards" presently.

Much ink has been shed in an effort to solve the *Mystery of Edwin Drood*, but I never heard of anyone attempting to guess how A *Sentimental Journey* would have ended had its author lived to finish it. As it is, it ends—where it begins—in the middle: indeed, in the middle of a paragraph. Alas! Poor Yorick: his life ended in the middle, too. He always enjoyed poor health: listen to him on the subject:

> "O blessed Health! thou art above all Gold and Treasure, 'tis thou who enlargest the Soul,—and openest all its Powers to receive instruction, and to relish Virtue—He that has thee, has little more to wish for! and he that is so wretched as to want thee,—wants every thing with thee."—STERNE.

The desire to supplement his clerical income led Sterne—who had already published several volumes of *Sermons* and the like—to publish in 1760 two volumes of *Tristram Shandy*. These volumes bear no publisher's imprint or place of publication. Dr. Cross of Yale, the one great authority on Sterne, does not know whether these two volumes were printed in London or in York, therefore it is useless for us to guess about it; but on January 1, 1760, *The London Chronicle* makes this announcement: "This day was published, printed on a superfine Writing Paper, and a new letter, in two volumes, Price 5 Shillings, neatly

Frontispiece of the second edition of the first part and the first edition of the second part of the world's greatest novel

"Tristram Shandy"

in "boards"   *in full levant*

bound, *The Life and Opinions of Tristram Shandy."*
"Neatly bound" can mean nothing but calf. The
remaining volumes were published in London, the last
appeared in 1767, and it is usual to find Sterne's
signature in volumes 5, 7, and 9. Occasionally un-
scrupulous booksellers suggest that these were Sterne's
own copies, whereas this was merely Sterne's way of
indicating to his customers that they were buying
the authorized edition of his book, which was so
enormously successful that a pirated edition, printed
in Dublin, almost immediately made its appearance
on the London market.

Tristram is a trifle smaller than either *Pamela* or *Tom
Jones*, my bound copy being exactly the size of my
bound *Rasselas*. The earlier book may indeed have
served as a model for the later, both having the same
page appearance and twenty lines to the page. Sweet
little books they are and only now beginning to be
appreciated by the collector. It is curious that for so

many years eighteenth-century prose has been so neglected. The avidity with which scarce seventeenth-century drama has been sought by collectors who hardly read a line of it,—the very titles of which would bring a blush to the cheek of a girl in the "Follies,"—meantime neglecting some of our greatest prose, which is a delight to read — this is one of those vagaries of col-

A fine "unpressed" copy of "The Sentimental Journey," in blue-gray wrappers; two volumes

lecting for which no explanation is offered.

The small calf-bound book continued to be the fashion until after the turn of the century; then, with the increasing number of readers, it was discovered that leather was expensive and paper boards came into use. The exact moment that the change took place it is impossible to say; no doubt it was gradual and the two types overlapped, but a new generation of novelists had come upon the scene—Jane Austen, Sir Walter Scott, Peacock, Bulwer Lytton, and our own Fenimore Cooper, all published in boards with a paper label. The poets of the period—Byron, Keats, Shelley, and the early Tennysons—were all published in boards.

The reasoning of the publisher was doubtless this.

THE

VICAR

OF

WAKEFIELD:

A TALE.

Suppoſed to be written by HIMSELF.

Sperate miſeri, cavete fælices.

VOL. I.

SALISBURY:
Printed by B. COLLINS,
For F. NEWBERY, in Pater-Noſter-Row, London.
MDCCLXVI.

Authors are a rapacious lot: if we have to pay them what they demand, we must bring out their books in cheaper format; instead of calf we shall use paper boards, and the little leather label stamped in gold must give way to a paper label printed in black. Instead of having to trim the book with the binder's knife, we shall leave it uncut; the reader can cut the pages with a paper-knife, and if after reading he wants to have the book properly bound, there will be plenty of margin. This was excellent reasoning, and doubtless the Napoleonic Wars made certain economies desirable if not necessary; in any event, by the time Jane Austen had begun to publish, boards were the style, and the fashion spread from the novel to the volume of poetry. Then, just as the novel in its negligé became established, an entirely new style arose. Enter the Age of Parts.

Early Tennysons, in boards

"Emma." A perfect copy of a perfect book

Who does not delight to look at pictures—pictures that tell a story? The English certainly do, and with the final overthrow of Napoleon they had a lot of money to spend, and some of it they spent on books published in monthly parts. Albert M. Cohen—with whom I have crossed swords as to the first issue of the first edition of *A Christmas Carol*—is of the opinion that

"Lamia" in boards

the *Annals of Gallantry* is the first book of any importance to be so published, but this is hardly a novel. It may be that Mr. Cohen is not aware that *Robinson Crusoe* was published in parts. It appeared in the *Original London Post or Heathcot's Intelligence*. The story begins in the number of Wednesday, October 7, 1719 (the year of publication in book form), and ends in the issue of October 19, 1720. The book is extremely rare. Only three copies are known: the Grenville copy, in the British Museum, which is very imperfect; my own copy, which has but one leaf in excellent facsimile (by Harris?); and one which was sold at auction in Sotheby's, in March 1928, when it brought with a few unimportant Defoe items about fifteen thousand dollars.

But this is hardly publication in parts in the accepted sense of the word: it is really the first serial publication of a novel in a newspaper. But *Life in London*, by Pierce Egan, undoubtedly is. This famous book,

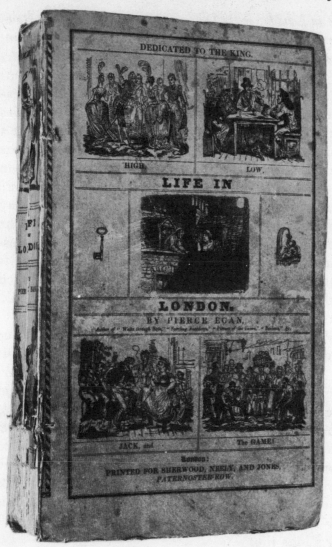

"Life in London," in pictorial boards

Life in London; or the Day and Night Scenes of Jerry Haw-thorne, Esq. and His Elegant Friend Corinthian Tom, Accompanied by Bob Logic, the Oxonian, in Their Rambles and Sprees through the Metropolis,—to give it its full title,—was dedicated by permission to His Most Gracious Majesty King George the Fourth. This work was the earliest important example of monthly parts, at a shilling each. It was enormously popular; for years there was not a man—not a gentleman, that is—in England but knew the book almost by heart. And there were many in this country who knew it as well. To-day it is valued for its description of what is called the sporting life of a century ago, and for its excellent illustrations by Cruikshank. As soon as its issue in parts was completed, it came out in illustrated boards, which is the form in which the collector will want the book, parts being utterly impossible.

From this rather questionable origin sprang the issue of many books in parts, which reached their apotheosis in *Pickwick*, but this was not until some years later. Meantime Rudolph Ackermann had taken a hand in the game. His *Tours of Dr. Syntax*, the joint work of Rowlandson and Combe, are really novels in verse. Rowlandson's drawings gave point and humor to Combe's text, and between artist and artisan they "Syntaxed" the world. It is sad to think how little fun there is on this planet of ours; I suppose that is why a book with a trace of the real article has a chance for a long life.

By the end of the first quarter of the nineteenth century a great change had come over England. Wealth was pouring in, and with the use of steam power and

"Sketches by Boz"

the growth of manufacturing—mass production for the
first time—this wealth was no longer exclusively in the
hands of the great county families: it was widely dis-
tributed. The public, which a generation earlier had
bought but few books, came into the market, and books
in parts became so fashionable that several which had
been originally issued in cloth—which was just coming into use—were reissued in parts, a notable instance
being *Sketches by Boz*.

    And now, at the outset of the consideration of parts,
one comes upon one of the several difficulties which

A prime "Pickwick" in parts

confront the collector. The paper on which the parts were printed was not too good. They contain "plates,"—that is to say, illustrations printed from copper plates,—and copper was very soft in those days; they have "advertisements," and they have "covers:" and all of these must be right—the difference between a right and wrong *Pickwick*, say, is to-day about fifteen thousand dollars.

To return to *Sketches by Boz:* it was issued in twenty parts in pink paper wrappers; it had forty illustrations by George Cruikshank; Part II should contain a two-

"The Way We Live Now"

page address of the publishers, apologizing because
there was less printed matter in the parts than there was
in *Pickwick*, and Part V should contain a three-page
proclamation signed "Boz." If one does not know these
"points," and buys a copy bound up from the parts,
these advertisements will almost certainly be omitted,
even if some of the covers are bound in, as a sort of
guarantee of good faith.

Harry B. Smith, who once owned what I consider
the most interesting *Pickwick* in the world,—which
now belongs to my friend William M. Elkins of Phila-

delphia,—tells in his catalogue, entitled *A Sentimental Library*, of the early wanderings of this famous book: how it went to India with its owner, who died there; whereupon his widow, returning to England, thought it would be nice to have the parts bound up "for the children to read;" and how the binder inquired *whether the covers were to be discarded—each of which bore an inscription from Charles Dickens!* It is these covers which give the Elkins *Pickwick* its unique interest to-day.

It is impossible for one—for me, at least—to overcome the prejudice of a lifetime, and fearing that I shall not be fair to the subject of Books in Parts, which give other—and it may be wiser—collectors than myself such a thrill, I shall again quote a writer who has said: "When A. Edward Newton talks about books in parts do not listen to him." If not to him, then listen to my critic on the subject. "To one who appreciates a book as it left the loving hands of the author from whose brain it sprang, a work in the paper parts . . . possesses a flavor that is unsurpassed even by original boards uncut. Each page is a joy unto itself, and should there be a leaf of the advertisement lacking, there will be the hunt of an odd part to supply the defect—it is a game not without the excitement of the chase, for the wanted oddment is very elusive, and the pleasure of finding it very great. How fascinating it is to turn the pages of those old advertisers . . . whose perfect presence may alter the value of a copy from fifty pounds to a thousand."

We have been told so frequently that advertising is an American art that we have come to believe it. Our great magazines are, indeed, bought and read quite as

much for their advertising pages as for their reading
matter; the national advertiser, as he is called, draws
attention to his wares with such superlative skill that
we are apt to feel that everything has been, is, and will
continue to be wrong with us until and unless we take
his advice. How often have I wished that my gar-
ments had the distinguished cut and fit of those
advertised in certain popular monthlies—which they
never have because I buy them in London and not in
Chicago. I ponder would it not be wise for me to
spend my remaining days polishing my remaining
teeth with Blank's Dental Cream, and I have gone so
far as to consider whether I should not take to smoking Dromedary Cigarettes that I might get that look
of splendid determination which seems to result from
their use—although smoking a cigarette is, to me,
like kissing a girl through a pane of glass: it is very
hygienic and all that sort of thing, but with little
"kick" to it.

We think we are very clever in our advertising, but
take down from your shelves, if you can, a faultless
Pickwick—mine, for example, if I may say so—and
read the advertisements therein. I read and wonder
whether "Parker's Grecian Compound" will change
my hair from its present gray to its original lustrous
black—which it never was; whether I ought not to
lay in a supply of "Russian Corn Cure" against an
hour of pain; whether it is not my duty to buy a
bottle of the "Bloom of Ninon de l'Enclos" with
which my wife may restore that schoolgirl complexion
—which a certain soap of our day has been unable to
do; whether we ought not to have a box of the

"Widow Welch's Female Pills" in the house, the recipe for which was bequeathed to her by her late husband, as she swore it was before the Lord Mayor at the Mansion House on the third day of November, 1798.

All these things and a hundred more must be "right" before one hands over his check for the price of a small house, and receives in exchange a little bundle of nineteen tender pamphlets which can never again be touched, for fear of injury. The accepted authority on *Pickwick* is my friend John C. Eckel; he keeps a bibliographical stud-book—for each great *Pickwick* has a pedigree—which is always at the service of his friends; the latest news is that he has published it.

It may be that I have treated with too great levity some of the necessary advertisements of a perfect *Pickwick*, and I may also fail to refer to the "plates" with the reverence they deserve. It is supposed by Mr. Eckel that there were printed about four hundred copies of the first "part," which appeared on the last day of March, 1836. In its early numbers *Pickwick* was not a success. Indeed it was not until the appearance of Sam Weller that the book caught the taste of the town; then there was a rush for the early parts. Much has been written about the genesis of the book. The idea of a cockney sportsman on tour seems to have been suggested to the publishers, Chapman and Hall, by Robert Seymour, the first illustrator and the creator of the accepted portrait of *Pickwick*. Mr. Hall took up the idea and sent for Dickens—then an obscure journalist—and asked him to do the text. He ac-

"Vanity Fair," in parts

cepted the commission. He was at the time only twenty-four, and he was, as he remained all his life, very "touchy." Promptly he quarreled with the illustrator, who, to the horror of all, committed suicide; and another illustrator, Buss, took up the work, his plates appearing in Part III. But it was immediately seen that Buss had not caught the spirit of *Pickwick*, and he disappeared—to the satisfaction of the author, the publisher, and the public. Thackeray himself is our authority for the statement that he applied for the job of illustrator after Seymour's death, but his sketches did not please Dickens and were declined—luckily, as it turned out, else we might have had no *Esmond* or *Vanity Fair;* and, luckier still perhaps, Hablot K. Browne ("Phiz") was accepted and was able to merge his inimitable genius in that of the author.

The copper plates on which the original sketches were etched almost immediately began to show signs of wear, and, with the increased and ever-increasing demand for parts, were engraved and reëngraved several times, and seemingly unimportant changes in them were made. And at this point the fun—or perplexity—begins again.

Turn to Part I. Have the inside covers advertisements thereon? If they have, throw them away; they are no good—they should be blank. In the plate, "Mr. Pickwick addresses the Club,"—one of the most famous illustrations in any book,—are the buttons of Mr. Pickwick's vest on the right side or the left? This makes a lot of difference. In the second plate, is the milkmaid well defined? If she is faint—well, it's not a crime, but it's a great misfortune. Has the gamekeeper's gun a lock and trigger, in the third plate? It should have; most copies have not. In the next plate, is the floor composed of ten boards or eleven? If eleven, have a carpenter in and remove one. And so throughout the book.

We can hardly realize to-day the immense furore created by *Pickwick*. In its infancy it was not a lusty child, but as it approached manhood it outgrew almost the strength (resources) of its creators. In Number XIV the publishers announced that twenty thousand copies were being printed, and this was increased to twenty-nine thousand for the final numbers. The world had never seen anything like it before, and the rage in almost a hundred years has not yet subsided; when a great copy comes up for sale —as there did on the evening of December 7, 1927, at the American Art Association— there is great to-do among bibliophiles and collectors, and only mild amazement is expressed when a copy fetches a record price of sixteen thousand, three hundred dollars.

"Comic History of England"

A superlatively fine *Pickwick* "in parts" is a heritage for one's children: this in spite of the fact that, as Edmund Lester Pearson has said, a novel in original parts is about as useful as an automobile in parts. And was it not Carolyn Wells who called this sort of collecting "The Idiot's Delight?" Well, so is playing solitaire, and yet wise and busy men recreate themselves with the game.

If I have enlarged upon *Pickwick* it is not only because it is the greatest book that ever appeared in parts, but because it has more "points" than any other book of its kind and has been more closely studied. But *Vanity Fair*, with illustrations by the author, should not be forgotten; it made its appearance in parts some ten

"Mr. Romford's Hounds," a scarce book in parts

years later than *Pickwick*, and, like it, has a complicated
bibliography. As a book in parts, neither *Pickwick* nor
Vanity Fair is beautiful; the distinction of beautiful
"books in parts" belongs, it seems to me, to the Surtee's novels, to *The Comic History of Rome* and *The Comic
History of England*, perhaps because of their fascinating
colored plates by Leech. These, the Surtee's novels; I
have them all, but all in cloth, except *Mr. Romford's
Hounds*, of which I have two, "in parts," on account

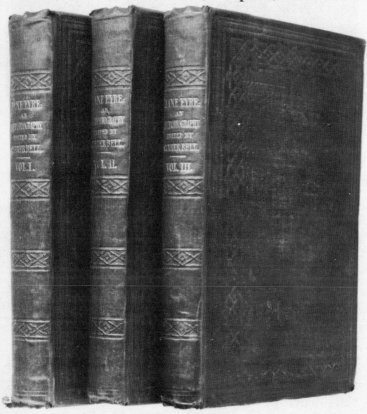

A fine three-decker, "Jane Eyre"

A Group of three-deckers

of interesting variations. My *Rome* and *England* are as fresh as the day of issue—presentation copies signed by both author and illustrator. It was possible to get such things once.

As the Age of Calf overlapped the Age of Boards and Boards overlapped Parts, so Parts overlapped the three-volume novel in cloth—the three-decker.

It was just about a hundred years ago that publishing conditions became modern, if I may use the word. It had been customary for a country gentleman, immediately upon his arrival in town, to visit "Ackermann's." The country gentleman's tastes were not overrefined—Squire Western in *Tom Jones* is not overdrawn. He was a sportsman given to robust living; he thought of himself—when he thought at all—as a lord of creation, and he would have been bewildered had he been told

that he was on the verge of an era when books would
be written by women for women; but so it was. Hannah
More, Jane Austen, Miss Edgeworth, Mrs. Gaskell, the
Brontës, George Eliot—these were the writers who
revolutionized the reading world. The end of the colored-plate book was just about coincident with the
end of the first third of the nineteenth century, and
about the same time "lending libraries" began to play
an important part in the success or failure of a novel.
They sprang up all over England, but they were quickly
outdistanced by the metropolitan libraries; and by the
time that the Brontës and George Eliot had reached the
fullness of their fame an institution such as "Mudie's"
had become more powerful than any publisher or group
of publishers.

All was running like clockwork. The length of the
novel was prescribed by the libraries: it must be three
volumes. The royalty was to be—what it was. The
publisher was to see to that and make the best terms
with the author he could, but the price was established:
thirty-one shillings and sixpence, which made it practically prohibitive for anyone but the very rich to buy
a novel outright—so few did. Finally Mudie became so
arrogant that he presumed to dictate the manner in
which the author should handle his material. Love, of
course, was to continue to motivate the novel, but
there were to be no low amours. A duchess might have
a love affair, but not a servant girl. Queen Victoria was
on her throne and was very particular, as was an old
lady who wrote to William Mudie, the would-be cen-
sor of public taste, and told him that a novel by George
Moore, *A Modern Lover*, had offended her taste and that

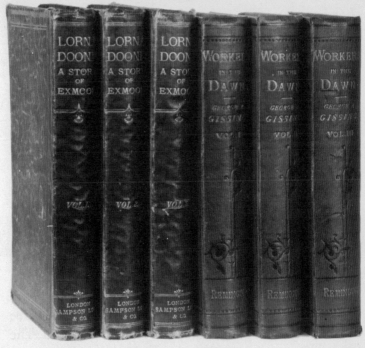

Two scarce three-deckers

of another lady she knew. *A Modern Lover* had been published in 1883, by "old Tinsley," the sponsor for many other famous novels. For half a century the three-decker, well printed in bold type on good paper and substantially bound in cloth and lettered in gold, had weathered all gales. A fleet of battleships would hardly seem more enduring than a fleet composed of such units as *Lady Audley's Secret*, *Jane Eyre*, *Adam Bede*, *The Moonstone*, *Richard Feverel*, and *Lorna Doone*, to mention only a few. But a submarine had been invented which was destined to blow the fleet sky-high: George Moore was it.

George Moore is Irish: an Irishman loves a fight. When he found the shelves of Mudie's closed to him, he scented a fight and was in his element. "What ho!" he cried. "The libraries closed to me! Very well: never again shall I publish a three-volume novel; hereafter I make my appeal direct to the public; my next novel shall be in one volume, and shall sell for six shillings." Mudie sent for him and begged him to stop rocking the boat, he tried by persuasion and by threats to force him to see the error of his ways, but in vain. "Don't you think," said Moore, "the Lord is just as much interested in the amours of a servant girl as He is in the indiscretions of a duchess?" Mudie, however, had not sent for Moore to discuss ethics; he had sent for him to tell him what he was to do and when. It soon became a free-for-all fight, and many entered or were drawn in. *A Mummer's Wife* came out in one volume at six shillings, and was an immense success. Four editions appeared within the year: people were glad to get a book which they could own and take their time over and finally place on their shelves. The whole story is told in an interesting pamphlet called *Literature at Nurse or Circulating Morals*, a copy of which, inscribed to William Wilde (Oscar's brother) with George Moore's compliments, is before me.

The battle became a general engagement; one by one, the three-deckers went down. Publishers began to look the libraries in the face and tell them where to go. The sea had been in some measure prepared for the slender craft soon to be launched upon it: it had been customary for publishers to issue cheap one-volume editions of a book after its sale in three luxurious

To William Wilde with George Moore's Compliments

PRICE THREEPENCE

Literature at Nurse

OR

CIRCULATING MORALS

By GEORGE MOORE

AUTHOR OF "A MUMMER'S WIFE," "A MODERN LOVER," ETC.

"They stand there, Respectable; and—what more? Dumb idols; with a skin of delusively-painted waxwork, inwardly empty, or full of rags and bran. Such bounties, in this as in infinitely deeper matters, does Respectability shower down on us. Sad are thy doings, O Gig; sadder than those of Juggernaut's Car; that, with huge wheel, suddenly crushes asunder the bodies of men; thou in thy light-bobbing Long-acre springs, gradually winnowest away their souls!"

"One day the *Mudie* mountain, which seemed to stand strong like the other rock mountains, gave suddenly, as the icebergs do, a loud-sounding crack; suddenly, with huge clangour, shivered itself into ice dust; and sank, carrying much along with it."—*Carlyle's Essays.*

LONDON

VIZETELLY & CO., 42 CATHERINE STREET, STRAND

1885

A very scarce pamphlet, by George Moore

volumes had ceased. Now, instead of waiting a year or two for a popular novel to appear "at a price within the reach of all," it came out, at that price, upon the date of first publication. And the competition between rival publishers made them spare no pains to give the most they could for the money, in paper, type, and binding; with this further advantage, that interminably long novels almost ceased to be written. The fight was not won at once: it took time. It seems perfectly clear now that there could have been but one result, but thirty-five years ago it required courage, persistence, and a series of good novels to break down a tradition almost as old as the novel itself; fortunately, of courage there was sufficient, and good novels were forthcoming as needed. So it is to George Moore, rather than to any other man, that we owe the one-volume novel, printed on good paper, in clear, legible type, and at a price within our reach. And with the change from three volumes to one there came another change. When novels were published in parts, they were infernally padded; a certain amount of space had to be filled each month; if the story had been carried as far as it was wise in that "part," a good incident was kept for the following issue. Pick up *The Virginians*, say, and you will see the padding sticking out.

The three-volume novel also was too long, too full of words masquerading as ideas; with the one-volume novel a man—or a woman—said what he had to say and quit. The change in form, then, is at least to some extent responsible for the change in style. It may be treason to say so, but the candid reader will admit that most of the great Victorian novels would be much improved if they were shorter. Novelists wrote under pressure and for money, just as Shakespeare wrote his plays, and as novelists do to-day; and when parts went out of style and the three-decker became the vogue, one had still to fill a certain number of pages: this accounts for the unnecessary length of countless excellent novels, including those of my favorite author, Anthony Trollope. To-day we ask that a writer tell his story, one story at a time, and have done. Of course long novels still appear, but they are *tours de force*, as it were; or, if they are very long, they are broken up into sections or epochs, each complete in itself, as in Galsworthy's *Forsyte Saga*. And even this work of genius came out in sections over a period of years, and is now long enough.

An interesting question for debate would be, Are we to-day producing novels that will be read a hundred years from now?—as we are to-day reading *Emma*, say, or *Cranford*. I think that we are: looking back to see that the continuity of English literature is unbroken. If I may venture to prophesy, I should say that *The Forsyte Saga* will probably be read a hundred years hence with more interest than it is to-day. Consider *The Damnation of Theron Ware*, *Colonel Carter of Cartersville*, *Casuals of the Sea*, *Joanna Godden*, *Ethan Frome*—lots of good stories are being written; the difficulty is that the average is so high that to write an outstanding novel is to-day almost impossible. *Moby Dick*, the greatest book written on this continent, is sure to live, if one may speak of that great epic as of to-day—it is seventy-five years old, but is only now coming into its own. Of Conrad, I, who cannot read him, say nothing because I know nothing.

One drawback to collecting the novels of to-day should be mentioned: with the cheap and pulpy paper now almost invariably used, where will these books be, physically, a century hence? The paper will turn to dust and the book will come to pieces— in most cases this is not to be regretted. A new note in bibliography was introduced into the book-collecting game with the publication of books in cloth. What cloth binding was used on the original first edition, and what on following editions or remainders? When boards were in vogue, they were indeed little more than cases for the sheets or quires which go to make up the book; when, however, cloth bindings became elaborate and in-creasingly expensive, publishers ordered only a limited number bound up in the first instance, then they ordered further copies from the binder as the demand for the book warranted. Here one has a clue—or a problem, as the case may be—as to what is the first issue of the first edition, supplied by the binding as well as by the sheets.

Moby Dick
First American edition

I collect Hardy, and I have two copies of the first edition of *The Woodlanders*, three volumes, green cloth; Macmillan 1887. Seemingly they are identical, but one is bound in pebbled green cloth with a heavy border

An excessively rare novel, "Desperate Remedies," and its "pull-off" case

within a narrow border, both borders having square corners; the other is in smooth green cloth, and the inside border is much narrower than the one first mentioned, and has round corners. It makes no difference to me which is accredited the first edition—I have both. But what if some careful student of the novel—like my friend Morris L. Parrish—rises up and says, "The first issue of *The Woodlanders* should have no side stamp whatever." Then what? I ask you.

One has to be very careful in the matter of what may

be called "remainder" binding, which is always cheaper in character than that used originally. A "remainder" binding is an abomination—to be avoided. In a "remainder" it may be that a large volume has, by trimming away its margins, been turned into a small one, or a three-volume novel may be bound up in two or even in one volume. Such volumes are not to be touched by the discriminating collector at any price—unless indeed, as Michael Sadleir says, it might perchance be Hardy's *Desperate Remedies*, which one might then take on, "pending the millennium or the death of a rich relation." A "remainder" looks about as much like a proper "first" as a counterfeit bill looks like a genuine one.

The end papers of a cloth-bound volume call for a word of comment. Originally end papers and blank leaves (which in the case of very rare books are matters of the greatest importance) were once an integral part of the signature or quire, but gradually surfaced or colored or flowered end papers came into vogue, and afford another subject for discussion; indeed the battle still rages as to the priority of green or lemon end papers in the case of the first issue of *A Christmas Carol*. Sadleir says the Victorian end papers were frequently something between a cream and a yellow in shade, with an opaque and chalky surface, and afford another clue as to whether the volume is remaindered or not. General advertisements, too, and publishers' announcements, dated and otherwise, still remain to perplex the tyro. Usually these are a part of a separate printing and immediately precede the end papers at the back of the book; only experience, a good bibliography, or the advice of a reliable bookseller will be of service here; to generalize is to bewilder. Indeed to collect Stevenson, Hardy, Conrad, or Kipling—especially Kipling—without a good bibliography is to head straightway for a lunatic asylum. Only the close student can have any idea of the years of study and work which go to the making of a modern bibliography. In support of this statement, see Henry Clinton Hutchins's *Robinson Crusoe and Its Printing*.

Modern books in beautiful cloth bindings, published by Macmillan—such binding is almost a lost art

Some modern books are very beautiful; others are inexcusably ugly. With the general use of fine, smooth cloth, it is possible to use heavy gold ornamentation with good effect. For certain classes of books—books containing illustrations, usually—beautiful stampings sometimes decorate the front cover. We bound books beautifully in cloth in this country seventy-five years ago, and a series of lovely little volumes illustrated by Hugh Thomson occurs to me. In this type of binding no one excelled the publications of Macmillan. On the other hand, *Moby Dick*, published by Harper and Brothers, is, with the possible

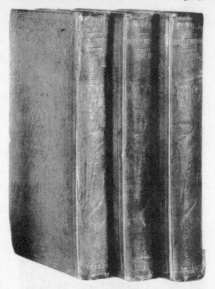

"The Whale"

exception of *The Education of Henry Adams*, the ugliest book I know. An English edition of Melville's book, under the title of *The Whale*, was published in three volumes in 1851 by Richard Bentley. Michael Sadleir, in his excellent *Excursions in Victorian Bibliography*, says that the English edition predates the American edition. I had unsuccessfully sought this edition for years, and had just about made up my mind to live and die without a copy of this excessively scarce book when I heard that a rival collector, B. George Ulizio of Atlantic City, had one. Knowing that money would not tempt him to part with it, I wrote and suggested an exchange. He declined what I offered, but added, "Since you want *The Whale* so badly, I am sending it to you with my compliments." I believe this incident to be unique in book-collecting annals.

A Trollope, in cloth

It is now admitted that *Moby Dick* or *The Whale*, call it as you will, is one of the finest pieces of literature in the English language. The first English edition was five hundred copies; it may be that the first New York edition was no larger. A few people read the book and threw it aside. For seventy years the book and the author were forgotten; then came the awakening—and immortality. Tomlinson, who writes of the sea as no other man now living does, says *Moby Dick* is the greatest thing written in America since the Declaration of Independence. Why lug in the Declaration? But let us be calm.

Since the war, the cost of all the items that go into bookmaking has risen so enormously that publishers have been forced once again to the too general use of books in boards with a cloth back strip with a paper label. This, even if it cannot be helped, is much to be regretted, for books so bound will not last even the brief period that time allots to the modern book.

I know no pleasanter occupation than collecting the great novels of our language. The seventeenth-century poets, so much esteemed, are practically unobtainable.

The great poems of the eighteenth century are priceless: it is hardly worth while to tell the average collector to get the *Travellers* and the *Villages* and the *Elegies;* but he can still find the eighteenth-century novels in calf, and some desirable books in boards, and some of the great books in parts. When he comes to the three-deckers, he will find his work cut out for him—but if the game were easy there would be no sport in it. And while you are buying the great novels, read them: they are good reading. Our fiction may not be as tremendous as Russia's, but who would live forever in an atmosphere of *Crime and Punishment?* There is something to be said for *John Halifax, Gentleman,* and here's good luck to Wilkins Micawber!

Mr. Micawber

ONE HUNDRED GOOD NOVELS

"You seem to get a lot of pleasure out of book-collecting. I am a man" (or woman) "of some little means and ordinary intelligence; I have always been fond of books and reading. Can you give me any suggestion as to what to collect?"

Having received hundreds of letters of this general tenor, after due consideration I venture to suggest the collection of good novels. The novels I recommend must be written in English; they should have a certain bibliographical interest, and for the most part be fairly accessible in first editions; they must be readable to-day, and if they were once popular—so much the better.

I have been told and I have reluctantly come to believe that the greatest novels have been written in the Russian language. I admit their greatness, but I do not much care for them: they are immense canvases—like Tintoretto's—and they are almost certainly gloomy, when they are not tragic. But, however great, foreign novels have no place either in my life or in my list.

I shall not attempt to make any distinction between a novel and a romance. Someone has said that a story filled with tea fights is a novel, while if it is filled with sea fights it is a romance; this distinction will serve as well as any other. We all know what we mean when we use the word "novel:" it is the literary form that to-day makes the widest appeal the world over. People can and do read novels who read little else; they are suited to every taste and age, and, speaking generally, they are read and forgotten.

Anticipating the further question, "What novels shall I collect?" I have with the advice of several eminent writers of fiction, and with the suggestions of many friends and the aid of a bookseller or two, prepared my list of

ONE HUNDRED GOOD NOVELS

1. Adam Bede.................................Eliot
2. Adventures of Sherlock Holmes, The.........Doyle
3. Alice in Wonderland.....................Carroll
4. Babbitt.................................Lewis
5. Barchester Towers.......................Trollope
6. Ben-Hur................................Wallace
7. Caleb Williams.........................Godwin
8. Captains Courageous.....................Kipling
9. Cashel Byron's Profession................Shaw
10. Casuals of the Sea......................McFee
11. Children of the Mist...................Phillpotts
12. Cloister and the Hearth, The.............Reade
13. Colonel Carter of Cartersville...........Smith
14. Conqueror, The.........................Atherton
15. Conrad in Quest of His Youth...........Merrick
16. Cranford..............................Gaskell
17. Crisis, The...........................Churchill
18. Crock of Gold, A.......................Stephens
19. Cruise of the "Cachalot," The............Bullen
20. Damnation of Theron Ware, The..........Frederic
21. David Copperfield......................Dickens
22. Democracy.............................Adams
23. East Lynne............................Wood
24. Emma.................................Austen
25. Esther Waters.........................Moore
26. Ethan Frome...........................Wharton
27. Evelina...............................Burney
28. Sir Richard Calmady....................Mallet
(Mary St. L. Harrison)
29. Frankenstein.........................Shelley Mrs.

30. Green Mansions...........................Hudson
31. Handy Andy...............................Lover
32. Heart of Midlothian, The..................Scott
33. Henrietta Temple........................Disraeli
34. History of Sandford and Merton, The.........Day
35. Honorable Peter Sterling, The....'..........Ford
36. Honour of the Clintons, The.............Marshall
37. Huckleberry Finn...................Mark Twain
38. Humphrey Clinker.....................Smollett
39. Jane Eyre.............................Brontë (C.)
40. Joanna Godden......................Kaye-Smith
41. John Halifax, Gentleman.................Mulock
42. Joseph Vance........................De Morgan
43. Lady Audley's Secret....................Braddon
44. Last Days of Pompeii, The........Bulwer-Lytton
45. Last of the Mohicans, The................Cooper
46. Lavengro................................Borrow
47. Life and Adventures of Peter Wilkins, The..Paltock
48. Life and Opinions of Tristram Shandy,
        Gent, The.............................Sterne
49. Little Minister, The.....................Barrie
50. Little Women...........................Alcott
51. Lorna Doone.........................Blackmore
52. Luck of Roaring Camp, The...............Harte
53. Man of Property, The...............Galsworthy
54. McTeague..............................Norris
55. Moby Dick............................Melville
56. Monsieur Beaucaire..................Tarkington
57. Moonstone, The.........................Collins
58. Mr. Midshipman Easy...................Marryat
59. Mr. Facey Romford's Hounds.............Surtees
60. New Grub Street........................Gissing
61. Mr. Britling Sees It Through ....Wells
62. Nigger of the Narcissus, The.............Conrad
63. Nightmare Abbey......................Peacock
64. Of Human Bondage....................Maugham
65. Old Wives' Tale, The...................Bennett

66. Ordeal of Richard Feverel, The...........MEREDITH
67. Pamela...............................RICHARDSON
68. Parnassus on Wheels....................MORLEY
69. Peter Ibbetson......................DU MAURIER
70. Picture of Dorian Gray, The..............WILDE
71. Portrait of a Lady........................JAMES
72. Prisoner of Zenda, The.................HAWKINS
73. Rasselas.................................JOHNSON
74. Red Badge of Courage, The................CRANE
75. Rise of Silas Lapham, The...............HOWELLS
76. Robert Elsmere............................WARD
77. Robbery Under Arms................BOLDREWOOD
78. Romantic Comedians, The.............GLASGOW
79. Scarlet Letter, The...................HAWTHORNE
80. Story of a Bad Boy.....................ALDRICH
81. Story of Kennett, The...................TAYLOR
82. Ten Thousand a Year....................WARREN
83. Tess of the D'Urbervilles.................HARDY
84. Thaddeus of Warsaw.....................PORTER
85. Three Black Pennys, The...........HERGESHEIMER
86. Tom Brown's School-Days...............HUGHES
87. Tom Burke of Ours........................LEVER
88. Tom Cringle's Log.........................SCOTT
89. Tom Jones.............................FIELDING
90. Treasure Island.......................STEVENSON
91. Two Years before the Mast.................DANA
92. Uncle Remus............................HARRIS
93. Uncle Tom's Cabin........................STOWE
94. Vanity Fair..........................THACKERAY
95. Vicar of Wakefield, The...............GOLDSMITH
96. Virginian, The...........................WISTER
97. Way of All Flesh, The....................BUTLER
98. Westward Ho!..........................KINGSLEY
99. Wuthering Heights...................BRONTË (E.)
100. Zuleika Dobson.......................BEERBOHM

I could say why I admit a certain author or a certain book and exclude another, but I do not wish to be asked to give my reasons. I suggest that every collector make his own list.

Let it be understood that by collecting novels I mean collecting the books in first edition, as they were originally published, whether in calf, boards, parts, or cloth, and in good condition. Good is a relative term: it will be practically impossible to find an old and popular novel in fine condition. Books which have passed into and out of "lending libraries," or books which have been read by a whole generation of readers, invariably show grievous signs of wear. Every collector will decide for himself whether he will take on a poor copy of a book, hoping to get a better one later, or wait until a good copy turns up. I recommend both courses.

It was an easy matter to select sixty volumes for my list: there could be little or no disagreement as to the best sixty novels. The next twenty occasioned difficulty and much discussion, but it was carried on without undue acrimony: "It's your list, not mine," a man would say. The last twenty brought about a pitched battle: "No sane man would omit Marie Corelli and Ouida and include Tarkington and Owen Wister, and why in heaven's name do you omit *Pickwick?*" My first thought was to place an asterisk (*), à la Baedeker, after the title of the sixty novels about which there was no question; a question mark (?) after the title of the next twenty—the doubtful titles; and an exclamation point (!) after the last twenty—"which no sane man would think of." But why deprive my reader of the pleasant

feeling of superiority which he might have in himself
appraising the comparative value of all the books in
my list? It seemed that a pleasant hour might be
passed in placing here a star, there a question mark,
and elsewhere an exclamation point. Then it occurred
to me that my reader might not be provided with
sixty stars, twenty question marks, and twenty exclamation points. Whereupon, taking a leaf out of the
eccentric Lord Timothy Dexter's famous book,—in
which he massed the punctuation marks on one page,
that his readers might pepper and salt his work as
they pleased,—I secured from my publisher the space
necessary to provide the given number of "points,"
and here they are, very much at my reader's service.

          * * * * * * * * * *

          * * * * * * * * * *

          * * * * * * * * * *

          * * * * * * * * * *

          * * * * * * * * * *

          * * * * * * * * * *

          ? ? ? ? ? ? ? ? ? ?

          ? ? ? ? ? ? ? ? ? ?

          ! ! ! ! ! ! ! ! ! !

          ! ! ! ! ! ! ! ! ! !

The novels I have selected have at one time or another enjoyed great popularity or had some special significance. I include *Uncle Tom's Cabin* and omit *Old Town Folks*, which is a better novel. The thoughtful reader will soon discover why I have included Conan Doyle and Joel Chandler Harris, and omitted Poe and O. Henry.

It is hardly worth while recommending a book which in first edition is practically nonexistent, like *Pamela*, but it can be had, at a price, and as it is the corner stone or capstone of any collection of modern English novels, I have included it in my list. Some very rare books can be had cheaply—with luck. An excellent copy of *Lady Audley's Secret* was sold for almost nothing not long ago; and a correspondent writes me that he recently bought a first edition of *Moby Dick* for ten cents and sold it to a bookseller for sixty dollars; he asked me what I thought of the transaction. I told him that I should have respected him more if he had doubled both his buying and his selling price.

My list is designed to suggest the collection of other books by the same author, or similar books by various authors. *Zuleika Dobson* never had the success of *David Harum*, but it will be read when *David Harum* is forgotten, on account of its enduring fantastic charm; and if Beerbohm's novel leads the reader to collect Max, it will have earned its place in this list. It will be observed that only one book by each author is indicated: a better and less interesting list could be made if some authors were permitted two or more books. There are one hundred great novels in the

English language, but there are not a hundred great novelists—not by any means.

If I were asked how these novels can be obtained, and how one is to tell a first from a second or twenty-second edition, I should reply: Consult the booksellers' catalogues. It won't be long before the arrival of a catalogue will mean a pleasant thrill, especially if the catalogue has been compiled with care. The secondhand booksellers of London and the English provinces will be found the cheapest, but one may read many catalogues before coming across a book which he will care much to own, and by the time the order is received on the other side the item will almost certainly have been sold. On the other hand, not only are most of the catalogues published in this country well printed, but they are mines of bibliographical information: they may, indeed, be regarded as textbooks of literature, and as such they may be profitably studied. Even with good catalogues, you will make mistakes at first: we all do, but keep right on, studying as you go.

I put Dickens at the top of my list of novelists, but for steady reading Trollope gives me more pleasure. With no single masterpiece to his credit, he has written a greater number of thoroughly readable novels than any other English author.

I do not undervalue humor; it is only too rare. It is easy to be tragic; tragedy lives just around the corner from most of us. I am, with Sterne, "firmly persuaded that every time a man smiles—but much more so when he laughs—it adds something to this fragment of life."

It is very sad to think that, out of our population of over one hundred and ten million people, it has been estimated that only about two hundred thousand are consistent book-buyers. Too few people understand the joy of buying books, and too few people know how to sell them. People are taught to sell bonds and automobiles and washing machines, but books are supposed to sell themselves. Bessie Graham should be teaching the art of bookselling, not to fifty people, but to five thousand. A correspondence course could be instituted: let the publishers club together and establish a School of Bookselling.

Too many people believe that it is an extravagance to buy books. "He has a book; in fact, several:" well, the more he has the more he wants, usually. Too much that has been written about books is very "high hat" indeed. "A book is a window through which the soul looks out:" such a statement only bewilders the average man. Lord Grey of Fallodon voices my opinion very simply. "Books are the greatest and most satisfactory of recreations. I mean the use of books for pleasure: without having acquired the habit of reading for pleasure, none of us can be independent."

As life tends to become more and more distracting, let us firmly hold on to books. We move to the country to escape interruptions of the city, and the damned telephone keeps ringing all the time, and now the radio has added to its distractions. For myself, I have no desire to hear a political speech, a concert, a sermon, some cheap jokes, and a lot of "static," all in one evening— or, indeed, any of them in any evening. I prefer to live behind the times with a good book—not too far from a wood fire in winter, in the shade of a tree in summer;

but it is difficult to read out-of-doors: Nature, in her quiet way, has a way of interrupting us.

To come back to my list of novels. I have changed it again and again; it is not right now and never will be. There are fashions in novels as there are in plays; a twenty-year-old play is rather silly: "it dates," we say, meaning thereby that its machinery creaks. At a recent revival of *The Two Orphans*, girls whose knees were "overexposed" as the photographers say; with bobbed hair, and whose skirts were a mere flounce, laughed at scenes which had caused their mothers to weep copiously—mothers whose crowning glory was their hair and who wore bustles to make their skirts "hang," — who upon leaving the theatre covered their red and swollen eyes with a veil, that no one should suspect how thoroughly they had been enjoying themselves.

Old Father Time, with his scythe and his whiskers, has seen so many things come and go that he is reluctant to express an opinion as to what is permanent. The novel of to-day is gone to-morrow: at the moment it is the fashion to praise *The Bridge of San Luis Rey;* where will it be in six months? I should have found a place in my list for a novel by Ouida; for *All Sorts and Conditions of Men*, by Besant; for *The Manxman*, by Hall Caine; for *John Inglesant*, by Shorthouse . . . There are certainly forty novels just as good as those to which the reader will append a question mark or an exclamation point.

One final word to collectors: avoid artificial rarities, most private press books, masterpieces of printing, reprints of famous books in expensive and limited edi-

tions. Stick to first editions; don't be afraid to pay a
good price, a high price, for a fine copy of any important book, but be sure that it is important. The better
the book, the higher the price, the better the bargain.
And a good rule for a beginner is to read every book he
buys: this will slow down his purchases somewhat,
but will make him a better collector in the end.

**Books are intended to be read; the collecting
of them is only an incident in their
lives as it is in ours,
saying which,
in the words of William Blake,
"The Scribe of Pennsylvania casts his pen
upon the earth."**

This interesting picture of George Bernard Shaw, by Augustus John, in the Fitzwilliam Museum, Cambridge, was received too late to be properly placed. It is a beautiful portrait, in pink and white, and simply could not be omitted.

INDEX

ABBOTT, JACOB, 59. *See* Rollo books.

ABBOTT, JOHN, *Life of Napoleon*, 9, 59.

À BECKETT, GILBERT, *The Comic History of England*, 367, 368; *The Comic History of Rome*, 367, 368.

ACKERMANN, RUDOLPH, publisher of *Tours of Dr. Syntax*, 356.

ACKERMANN'S, London, 210, 368; in Chicago, 211.

ADAM, R. B., of Buffalo, 184, 211; an "amenity" of, 319, 320.

ADAM (R. B.) SALE, 198–200, 316, 317.

ADAMS, HENRY. See *Education of Henry Adams*.

ADAMS, RANDOLPH, custodian of the William L. Clements Library, 36; *The Whys and Wherefores of the William L. Clements Library, or a Brief Essay on Book-collecting as a Fine Art*, 36; *History of the Foreign Policy of the United States*, 36.

ADDISON, JOSEPH, his *Cato*, first play produced in America, 92.

ADVERTISEMENTS, in first editions, 360–362, 364, 377.

ADVERTISING, 124.

ÆSCHYLUS, Payne's, 154.

AITKEN, THOMAS, publisher of first English Bible in this country, 75, 89; other books published by, 88, 89.

ALCOTT, LOUISA M., *Little Women*, 279.

ALDRICH, THOMAS BAILEY, letter of, to Austin Dobson, on English criticism of New England authors, 288.

ALLAN (JOHN) SALE, 192.

ALMANACS for 1639 and 1640, first set up and printed by Stephen Daye in Cambridge, Mass., 71.

AMERICAN ANTIQUARIAN SOCIETY, Worcester, Mass., 72, 86.

AMERICAN ART ASSOCIATION, auction rooms of, 16, 95, 193, 194, 205, 279, 365.

AMERICAN CHILDREN'S BOOKS, Dr. Rosenbach's collection of, 278.

AMERICAN LITERATURE, 274–293; not of first rank, 274, 275; a review of, 274, 275; uninteresting, 275; Wakeman collection of, 279–282.

AMERICANA, 193, 243, 278.

ANDERSON GALLERIES, 34, 97, 182, 193, 194, 198, 316.

ANDREWS, WILLIAM LORING, his study of Thomas Gosden (*An English Nineteenth-Century Sportsman and Biblio-phile*), 161, 163; *A Short Historical Sketch of the Art of Book Binding*, 187, 188. *Anecdotes on the Origin and Antiquity of Horse-Racing*, 162.

ANGLO-SAXONS, in early New England, 84.

Annals of Gallantry, 354.

APPLETON, MR., publisher, 299.

Arabian Nights, The, 59, 60.

ARBLAY, MADAME D'. *See* Burney, Fanny.

ARISTOTLE. See *Dialectica of Aristotle*.

ARNOLD, WILLIAM HARRIS, *A Record of Books and Letters*, 186; *A Record of First Editions*, 186; his collections, 186–189; mentioned, 195.

ASHHURST, JOHN, librarian of The Free Library of Philadelphia, 278.

Aspects of the Novel, 303.

Athenaeum, 285, 296.

"ATLAS FOLIO," 113.

AUCHINLECK, 183.

AUCTION SALES, the fun of, 39; the dangers of, 175, 176; in London and in New York, compared, 193, 194; the knock-out, 194–196; the romance of, 196; three ways of procedure at, 197, 198. *See also* Prices, Sales.

AUCTIONEERS: William Cooper, 176, 177; Millington, 177; John Danton, 177, 178.

AUCTIONEERS, INCORPORATED SOCIETY OF, 196.

AUCTIONEERS' CATALOGUES. *See* Catalogues.

AUSTEN, JANE, *Emma*, the perfect novel, 341, 374; published in boards, 351, 352; mentioned, 112, 369.

BACON, SIR FRANCIS, his first appearance in the New World, 84.

BAGFORD, JOHN, his collection, 150.

BAILEY, NATHANIEL, his dictionary, 328.

BAKER (G. A.) AND COMPANY, 290.

BALLARD, ELLIS AMES, 205.

BALLARD COLLECTION, 205.

BANGS AND CO., auctioneers, New York, 11, 186.

BARCLAY, ALEXANDER, *The Ship of Fooles*, quoted, 29.

BARRE, MASS., 85, 86.

BARRETT, ELIZABETH, 280.

BASKERVILLE, JOHN, printer, 117.

BATTLE, SARAH, her whist-playing with Charles Lamb, 14.

BAUMGARTEN, bookbinder, 156.

BAXTER, RICHARD, *Call to the Unconverted*, 77.

BAY, J. CHRISTIAN, lectures on "Incunabula of Chicago," 37, 38.

Bay Psalm Book, metrical paraphrase of, 70; published in 1640, by Stephen Daye in Cambridge, Mass., 71; existing copies of, 72; the most valuable and interesting book printed in America, 278.

BEACONSFIELD, BENJAMIN DISRAELI, Earl of. *See* Disraeli.

BEAUCLERK, TOPHAM, sale catalogues of his library, 178, 179; his "frisk" with Johnson and Bennet Langton, 178, 179; his death, 179.

BEDFORD, DUKE AND DUCHESS OF, 157.

BEDFORD, FRANCIS, bookbinder, 166.

BEDFORD MISSAL, 156–158.

BEEKMAN, CATHERINE, 93.

BEERBOHM, MAX, *Zuleika Dobson*, 388.

BELL, ROBERT, his edition of *Rasselas*, 88, 89; auctioneer and publisher, 90; early publishing ventures of, 90; his *Free Sale of Books*, 90, 91; his edition of *Paradise Lost*, 91, 92.

BEMIS, FRANK B., 164.

BENSON, ARTHUR C., *The Upton Letters*, quoted on the novel, 342, 343.

BENTLEY, RICHARD, 379.

BERTHELET, THOMAS, Royal Printer and Binder to Henry VIII, 138, 139.

BESANT, SIR WALTER, *All Sorts and Conditions of Men*, 391.

BIAGI, DR. GUIDO, custodian of the Laurentian Library, 270, 272.

BIBLE, in English, the first published in this country, 75; Eliot's Indian, 76, 77, 192; the first complete English (1535), 103; the Great, of Henry VIII (1539), 106, 221; the Matthews, 107; with embroidered binding, 144; of Doves Press, 169; of Martha Washington, 189, 190; Graingerized, 239; Coverdale (1535), 221, 226. *See* Gutenberg Bible.

BIBLIOGRAPHICA, 39, 378.

BIBLIOTHÈQUE NATIONALE, the world's worst library, 117.

BICKNELL, barrister, 47, 48.

BICKNELL, SARAH (SABRINA), 48, 53.

BINDERS, French, 138; Berthelet, 138, 139; Mearne, 148–152, 164; Payne, 152–154, 164; Edwards, 156–161; Gosden, 161–164; Hering, Kalthoeber, Charles Lewis, 164; Francis Bedford, 166; Thomas J. Cobden-Sanderson, 168, 169.

BINDING, a continental art, 128, 156;

flourished as an art under Charles II, 148.

BINDINGS, dos-à-dos, 115; tariff on, 129; two classes of, 130–134; "in boards," 134; Grolier, 134; example of, in boards (Boethius's *De Consolatione Philosophiæ*), 135; "in African fashion," 136; Henry VIII, 136–138; fragments of books rescued from, 138; leather, 138; Elizabethan, 139, 142; sample of, from Thomas Wotton's library, 140; of James I's time, 140, 142; done for Henry, Prince of Wales, 142; embroidered, 142–144; Little Gidding, 144–146; of Charles II's time, 148; Mearne ("rectangular," "allover," "cottage"), 150–152; "Edwards of Halifax," 156–161; in transparent vellum, 156, 158; in "Etruscan" calf, 158; in Levant morocco, 166, 167; tree calf, 167; Dutch and German silver, 167; in vellum "with ties," 168; in cloth, 169, 171 (cf. 18); effect of coal and illuminating gas on, 174; treatment of, with preservatives, 174; "remainders," 377. *See also* Format, Novel.

BINYON, LAURENCE, 23.

BIOREN AND MADAN, publishers, 93.

BIRMINGHAM, 117.

BIRRELL, AUGUSTINE, *Obiter Dicta*, "A Rogue's Memoirs" in, 270.

BLACKMORE, RICHARD D., *Lorna Doone*, 370.

BLACKSTONE, SIR WILLIAM, *Commentaries*, published by Bell, 90.

BLADES, WILLIAM, 111.

BLAIR, ROBERT, *Grave*, published in America, 89.

BLAKE, WILLIAM, collections of, 23, 268; biographical studies of, 25; mentioned, 28.

BLANDFORD, MARQUIS OF. *See* Spencer, George.

BLANK LEAVES, 377.

BLUESTOCKING PARTIES, Mrs. Vesey's, 317.

BOCCACCIO, GIOVANNI, *Decameron*, in Roxburghe Sale, 105.

BODLEIAN LIBRARY, 130, 268.

BOETHIUS, *De Consolatione Philosophiæ*, 135.

BONNER, PAUL HYDE, 203, 290, 291.

BOOK-COLLECTING, the game of, 1, 2; the by-product of, 2, 6, 23, 247, 248; delights of, 9, 23, 33, 245–247; skill and money demanded by, 14, 38, 255; a hundred years ago, 104; the best of indoor sports, 245, 247–249.

BOOK MARKETS, 39.

Book of Common Prayer, the Psalms and Bible, so-called "Little Gidding binding," 146.

Book of Kells, 157.

Bookman's Journal, referred to, 197; article on forgeries in, 222, 223.

BOOKS, sets of, 20–22; the kind to collect, 38; originally called "rolls," 97; of parchment, of vellum, and of paper, 97; the colophon, 97–99; incunabula, 100; title-page, 106; designs for, 107; watermark, 109, 110; made in their entirety by one man, 109, 110; half title, 111; signature, 111, 112; collation of, 112; names for designating size of, 113–115; printing, 116, 117; binding, 128–174; prices of, 186, 187, 192, 195, 202, 205; restoration of, 221, 223; forgeries of, 222, 223; bowdlerized, 234–236; Graingerized, 238–244; as an investment, cost, 249; the "condition" of, 255, 346, 386; colored-plate, 369; in cloth, 375, 377; with end papers and blank leaves, 377; beautiful and ugly, 378; the reading of, as a pleasure, 390. *See also* Bindings, Format, Novel.

"BOOKS OF A BUSTED BIBLIOPHILE, THE," sale of, 160, 205.

BOOKSELLERS AND PUBLISHERS, in Philadelphia, 88–96.

BOOKSELLERS' CATALOGUES. *See* Catalogues.

BOSWELL, JAMES, material, 183, 184; sale of his portrait, 184; letters of, expurgated, 236; on Grainger's *History*, 239; *A Tour to the Hebrides*, 329; mentioned, 13, 179, 309, 312, 320; *Life of Johnson*, first edition of, 13, 186, 314; the preparation of, 183; Graingerizing of, 239, 240; hard to sell before the *Dictionary* appeared, 313; a great biography, 329; mentioned, 10.

BOSWELL, JAMES, JR., auction catalogue of his library, 183–186; an extra-illustrated Boswell inscribed to, 240.

BOWDEN, A. J., 189–191, 193.

BOWDLER, TOM, 234–236.

BOWDLERIZING, 234–236.

"BOY STOOD ON THE BURNING DECK, THE," 43.

BRADDON, MARY ELIZABETH, *Lady Audley's Secret*, 370, 388.

BRADFORD, WILLIAM, printer, 84.

BRADSTREET, ANNE DUDLEY, *The Tenth Muse lately sprung up in America* (English title), *Several Poems, Compiled with Great Variety of Wit and Learning by a Gentlewoman in New England* (Colonial title), 80.

BRANNON AND MONFORD, 94.

BRAWNE, FANNY, Keats's letters to, 236.

BRAY, silversmith, 212.

BRINLEY (GEORGE) SALE, 82, 192, 278.

BRITISH MUSEUM, 19, 130, 135, 138–140, 144, 150, 154, 158, 161, 221, 222, 268, 354; the world's best library, 117.

BRONTË, CHARLOTTE, *Jane Eyre*, 370.

BRONTË, SISTERS, 369.

BROWN, CHARLES BROCKDEN, 275.

BROWNE, HABLOT K. ("Phiz"), illustrator of Dickens, 364.

BROWNING, ROBERT, 31, 320.

BRYAN, WILLIAM JENNINGS, 37, 235.

BRYANT, WILLIAM C., *The Fountain*, 280; *Thanatopsis*, 280, 291; *The Embargo*, 280; poems (1821), 290, 291: mentioned, 275, 279.

BUCKLE, HENRY THOMAS, 320.

BULLEN, ANNE, 139.

BULWER-LYTTON, SIR EDWARD, 351.

BUNYAN, JOHN, his *Pilgrim's Progress*, earliest New England edition of, 81; first edition of, 81; second part, first edition of, published in America, 82; instantly popular, 256.

BURKE, EDMUND, 317.

BURLINGTON FINE ARTS CLUB, 115.

BURNEY, DR. CHARLES, his interest in Johnson's *Dictionary*, 321, 322; on Dr. Johnson, 309.

BURNEY, FANNY (Madame d' Arblay). Johnson's interest in, 320, 321; *Evelina*, 321, 346.

BURNS, JOHN, his interests, 25; anecdote of, 25, 26.

BURNS, ROBERT, *Poems Chiefly in the Scottish Dialect*, published in Philadelphia in 1788, 94; Kilmarnock copy of, 192; his "hand" readily imitated, 222; mentioned, 31.

BURTON, ROBERT, *Anatomy of Melancholy*, 182.

BUSS, MR., his plates in Part III of *Pickwick*, 363.

BUTLER, SAMUEL, *Hudibras*, 151, 152.

BUYING, caution necessary in, 207–212; rules to be observed in, 208.

BYRON, GEORGE GORDON, LORD, *English Bards and Scotch Reviewers*, first American edition of, 94; his works early reprinted in Philadelphia, 94; his "hand" readily imitated, 222; journals and letters of, destroyed, 237; published in boards, 351.

CAINE, HALL, *The Manxman*, 391.

CAMBRIDGE, MASS., early printing done in, 71.

CAMPBELL, BARTLEY, *The White Slave*, 337.

CAREY, CAREY LEA AND CAREY, CAREY AND HART, publishers, 95.

CARLYLE, THOMAS, on Johnson's *Dictionary*, 327.

CARROLL, LEWIS, *Alice in Wonderland* (1865), 201, 202, 255.

CARSON, HAMPTON L., lawyer and collector, 59, 60.

CARTER, THOMAS FRANCIS, *The Invention of Printing in China*, 97.

CASSEL, publisher, 285.

CATALOGUES, booksellers', 39, 389; auctioneers', 39.

CAVALIERS, of the South, 70.

Caveat emptor, 207, 208.

CAXTON, WILLIAM, *The Recuyell of the Historyes of Troye*, 103; *The Recuyell* containing written signature, 112; *The Game and Playe of Chesse*, 103; *The Dictes and Sayings of the Philosophers*, 103; his books not beautiful, 117.

CELLINI, BENVENUTO, *Autobiography*, the interest of, 270; manuscript of, 272; mentioned, 10.

CERVANTES, MIGUEL, *Don Quixote*, 286.

CHAPIN, MR., his collection in Williams College, 31.

CHAPMAN, R. W., of Oxford University Press, 118, 183.

CHAPMAN AND HALL, publishers, 362.

CHARLES I, KING, 147.

CHARLES II, KING, the art of binding under, 148; *Hudibras* his favorite poem, 151, 152; mentioned, 77, 178.

CHARLOTTE, Queen Consort of George III., Prayer Book with arms of, 161.

CHATTIN, JAMES, 88.

CHAUCER, GEOFFREY, Morris's edition of, 119.

CHESTERFIELD, EARL OF, and Johnson's *Dictionary*, 312, 313.

CHEW, BEVERLY, 146, 154, 167.

CHICAGO, growth of, 38.

CHISWICK PRESS, 117.

CHOATE, RUFUS, jest of, 85.

CHRISTIE'S, 328.

CHURCH OF ENGLAND, 87.

CHURCHILL, WILLIAM, bookbinder to Charles II, 150.

CICERO, his *Cato Major*, first classic of which translation was published in this country, 21, 82; first edition of, 263.

CLARENDON, LORD, his *Rebellion* Graingerized, 239.

CLARKE, inventor of tree calf, 167.

CLASSICS, English, 81; Latin, 82.

CLAXTON, REMSEN AND HAFFELFINGER, 96.

CLEMENS, SAMUEL LANGHORNE, *Huckleberry Finn*, a great book, 8, 293; *Huckleberry Finn*, source of story in, 270; should be collected, 274, 293; *Life on the Mississippi*, 293; *Tom Sawyer*, 293; *Personal Recollections of Joan of Arc*, 293.

CLEMENTS, WILLIAM L., his collection at University of Michigan, 31; essay of; quoted on book-collecting, 35.

CLEMENTS (WILLIAM L.) LIBRARY, University of Michigan, 35, 36.

CLOVIS, binder, 138.

CLUB BINDERY, 128.

COBDEN-SANDERSON, THOMAS J., bookbinder, 168, 169.

COCHRAN, MR., his collection at Yale, 31.

CODINGTON, DR., 136.

COHEN, ALBERT M., 353.

COLLATION OF BOOKS, 112.

COLLECTIONS, disposition of, 272.

COLLECTORS, advice to, 391, 392. *See Caveat emptor*.

COLLET, JOHN, 145.

COLLETS, THE, 145, 146.

COLLINS, WILKIE, *The Moonstone*, 370.

COLOPHON, 97-103; gives way to title-page, 106.

COLUMBIA UNIVERSITY PRESS, 260.

COMBE, WILLIAM, *Tours of Dr. Syntax*, 356.

Comic History of England, The, 367, 368.

Comic History of Rome, The, 367, 368.

Concise Oxford Dictionary, 330, 332, 343.

CONCORD, MASS., 279.

"CONDITION," 255, 346, 386.

CONGREVE, WILLIAM, *Incognita, or Love and Duty Reconciled, A Novel*, offers first use of word "novel" in our sense on title-page, 7, 8; artificial comedies of, 12.

CONRAD, JOSEPH, *Lord Jim*, 301; *The Nigger of the Narcissus*, 301; *Ave*, 301; the collecting of, 378; mentioned, 374.

COOPER, JAMES FENIMORE, published in boards, 351; mentioned, 274.

COOPER, WILLIAM, auctioneer, 176, 177.

CORELLI, MARIE, 386.

COTTON, JOHN, *Spiritual Milk for Boston Babes in either England, Drawn out of the Breasts of Both Testaments for their Souls' Nourishment*, 71, 72.

COVERDALE BIBLE, 221, 226.

CRABBE, GEORGE, 31.

CRACHERODE, REV. CLAYTON, patron of Roger Payne, 154.

CRAIK, MRS. *See* Mulock, Dinah Maria.

CRASHAW, RICHARD, 31.

CROCKER, TEMPLETON, 134, 140, 146.

CROKER, JOHN WILSON, 183.

CROSS, WILBUR L., on the English novel, 336; authority on Sterne, 348.

"CROWN OCTAVO," 114.

CRUIKSHANK, DR., performs autopsy on Dr. Johnson, 211.

CRUIKSHANK, GEORGE, illustrator of Dickens, 3, 358; *Uncle Tom's Cabin* illustrated by, 285; *Life in London* illustrated by, 356.

CURRIE, BARTON W., 205.

CURRIER AND IVES LITHOGRAPHS, 275, 278.

CURTIS COMPANY, publishers, 96.

DALY, AUGUSTINE, 287.

Dance of Death, The. Miss Susan Minns's collection of, 16, 18.

DARLING, LORD (Mr. Justice), bill to prevent the knock-out introduced by, 195, 196.

DAVENPORT, CYRIL, 139.

DAWES, CHARLES GATES, 316.

DAY, MRS. THOMAS, 49, 54.

DAY, THOMAS, sketch of, 45–50; *Sandford and Merton*, first edition of, 50, 52, 53, 60; the story of, 52, 53; mentioned, 9, 45, 54.

Day of Doom, The, 278.

DAYE, STEPHEN, his press in Cambridge, Mass., 71.

DAYTON AND WENTWORTH, Boston, 171.

De Amore Conjugali, in Elizabethan binding, 139.

DECLARATION OF INDEPENDENCE, "Signers" of, 200.

DE COVERLEY, bookbinder, 169.

DEERING, FRANK C., letter of, on extra-illustrating, 242–244.

DEFOE, DANIEL, *Robinson Crusoe*, compared with *Swiss Family Robinson*, 64, 65; copy of, with a page of Harris's work, 222, 354; full of points, 259, 260; first half of, 303; published in parts, 354, rare copies of, 222, 354; mentioned, 9, 60, 278, 333.

DE LA MARE, *Songs of Childhood*, 38.

DE RICCI, SEYMOUR, French bibliographer, 80.

DEROME, binder, 138.

DEVONSHIRE, DUKE OF, patron of Roger Payne, 154.

DEXTER, LORD TIMOTHY, 387.

Dialectica of Aristotle, 107.

DIBDIN, THOMAS FRAGNALL, *Bibliographical Decameron*, 104, 105; mentioned, 154, 239.

DICKENS, CHARLES, copy of Bryant's *The Fountain* inscribed to, 280; his language, 304; his copy of Johnson's *Dictionary*, 316; his rank as a novelist, 389; mentioned, 10, 21; *A Christmas Carol*, first edition of, 353; end papers of, 377; mentioned, 3; *David Copperfield*, reference to, 381; *Great Expectations*, the joy of reading, 9, 57, 58; *The Mystery of Edwin Drood*, 348; *Nicholas Nickleby*, interpolated narratives a blemish in, 342; *Pickwick Papers*, points of, 260, 364, 365; prices of, 273; quoted, 287; published in parts, 356; omitted from list of one hundred good novels, 386; difference between a right and wrong, 358; the Elkins, 359, 360; advertisements in, 361, 362; the first part of, 362; genesis of, 362; the accepted portrait of Mr. Pickwick in, 362; plates of, 362–364; the furore created by, 364, 365; "in parts," 365, 367; mentioned, 291, 346, 359; *Sketches by Boz*, issued in parts, 357, 358; points of, 358, 359.

DISRAELI, BENJAMIN, *Henrietta Temple*, 56, 57.

DOBSON, AUSTIN, article on, 288; his lines on Johnson, 329.

DODGSON, CHARLES LUTWIDGE. *See* Carroll, Lewis.

DODSLEY, ROBERT, publisher of Johnson's *Dictionary*, 309, 321; suggests the *Dictionary*, 309.

DONNELLEY (R. R.) AND SONS COMPANY, of Chicago, 53.

DOS-À-DOS BINDING, 115.

DOSTOEVSKY, F. M., 304; *Crime and Punishment*, 381.

"DOUBLE ELEPHANT," 113.

DOUBLEDAY, PAGE AND COMPANY, 129.
DOVES BINDERY, 169.
DOVES PRESS, 169.
DOYLE, CONAN, 388.
DRAKE, JAMES F., 231, 291, 297.
DRAPER, JOHN, publisher, 81.
DREER, FERDINAND J., collector of autographs, 41.
DRING, E. H., of Quaritch, 226.
DUFF, GORDON, *The Great Mearne Myth*, 150.
DUNLAP, W., 88.
DUNTON, JOHN, auctioneer, 177, 178.
DUODECIMO, 114, 115.
DUPLICATES, to be kept, 205.
DURANT, SARAH VIRGINIA, 282.
DÜRER, ALBRECHT, borders for title-pages designed by, 106.
DUTCH AND GERMAN SILVER BINDINGS, 167.
DYER, GEORGE, 266.

EAMES, WILBERFORCE, of the New York Public Library, 138.
ECKEL, JOHN C., on Hardy's *Desperate Remedies*, 202, 203; on copy of *Tess of the D'Urbervilles*, 231, 232; Dickens's bibliographer, 260; *Prime Pickwicks in Parts*, 260; authority on *Pickwick*, 362.
EDGEWORTH, MARIA, 46, 47, 369; her *The Parent's Assistant*, 47.
EDGEWORTH, RICHARD LOVELL, father of Maria Edgeworth, 46, 47.
Education of Henry Adams, The, 288, 379.
EDWARD VI, PRAYER BOOK, title-page of, 107; books bound for, by Berthelet, 139.
EDWARD VII, KING, 148.
EDWARDS, FRANCIS, bookseller, 60, 61, 216-221.
EDWARDS, JAMES, son of William, 156; his patent for vellum bindings, 156; his great possession (Bedford Missal), 156-158; secures patent for transparent vellum, 159; death of, 161; tablet to memory of, 161.
EDWARDS, JOHN, son of William, 156.
EDWARDS, THOMAS, son of William, famous for fore-edge paintings, 158.
EDWARDS, WILLIAM, 156, 158.
EDWARDS AND SONS, 156.
EDWARDS OF HALIFAX, 156-161.
EGAN, PIERCE, *Life in London*, earliest important example of monthly parts, 354, 356.
"ELEPHANT FOLIO," 113.
ELIBANK, LORD, 325.

ELIOT, GEORGE. *See* Evans, Mary Ann.
ELIOT, JOHN, his Indian Bible, 76, 77, 192; other Bibles of, in Indian language, 77; his *Call to the Unconverted* by Richard Baxter, 77, 78.
ELIZABETH, QUEEN, books bound for, by Berthelet, 139; offers knighthood to Thomas Wotton, 140; embroidery of, 144.
ELIZABETHAN BINDINGS, 139, 142.
ELKINS, WILLIAM M., his *Pickwick*, 359; his catalogue, entitled *A Sentimental Library*, 360.
EMERSON, R. W., 95, 274, 279, 280.
END PAPERS, 377.
ENGLAND, slow to make use of art of printing, 99, 103.
ENGLISH, the, ignorant of American achievements, 288; their dislike of Americans, 289; always look out for Number One, 302.
ENGLISH LANGUAGE, the glory of, 41; the first book printed in, 103; the first book in, with an illustration, 103; the first book in, with a colophon, 103; the first book in, with a title-page, 106.
ENGLISH-SPEAKING UNION, 289.
EPICTETUS, his *Morals* published by Keimer, 82.
"ETRUSCAN" CALF, 158.
EVANS, his bibliography of early American imprints, 77.
EVANS, MARY ANN, *Adam Bede*, 342, 370; mentioned, 369.
EVE, NICHOLAS, binder, 138.
EXCHANGE PROFESSORSHIPS, 289.
"EX-LIBRARY" COPIES, 18.
EXTRA-ILLUSTRATED BOOKS, 238-244.

FAKES, 213-221.
FERRAR, NICHOLAS, founder of the Little Gidding nunnery, 145, 146.
FIELD, EUGENE, 286.
FIELD, R., 94.
FIELDING, HENRY, his library, 178; discovers Mr. B's (in *Pamela*) name, 338; *Shamela*, 338; *Joseph Andrews*, 338; published in small volumes, 346; mentioned, 321; *Tom Jones*, prices of, 178, 188; agreement for copyright of, 178; greatest of English novels, 339; publication of, 339-341; Gibbon on, 341; unbound copies of, 341; a blemish in, 342; Squire Western, 368; mentioned, 350.
FIRST EDITIONS, "read to pieces," 257;

distinguishing eccentricities of, 257; first issues of, 375; to be sought, 392.

"FIVE INTOLERABLE ACTS," 76.

FOLGER, H. C., his collection, 31.

"FOLIO," 113.

FOOTE SALE, 281.

FORE-EDGE PAINTINGS, 158, 159.

FORGERIES, 222, 223.

FORMAT of the English novel, 333-381; the word, 343. See Novel.

FOXE, JOHN, Martyrs, 314.

FRANKLIN, BENJAMIN, his career as a printer, 89, 90; letters of, 237; and Johnson, 310; mentioned, 246; Autobiography, original manuscript of, 21, 263; the puzzle of, 62, 293; Cato Major, the first classic translated and published in America, 21, 82; in original binding, 21; published by Franklin, 82; first edition of, 263.

FREDERIC, H., The Damnation of Theron Ware, 374.

FREEMAN, JOHN, his book about George Moore, 308.

FREEMAN'S OATH, first set up and printed by Stephen Daye in Cambridge, Mass., 71.

FRENCH, the, 63, 64.

FRENCH LANGUAGE, the language of the court and the law courts in England, 103.

FRIENDS, the by-product of book-collecting, 2, 6, 23, 247, 248.

FRONTISPIECE, engraved, 106.

FROSCHOVER, first complete English Bible printed by, 103.

FURNESS, DR. HORACE H., 320.

GALSWORTHY, JOHN, his opinion of Huckleberry Finn, 8, 293; a cross between Thackeray and Trollope, 301; Forsyte Saga, 301, 374.

"GAME," the word in the English and the American sense, 9.

Gammer Gurtons Nedle, 268.

GANNON, MR., 203.

GARRICK, DAVID, letter of Goldsmith to, relative to first production of She Stoops to Conquer, 192; lines of, on Johnson's Dictionary, 323.

GASKELL, ELIZABETH C., Cranford, 346, 374; mentioned, 369.

GEE, E. R., specialist on Sporting Books, 4.

GEORGE I, KING, 148.

GEORGE II, KING, 148; bibliophile, 142.

GEORGE III, KING, a collector of books, 148; bids on Bedford Missal, 157.

GEORGE IV, KING, 148.

GEORGE V, KING, 148.

GERMAN SILVER BINDINGS, 167.

GIBBON, EDWARD, bowdlerized, 234, 235; at times squeamish, 236; quoted on Tom Jones, 340, 341; mentioned, 286.

GILBERT, WILLIAM S., quoted, 293.

GILBERT AND SULLIVAN, Patience, 48; mentioned, 23.

GODWIN, MARY JANE, publisher of Swiss Family Robinson, 61.

GODWIN, (M. J.) AND COMPANY, publishing firm, 61.

GODWIN, WILLIAM, 62.

GOLDSMITH, OLIVER, Vicar of Wakefield, 13, 89, 278, 346; a phrase of, 53; Traveller, 88; Deserted Village, "second" edition, 188, 189; letter of, to Garrick, relative to first production of She Stoops to Conquer, 192, 201; Goody Twoshoes, 86, 87, 257; mentioned, 12.

GOODSPEED, of Boston, 241.

Goody Twoshoes. See History of Goody Twoshoes.

GOSDEN, THOMAS, sportsman and antiquarian, 161, 162; Anecdotes on the Origin and Antiquity of Horse-Racing, 162; drawings of, 162; bindings of, 162, 163; engraving of "The Jovial Fox Hunters" published by, 163; death of, 164.

GOSSE, EDMUND, 303.

GOUDY, printer, 124.

GRAHAM, BESSIE, 390.

GRAINGER, DR. JAMES, 238-242; Biographical History of England, 238, 239; The Sugar-Cane, 241.

GRAINGERIZING, 238-244.

GRAMONT, COUNT, Memoirs of, 239.

GRANT, COLONEL, Johnsonian scholar and collector, 181.

GRASBERGER, GEORGE, 256.

GRAY, THOMAS, An Elegy Written in a Country Churchyard, 89, 278; Poems, with fore-edge painting, 159.

GREAT BIBLE OF HENRY VIII. See Henry VIII.

GREEK AND LATIN, universal languages, 103.

GREEN, SAMUEL, his press in Boston, 72, 76.

GREENE, BELLE DA COSTA, librarian of Morgan Library, 33, 34, 236, 237.

GREY, LORD, of Falloden, remark of, on books and reading, 390.

GRISWOLD, RUFUS WILMOT, literary executor of Poe, 282; *Prose Writers of America*, 282, 283.

GROLIER, JEAN, his motto, 140.

GROLIER CLUB, 25, 124, 128, 167; bindings of, 134.

GUNTHER, C. F., 190.

GUPPY, DR. HENRY, Librarian of the Rylands Library, 153.

GUTENBERG, JOHANNES, 97.

GUTENBERG BIBLE, the boy who wanted to see, 34; record price for, 97; Melk copy, 97, 198–200; the paper of, 109.

GWINNETT, BUTTON, his signature, 200, 201, 202.

GWYN, NELL, 178.

HAIN, LUDWIG, his book on incunabula, 100.

HALF TITLES, 111.

HALL, DAVID, partner of Benjamin Franklin in the printing trade, 90.

HARDING, S., publisher, 154.

HARDY, THOMAS, *Desperate Remedies*, 18, 202, 377; *The Dynasts*, 201, 203, 205, 255; *Tess of the D'Urbervilles*, 231, 232; rank of, as a novelist, 300, 301; *Jude the Obscure*, 301; *The Woodlanders*, 375, 376; the collecting of, 378; mentioned, 15, 273.

HARKNESS, MRS., presents Gutenberg Bible to Yale University, 97, 199.

HARPER, LATHROP, 37.

HARPER AND BROTHERS, 379.

HARRIS, JOEL CHANDLER, 388.

HARRIS, JOHN, repairer of old books, 221, 222.

HARRISON, CHARLES, 81.

HARRISON, GABRIEL, his painting of Poe, 282.

HARROW GROVE, manor house, 157.

HARTE, BRET, 275.

HARVARD UNIVERSITY, Amy Lowell's collection of Keats in, 27, 28; collection of Harry E. Widener given to, 31.

HARZOF, MR., 290.

HAWKINS, SIR JOHN, disposer of Johnson's belongings, 211, 212.

HAWTHORNE, NATHANIEL, *Fanshawe*, 279, 280; *Twice-told Tales*, 280; *The Scarlet Letter*, 280; is becoming collected, 291; *Grandfather's Chair*, 291; *Famous Old People*, 291; *Liberty Tree*, 291; mentioned, 95, 274.

HAYDAY, bookbinder, 156.

HEARN, LAFCADIO, manuscripts of, destroyed, 236.

Heart of New England Rent, The, 72.

HEBER, collector, 206, 240.

HENLEY, MR., 306.

HENRY, O., 388.

HENRY VIII, KING, Great Bible of, 106, 221; Berthelet his printer and binder, 138; bindings of, 134–138.

HENRY, PRINCE OF WALES (son of James I), his bindings, 142.

HERBERT, GEORGE, 28.

HERFORD, OLIVER, anecdote of, 16.

HERING, bookbinder, 164.

HERRICK, ROBERT, 28, 75.

HILL, BIRKBECK, 183, 184.

HILL, WALTER M., bookseller, 18, 53, 62, 316.

HIRST, HENRY B., accuses Poe of plagiarism, 282.

HISTORICAL SOCIETY OF PENNSYLVANIA, 42, 84.

History of Goody Twoshoes, The, 86, 87, 257.

HOBBIES, 32, 33, 41, 42, 245.

HODGSON AND SON, of Chancery Lane, 197.

HOE, ROBERT, sale of his collection, 128, 190, 192, 193; and the Club Bindery, 128.

HOLBEIN, HANS, borders for title-pages designed by, 106.

HOLFORD, SIR GEORGE, 226.

HOLMES, OLIVER W., *Memoir of Emerson*, 281; mentioned, 95, 274, 279.

HOMER, Pope's translation of, 10; *Odyssey*, Palmer's translation of, 27.

HORACE, Baskerville's edition of, 117.

HOUGHTON MIFFLIN COMPANY, 22.

HOUSMAN, ALFRED EDWARD, *Shropshire Lad*, 38, 254, 290; a letter of, 254.

HOWARD, SIR ESME, British Ambassador, 288.

HOWELLS, WILLIAM D., writes introduction to *Swiss Family Robinson*, 64.

HUGO, VICTOR, *The Count of Monte Cristo*, 59.

HUNEKER, JIM, 295.

HUNTER, DARD, his *Old Papermaking*, 109; makes books in their entirety, 109, 110.

HUNTINGTON, HENRY E., collector, 21, 31, 34, 77, 80, 193, 263.

HURST SALE, 282.

HUSBAND, *Miscellany*, 268.

HUTCHINS, HENRY CLINTON, *Robinson Crusoe and Its Printing*, 259, 260, 378.

HUTH, ALFRED, his collection, 115.

INCORPORATED SOCIETY OF AUCTIONEERS, 196.

INCUNABULA, 100.

INDULGENCE, ENGLISH CATHOLIC, 137.

"INFANT INDUSTRIES," 130.

IRVING, HENRY, 23.

IRVING, WASHINGTON, 275.

ISHAM, COLONEL RALPH, 181, 268.

JAMES, HENRY, 342, 343.

JAMES I, KING, Counterblaste to Tobacco, 140; Basilikon Doron, 140; books bound for, 140–142; mentioned, 147.

JASTROW, MORRIS, 266.

Jessica's First Prayer, 44, 45.

JEWETT (JOHN P.) COMPANY, of Boston, publishers, 284.

JOHNSON, MARMADUKE, Colonial printer, 76, 78, 80.

JOHNSON, SAMUEL, on Congreve's Incognita, or Love and Duty Reconciled, A Novel, 8; remark of, on dictionaries, 39; remark of, on Shakespeare, 42; a saying of, 43; Rasselas, 88, 89, 256, 314, 345, 346, 350; first occurrence of "Rasselas" on title-page, 88; his ire at American treatment of Stamp Act, 89; on Paradise Lost, 91; Variety of Human Wishes, 111; Life of Savage, 111; on sizes in books, 116, 345; and Thomas Osborne, 152; Gosden's drawing of the stone covering his grave, 162; his "frisk" with Bennet Langton and Beauclerk, 178, 179; sale catalogue of his library, 181–183; items of, seeping into the market, 183, 184; portrait of, by Reynolds, 183, 184; silver teapot of, 208–213; disposal of his possessions, 211, 212; on James Grainger, 238; on Grainger's History, 239; on Grainger's The Sugar-Cane, 241; on the happiest life, 242; on the art of life, 246; Lobo's Voyage to Abyssinia, 268; was not a complainer, 309; arrested for debt, 310; and Millar, 311; his letter to Earl of Chesterfield, 312, 313; depression of, 313, 321, 322; remark of, on the effect of a good dinner, 314; remark of, on his laziness, 320; his interest in Fanny Burney, 320, 321; Rambler, 321; writes to Dr. Burney regarding Dictionary, 321, 322; his habit of procrastination, 321, 322; his library, 328; Austin Dobson's lines on, 329; Latin ode of, 329, 330; on Richardson, 335; on Millar, 340; mentioned, 78, 308; Dictionary, the "Plan" of, 184, 311;

prices of, 189; the work of "an obscure young man," 309; suggested by Dodsley, 309; Johnson's remuneration for, 309; Johnson's amanuenses in work of, 309, 311; seven years spent on, 310; work on, done in 17 Gough Square, 310; the printer of, 310; and the Earl of Chesterfield, 311-313; publication of, 313; demand for, 313; first editions of, 313, 314, 316, 317; Mrs. Thrale-Piozzi's copy of, 314; a copy of, in boards, 314; Dickens's copy of, 316; reprint from author's last folio edition of (E. Coppee Mitchell's reprint), 316; Mrs. Vesey's copy of, 317-320; circumstances under which it was composed, 320; to be read with pleasure and profit, 320; quotations in, 320; Dr. Burney's interest in, 321; a best seller, 322; retorts of Johnson concerning, 322, 323; lines of Garrick on, 323; definitions in, 323-327; the "Grammar of the English Tongue," 327; judgments of, 327; based on Bailey's dictionary, 328; Johnson's copy of the last edition of, published during his lifetime, 328; copy of, sold after Johnson's death, 328.

JOHNSONIANS, 314.

JOSEPH OF CHARING CROSS ROAD, 196.

"JOVIAL FOX HUNTERS, THE," sporting picture, 163.

KALTHOEBER, bookbinder, 156, 164.

KAYE-SMITH, SHEILA, Tramping Methodist, 38; Joanna Godden, 374.

KEATS, JOHN, Amy Lowell's Collection of, 27; Endymion, 159; Poems, 188, 195; his letters to Fanny Brawne, 236; published in boards, 351.

KEIMER, S., Benjamin Franklin's employer, 82, 90; Epictetus, His Morals, published by, in 1729, 82.

KELMSCOTT PRESS, 118, 119.

KENNERLEY, MITCHELL, 34, 182, 199, 328.

KERN, JEROME, 341.

KEYNES, GEOFFREY, his biographical studies of Blake, 25; mentioned, 112.

KIPLING, RUDYARD, on making a collection of, 14–16, 378; Schoolboy Lyrics, present value of, 14; Echoes, 14; Captains Courageous, the manuscript of, 14, 15; Captains Courageous, three first editions of, 14, 15; quotation from, 27; McCutcheon collection of, 202; prices of, 205; The Smith Administra-

tion, 205; as a writer, 301; hates Americans, 301; on Jane Austen, 341; mentioned, 273.

"KNOCK-OUT, THE," at London auctions, 194–196.

KOBURGER, his *Nuremberg Chronicle*, 119.

LAMB, CHARLES, and Sarah Battle, 14; the woman that he hated, 61; *Mr. H.*, 94, 95; *Elia*, 95, 159, 266; *Dream Children*, 241.

LANGTON, BENNET, his "frisk" with Johnson and Beauclerk, 178, 179.

LATIN AND GREEK, universal languages, 103.

LAURENTIAN LIBRARY, Florence, 272.

LAWLER, JOHN, his book on auctions, 176.

LEARY, his secondhand bookshop in Philadelphia, 9, 264.

LEE, SIDNEY, his census, 209.

LEECH, JOHN, 367.

LE GASCON, binder, 138.

LEMPERLY, PAUL, book-collector, 253, 254.

LENDING LIBRARIES, 369.

LEVANT MOROCCO, bindings in, 166, 167.

LEWIS, CHARLES, bookbinder, 164.

LIPPINCOTT (J. B.) AND COMPANY, publishers and booksellers, 96.

LITTLE BRITAIN, London, 176.

LITTLE GIDDING NUNS, 144–146.

"LITTLE SAMUEL WAKE," 44.

LIVING, the art of, 246, 247.

LLOYD, MRS. MARY, *Meditations on Divine Subjects*, 93.

LOBO, FATHER, his *Abyssinia* translated by Dr. Johnson, 268.

LONDON, as a book market, 39.

London Chronicle, 348.

LONGFELLOW, HENRY W., *Evangeline*, 256; as a poet, 274; mentioned, 279, 280.

LOVELACE, RICHARD, his *Lucasta*, 28.

LOWELL, AMY, an evening at her house, 26–29; her collection of Keats, 27; her love of Rollo, 60.

LOWELL, JAMES RUSSELL, *Commemoration Ode*, 279, 280; *A Year's Life*, 280; mentioned, 95, 274.

LUMLEY, LORD, his library, 142.

Lusitania, 241.

LYSONS, SAMUEL, antiquarian, 181.

LYTTON, EDWARD BULWER, EARL OF, *Lucile*, 57.

MACAULAY, THOMAS B., on John Baskerville's art, 117; on Johnson's etymologies, 327; mentioned, 297.

McCUTCHEON, GEORGE BARR, his collections, 202–205.

McFEE, WILLIAM, *Casuals of the Sea*, 374.

MACHLINIA, WILLIAM DE, printer, 106.

McINTOSH, CAPTAIN, 200.

MACMILLAN, publisher, 379.

MADIGAN, bookseller, 201.

MAGAZINE ARTICLES, difficulty of following an author through, 15.

MAGGS BROTHERS, of London, booksellers, 53, 136, 232.

MAIER, FRANK, his copy of Mitchell's *Reveries of a Bachelor*, 291.

MANNING, COLONEL, 201.

MANSFIELD, LORD, 325.

MAP, of Stevenson's Treasure Island, 65–68; of Battle of Bunker Hill, a fake, 218–221.

MARY, QUEEN, books bound for, by Berthelet, 139.

MARY, QUEEN OF SCOTS, embroidery of, 144.

MASEFIELD, JOHN, *Salt Water Ballads*, 38.

MATHER, COTTON, *The Nature, Number and Operations of the Devils*, 70.

MATTHEWS BIBLE, 107.

MAXWELL, J., printer, 94.

MEARNE, SAMUEL, binder, 148; our knowledge of, 148, 150; his bindings, 150, 151; a *Hudibras* of, 151, 152; his influence, 164.

MEDWIN, THOMAS, *Journal of Conversations*, 95.

MELVILLE, HERMAN, *Moby Dick*, 275, 286, 374, 380; English edition of, with title *The Whale*, 379, 380; first edition of, 388.

Memoirs of Count Gramont, The, Graingerizing of, 239.

MENZIE, WILLIAM, publisher, 89.

MEREDITH, GEORGE, his verse, 295; Benson's criticism of, 343; *The Ordeal of Richard Feverel*, 370.

MEREDITH, OWEN. *See* Lytton, Edward Bulwer.

MEXICO, CITY OF, first printing press in the New World set up in, 71, 107.

MICHIGAN, UNIVERSITY OF, William L. Clements Library at, 35.

MILFORD, HUMPHREY, of Oxford University Press, 118.

MILLAR, ANDREW, publisher, Fielding's

agreement with, for copyright of *Tom Jones*, 178; negotiates with Johnson for *Dictionary*, 309, 311; accepts *Tom Jones*, 339, 340.

MILLINGTON, auctioneer, 177.

MILNE, A. A., *When We Were Very Young*, first English edition of, 300.

MILNES, MISS, becomes wife of Thomas Day, 49. *See* Day, Mrs. Thomas.

MILTON, JOHN, Baskerville's edition of, 117; mentioned, 28; Epitaph on Shakespeare, forms of, 257; *Comus*, prices of, 39, 195; reading of title-page of first edition of, 39; mentioned, 256; *Paradise Lost*, published by Bell, 91; title-pages of, 257; mentioned, 278.

MINNS, SUSAN, her collection of "*The Dance of Death*," 16, 18.

"MINT STATE," 256.

MITCHELL, DONALD G., *Reveries of a Bachelor* (Frank Maier copy), 291.

MITCHELL, E. COPPEE, his copy of Dr. Johnson's *Dictionary*, 316.

MONTAIGNE, MICHEL E. DE, 41.

MONTGOMERY, DR., of the Historical Society of Pennsylvania, 84.

MONTOLIEU, BARONESS DE, and *Swiss Family Robinson*, 63.

MOORE, GEORGE, 294, 295; *Flowers of Passion*, 295; *Pagan Poems*, presentation copy of, to Oscar Wilde, 295; *Evelyn Innes*, 295, 296; *A Mummer's Wife*, 296, 371; *Esther Waters*, 296; *A Modern Lover*, 296, 369, 370; disciple of Zola, 297; supposed author of letter to Solicitor of the Treasury, 299; *Memoirs of My Dead Life*, English and American editions of, 299, 300; *The Brook Kerith*, 299, 300; *Avowals*, 299; 301, 303; *A Storyteller's Holiday*, 299; his rank, 300, 301; his ugly format, 301-303; his opinion of English fiction, 303; his prose, 304; his essays, 304, 305; *Modern Painting*, containing "Royalty in Art," 306; *Impressions and Opinions* (with errors on title-page and spine), 306; picture of, 306; his age, 308; his fight with Mudie, 371, 373; *Literature at Nurse on Circulating Morals*, 371.

"MOORE LITERARY CIRCLE, THE," 306.

MOORE SALE, 281.

MORE, HANNAH, 369.

MORE, SIR THOMAS, a collection of, 25; his *Utopia*, printed in Philadelphia in 1753, 88, 94.

MORGAN, JOHN PIERPONT, 31, 33, 237.

MORGAN LIBRARY, 15, 33, 34, 77, 131, 236.

MORLEY, KIT, *Parnassus on Wheels*, 38, 228.

MORRIS, MRS. WILLIAM, 168.

MORRIS, WILLIAM, founder of the Kelmscott Press, 118, 125, 168; *Aims in Founding the Kelmscott Press*, quoted, 118; his books, 118, 119.

MORRISON SALE, 192.

MOSHER, THOMAS BIRD, his books, 119-125.

MOTLEY, JOHN L., 10, 21, 270.

MUDIE, WILLIAM, of the "lending library," 296; dictatorial in matter of novel, 369; George Moore's fight with, 371, 373.

MUDIE'S LENDING LIBRARY, 296, 369, 371.

MULOCK, DINAH MARIA, *John Halifax, Gentleman*, 381.

MURRAY, JOHN, publisher, 186, 237, 240.

NAPOLEON, 9, 59.

NASH, printer, 124.

NEW ENGLAND, EARLY, religious and controversial literature of, 70-78.

NEW ENGLAND CONSCIENCE, 84.

NEW ENGLAND MOTHERS AND FATHERS, 85.

New England Primer, The, 81.

New English Dictionary, 330-332.

NEW YORK CITY, as a book market, 39.

NEWTON, A. EDWARD, how he became a book-collector, 9-13; his childhood, 43-45; on the Catalogue of Dr. Johnson's Library, 181-183; at Hoe Sale, 193; becomes owner of first folio of Shakespeare and Dr. Johnson's silver teapot, 208-213; *The Amenities of Book-Collecting*, a slip in, 262; a dinner given by, 316.

NEWTON, MRS. A. EDWARD, buys copy of Johnson's *Dictionary*, 316, 317, 319.

NICOLL, MR., Librarian of George III, 157.

NORMAN, J., 92.

NORTH, E. D., 119.

"NOVEL," the word, earliest instance of, in the English sense on title-page, 7, 8.

NOVEL, THE, the beginning of, 333; the format of, 333-381; in calf, 334-346,

350, 351; in boards, 334, 348, 351, 356; in parts, 334, 352–368; in three volumes ("the three-decker"), 334, 368–373 (cf. 18); of to-day (one volume), 334, 371–375; shortened, 373, 374; in boards again, since the War, 380; the collecting of, 380–382; the Russian, 382; and romance, 382.

NOVELS, list of one hundred good, 383.

"OAK KNOLL," Johnson's teapot at, 213. Library at, a holograph prayer in, 186; first edition of Boswell's *Johnson* in, 186; Goldsmith letter in, 192; Shakespeare folios in, 208; a conversation at, 294–308.

Oath of a Free Man, the first job of printing done in what is now the United States, 71.

"OCTAVO," 114, 115.

OGLETHORPE, GENERAL, 181.

Original London Post or Heathcot's Intelligence, 354.

Orphan, The, playbill of, 93.

OSBORNE, THOMAS, bookseller, 152.

OUIDA, 386, 391.

OXFORD DICTIONARY. *See* New English Dictionary, Concise Oxford Dictionary.

OXFORD UNIVERSITY PRESS, 117, 118.

PADELOUP, binder, 138.

PAIN, PHILIP, his *Daily Meditations*, the first volume of poems published in this country (1668), 78, 80.

PAINE, THOMAS, an employe of Bell, 90; *Common Sense*, 90; *The Age of Reason*, 152.

PALMER, ALICE FREEMAN, 29.

PALMER, GEORGE H., an evening with, at Amy Lowell's, 26–29; his translation of the *Odyssey*, 27; a past master in the art of book-collecting, 29; gives his first editions of English poetry to Wellesley College, 29; his *Notes on a Collection of English Poetry*, 29; his *Notes* quoted, 30; his ideas as to best arrangement of books, 31.

PAPERMAKING, 97, 109, 110.

PARKMAN, FRANCIS, 21.

PARRISH, MORRIS L., 172, 173, 376.

Passing Godle Lityll Boke Necessarye and Behovefull agenst the Pestilens, A, the earliest book in English with a title-page, 106.

"PAYNE, HONEST TOM," 152.

PAYNE, ROGER, bookbinder, 152–154, 164.

PEABODY, MISS SOPHIA A., copy of *Twice-Told Tales* inscribed to, 280.

PEACOCK, THOMAS LOVE, 290, 351.

PEARSON, EDMUND LESTER, 365.

PENNINGTON, JOHN, his bookshop, 96.

PENNSYLVANIA, religion in, 87.

PEPYS, SAMUEL, 210; *Diary*, expurgated, 235, 236.

PFORZHEIMER, CARL, 268.

PHELPS, WILLIAM LYON, on Trollope, 22.

PHILADELPHIA, as a publishing and book-selling centre, 88–96; Free Library of, 278.

PHILES, GEORGE P., authority upon Americana, 89.

PICKERING AND CHATTO, 151.

PICKWICK, MR., Seymour's original drawing of, 362.

PIERCE SALE, 281.

PILGRIM DINNERS, 289.

PLANTIN-MORETUS PRESS, at Antwerp, 107.

PLAYBILL, the first American, known to exist, 93.

PLINY THE YOUNGER, a copy of, 137.

POE, EDGAR ALLAN, has assured place in the world, 274; on collecting, 279; *Tamerlane*, 279, 280; *Al Aaraaf, Tamerlane, and Minor Poems*, copy of, used in preparing 1831 edition of *Poems* and given to Poe's cousin Elizabeth, 281; *Eureka*, Poe's own copy of, 281; *Tales of the Grotesque and Arabesque*, with five lines of writing in Poe's hand, 281; *Tales*, copy of, revised in Poe's autograph for new edition, 281; prices of, 282; esteemed abroad, 282; *Tales* unequalled in subtle horror, 282; *Poems*, finish and rhythm of, 282; has elements of "collected" author, 282; last lines of an attack of, on Henry B. Hirst, 282; painting of, by Gabriel Harrison, 282; his literary executor, 282; mentioned, 388; *The Raven and Other Poems*, dedication copy of, to Elizabeth Barrett, 280; presentation copy of, to Sarah Helen Whitman, 281; copy of, with autographed copy of last verse laid in, 281; presentation copy of, to Sarah Virginia Durant, 282.

POETRY, first volumes of, published in this country, 78–81.

POLLARD, ALFRED W., former Keeper of the Printed Books in the British Museum, on the colophon, 99.

POLLOCK, MOSES, bookseller, 96.

Pompadour, 345.

POPE, ALEXANDER, his *Essay on Man*, Colonial edition of, 88.

PORTER AND COATES, booksellers, 96, 192.

PORTRAITS, ENGRAVED, 238, 239.

PRAYER BOOK, EDWARD VI, title-page of, 107; with arms of Charlotte, Queen Consort of George III, 161.

PRESCOTT, WILLIAM H., 10, 270.

PRESENTATION COPIES, 279, 280.

PRICES OF BOOKS, 30, 39–41, 186, 187, 192, 195, 202, 205, 273, 280–282; no indication of scarcity, 290.

PRICHARD AND HALL, printers, Philadelphia, 92.

PRINCE CONSORT, 148.

PRINCE OF WALES (son of George V), 148.

PRINTERS' MARKS, 106.

PRINTING, the art of, 97, 99, 103, 116, 117.

PRINTING PRESS, the first in the New World set up in City of Mexico, 71, 107.

PRINTS, 215.

PROUST, MARCEL, 304.

PUBLISHERS AND BOOKSELLERS, in Philadelphia, 88–96.

Punch, 289.

PURITANS, of the North, 70; social life of, 84.

QUAKERS, 70.

QUARITCH, booksellers, 195, 226.

"QUARTO," 114.

READE, CHARLES, *The Cloister and the Hearth*, 10, 268–270.

REBINDING, to be avoided, 19, 171–173.

RELICS, 213.

"REMAINDER" BINDINGS, 377.

REPPLIER, AGNES, her essays, 289; *A Happy Half-Century*, 290.

RESTORATIONS, 221, 223.

REYNOLDS, SIR JOSHUA, his portrait of Johnson, 183, 184; mentioned, 241.

RHEAL, LOUIS, illustrator of *Swiss Family Robinson*, 64.

RHODES SCHOLARSHIPS, 289.

RICHARDSON, SAMUEL, his novels published in small volumes, 346; mentioned, 321; *Pamela*, a rare book, 226, 345, 388; starts the novel, 333; story of, 334–338; burlesques of, 338, 339; mentioned, 310, 350.

RIVERSIDE PRESS, 29.

RIVIERE AND SON, bookbinders, 129, 156, 166.

ROBERTS, WILLIAM, of The London *Times*, 209.

ROBERTSON, GRAHAM, his collections of Blake, 23–25.

ROBERTSON, WILLIAM, *Charles V*, published by Bell, 90.

RODD, MR., 240.

ROGERS, BRUCE, 124, 287.

ROGERS, JOHN, 107.

ROLLO BOOKS, 9, 50, 54–56, 58–60.

"ROLLO PARTY," 59.

"ROLLS," original name of books, 97.

ROMANCE, and novel, 382.

ROOSEVELT, THEODORE, 268.

ROSEBERY, LORD, on *Emma*, 341.

ROSENBACH ("Rosy"), bookseller, 37, 38, 77, 78, 202; his collection of early American children's books, 60, 278; how he obtained Philip Pain's *Daily Meditations*, 78, 79; buys Gutenberg Bible for Mrs. Harkness, 97, 199; at Adam Sale, 198–200; his signature of Button Gwinnett, 201; buys *Alice*, 202; buys *Dynasts* for Mr. Currie, 205; buys Smith Library, 241; gives picture of Moore to Newton, 306; mentioned, 80, 96, 104, 156, 193, 270.

ROSS, GORDON, a letter from, 3, 4; two sketches by, 3, 6; his portrait of Surtees, 4, 5.

ROWFANT CLUB, 253.

ROWLANDSON, illustrator of *Tours of Dr. Syntax*, 356.

ROYAL LIBRARY, at Windsor, 112.

"ROYAL OCTAVO," 114.

ROYAL SOCIETY, in London, 77.

ROXBURGHE, JOHN, DUKE OF, 105.

"ROXBURGHE FIGHT" (Roxburghe Sale), 105.

Rubaiyat of Omar Khayyam, The, 287.

RUDGE, printer, 124.

RUSSIAN WRITERS, 303, 304.

RYLANDS LIBRARY, in Manchester, 103, 130, 153, 154, 161, 328.

SADLEIR, MICHAEL, his book on Trollope, 22; on *Desperate Remedies*, 377; *Excursions in Victorian Bibliography*, 379.

SALE CATALOGUES. *See* Catalogues.

SALES: Adam, 198–200, 316, 317; Allan, 192; Brinley, 82, 192, 278; Foote, 281; Hoe, 128, 190, 192, 193; Hurst, 282; Moore, 281; Morrison, 192; Pierce,

281; Roxburghe, 105; Seaman, 177; Thomas, 201; Van Antwerp, 195; Wakeman, 279–282.

"Sales Fatigue," 16.

Sangorski, bookbinder, 129, 156, 164, 166, 167.

Sawyer's Bookshop, London, 25.

Scaliger, French scholar, 330.

Scott, Sir Walter, his works early reprinted in Philadelphia, 94; published in boards, 351; mentioned, 10, 21.

Seaman, Dr. Lazarus, his library, sale of, 177.

Seaman, Sir Owen, editor of *Punch*, 289.

Sedgwick, Ellery, 26.

Sessler, Charles, 178.

Sessler's Bookshop, in Philadelphia, 341.

Sets of Books, 20–22.

Seward, Anna, "The Swan of Lichfield," 326.

Seymour, Robert, first illustrator and creator of the accepted portrait of Pickwick, 362.

Shakespeare, William, remark of Johnson on, 42; first performance of, in America (*The Merchant of Venice*), 93; first published in America in 1795, 93; quoted, 114; first folio of, 117, 182, 208–213, 263, 328; folios of, 221; bowdlerized, 234, 235; Grangerized, 239; quartos of, 250, 252, 256; second folio of, variations in title-page of, 257; wrote under pressure and for money, 374; mentioned 12.

Shakespeare Society of Philadelphia, 320.

Shaw, George Bernard, 36, 273, 301.

Shelley, P. B., his stepmother-in-law, 61; *The Posthumous Fragments of Margaret Nicholson*, copy of, hidden in batch of sheet music, 197; his "hand" readily imitated, 222; *Adonais*, 223; *Hellas*, 223; published in boards, 351.

Sheridan, Richard B., his comedies, 12; *School for Scandal*, first edition of, 92; printed by Prichard and Hall in Philadelphia, 92.

Shorter, Clement, book-collector and editor of the *Sphere*, 177, 288.

Shorthouse, Joseph Henry, *John Inglesant*, 391.

Signature, 111, 112.

"Signers" of the Declaration of Independence, 200, 201.

Silver bindings, 167.

Size, importance of, in buying, 19.

Skinner, Mrs. Otis, 213.

Slater, Mr., 158.

Slip Case, 20.

Smith, George D., 190, 193, 281.

Smith, Harry B., "Sentimental Library" of, 241, 359, 360.

Smith, Harry Worcester, his *Sporting Tour*, 32; his presence, 32; his sporting distinctions, 163.

Smith, Hopkinson, *Colonel Carter of Cartersville*, 286, 287, 374.

Smith, Professor Robert Metcalf, *The Variant Issues of the Second Folio of Shakespeare*, 257.

Smith, Sydney, quoted on American productions, 274.

Smithsonian Institution, 110.

Smollett, Tobias, *Humphrey Clinker*, 260, 346; *Peregrine Pickle*, 346; published in small volumes, 346.

Society, the Best, 146–148.

Solander, Daniel Charles, "Keeper" in the British Museum, 19; case invented by, 19, 20.

Solander Case, 20.

Sotheby's Auction Rooms, 176, 183, 195, 354.

Spectator, 296.

Spencer, George, Marquis of Blandford, in the "Roxburghe Fight," 105; patron of Roger Payne, 153, 154; buys Bedford Missal, 158; founder of Rylands Library, 161; his librarian, 239.

Spencer Collection, 131.

"Spine," 135.

Spiritual Milk for Boston Babes in either England, Drawn out of the Breasts of Both Testaments for their Souls' Nourishment, 278.

Staggemeier, bookbinder, 156.

Stamp Act, The, 76.

Stedman, Edmund Clarence, 282.

Stephen, Sir Leslie, Johnsonian, 183.

Stern (Edward) & Company, Inc., printers, 125.

Sterne, Laurence, *Tristram Shandy*, 32, 348, 350; and Mrs. Vesey, 319; published in small volumes, 346; *Sentimental Journey*, 348; *Sermons*, 348; a remark of, 389; mentioned, 250.

Stevenson, Robert Louis, *Treasure Island*, story of origin of, 65, 67; original map of Treasure Island 65–68, 201; McCutcheon collection of,

202; *New Arabian Nights*, 256; the collecting of, 378.

STEWART (PETER) AND HYDE (GEORGE), 94.

STILLINGFLEET, MR., his blue stockings, 319.

STOCKDALE, JOHN, *Swiss Family Robinson* published by, 62.

STONE, WILBUR MACEY, 81, 174.

STORY, the artistic, 342.

Story of the Glittering Plain, The, printed by Kelmscott Press, 119.

STOWE, HARRIET BEECHER, *Uncle Tom's Cabin*, success of, 284–286; edition of, by Cassel, 285; illustrated by Cruikshank, 285; mentioned, 388; *Old Town Folks*, 388.

STRACHEY, LYTTON, *Life of Queen Victoria*, 288.

STRAHAN, WILLIAM, 310, 311, 345.

SUCKERMAN, gilder, 150, 154.

SULLIVAN, SIR ARTHUR. *See* Gilbert and Sullivan.

SURTEES, R. S., Ross's portrait of, 4, 5; his novels in parts, 367; *Mr. Romford's Hounds*, 367.

SUTCLIFFE, bookbinder, 129, 156, 164, 166, 167.

SWIFT, JONATHAN, *Gulliver's Travels*, 75, 286.

SWINBURNE, ALGERNON C., 205.

Swiss Family Robinson, translations and editions of, 60–64; authorship of, 63; and *Robinson Crusoe*, 64, 65; the fairyland of, 68; mentioned, 9.

TAINE, H. A., on Johnson, 329.

TARKINGTON, BOOTH, 386.

TAYLOR AND HESSEY, 159.

TEASING TOM, in *Patience*, 48.

TENNYSON, ALFRED, LORD, quoted, 125, 275; copy of Lowell's *A Year's Life* inscribed to, 281; early published in boards, 351.

TERRY, ELLEN, 25.

THACKERAY, WILLIAM M., *The Yellowplush Papers*, 95; his language, 304; applies as illustrator for *Pickwick*, 363; *Henry Esmond*, 364; *Vanity Fair*, 364, 365, 367; *The Virginians*, 373; mentioned, 10, 301.

THEATRICAL PERFORMANCE, the first in America, 92, 93.

Thersites, 268.

THOMAS, ISAIAH, founder of American Antiquarian Society, Worcester, Mass., 72; printer and publisher, 86; his private library, 86.

THOMAS SALE, 201.

THOMSON, HUGH, illustrator, 379.

THOMSON, JAMES, *Seasons*, published by Bell, 92; mentioned, 339, 340.

THOREAU, HENRY DAVID, *A Week on the Concord and Merrimac Rivers*, 279; *Walden*, 279; mentioned, 280.

THORPE OF GUILDFORD, 196.

THRALE-PIOZZI, HESTER LYNCH, her copy of the *Dictionary*, 314.

"THREE-DECKER," 18, 334, 368–373.

"TIES," 134, 168.

TINKER, CHAUNCEY B., a *Pilgrim's Progress* of, 82; his history of Bell's edition of *Rasselas*, 88, 89; and letters of Boswell, 236.

TINKER, MR., 236, 237.

TITLE, HALF, 111; on fore-edge, 135; on the spine, 174.

TITLE-PAGE, takes place of colophon, 106; the earliest book in English with, 106; development of, 106; printers' marks on, 106; engraved, 106, 107; humorous, 108.

TOMLINSON, MR., 286, 380.

TREE CALF, 167.

TREGASKIS, JAMES, 115, 154.

TROLLOPE, ANTHONY, a set of, complete in binding, 21, 22; his present vogue, 22; his *Autobiography*, 22, 23; *The Eustace Diamonds*, 23; length of his novels, 374; the readableness of, 389; mentioned, 301.

TURNER, WILLIAM JAY, 316, 317.

Two Orphans, The, 391.

TWO-VOLUMED WORKS, 256.

TWAIN, MARK. *See* Clemens, Samuel Langhorne.

TYPES, 99, 116.

ULIZIO, B. GEORGE, collector, presents book to Newton, 379.

UPDIKE, printer, 124.

VAN ANTWERP (WILLIAM C.) SALE, 195.

VANDERBILT, COMMODORE, 237.

VANDERBILT, MRS. CORNELIUS, 278.

VELLUM, transparent, 156, 158; "with ties," 168.

VESEY, MR., member of "The Club," 317.

VESEY, MRS., her copy of Johnson's *Dictionary*, 317, 319.

VICTORIA, QUEEN, 147.

VICTORIAN NOVEL, 334. *See* Novel.

VIRGIL, Baskerville's edition of, 117.

Virgins Complaint (*The*), *for the losse of their Sweet-Hearts by these present Wars. And their own long solicitude and keeping their Virginities against their Wills,* 108.

VIZETELLY, HENRY, publisher of Zola, arrested, 297.

VOLTAIRE, FRANÇOIS DE, Graingerized, 239.

WAGSTAFF, DAVID, collector, 162.

WAKEMAN, STEPHEN H., his collection of American authors, 279.

WAKEMAN SALE, 279–282; prospectus of, 281.

WALDEN POND, 279.

WALLACE, LEWIS, *Ben Hur*, dedication of, 260.

WALPOLE, HORACE, his bookplate, 142.

WALTON, IZAAK, *Life of Sir Henry Wotton*, 140; *Compleat Angler*, in Gosden binding, 163; *Compleat Angler*, first edition of, 256–259.

WARD, NATHANIEL, "The Simple Cobbler of Agawam," 81, 287.

WASHINGTON, GEORGE, letters of, destroyed, 236, 237.

WASHINGTON, MARTHA, her Bible, 189, 190.

WATERMARKS, 103, 109.

WATTS, ISAAC, *Divine Songs*, editions of, 81; Gosden's drawing of the tomb of, 162.

WELLESLEY COLLEGE, Professor Palmer's collection of first editions of English poetry given to, 29.

WELLS, CAROLYN, 365.

WELLS, EDGAR, 7.

WELLS, GABRIEL, bookseller, 199, 208–213, 272.

WESTCOTT, E. N., *David Harum*, 245, 388.

WHARTON, MRS. EDITH, *The Age of Innocence*, a slip in early issues of, 260–262; *Ethan Frome*, 287, 288, 374.

WHITE, GILBERT, *Natural History of Selborne*, Horace Walpole's copy of first edition of, 264–266; the specialist par excellence, 266.

WHITE, WILLIAM, and Dr. Johnson, 89.

WHITMAN, SARAH HELEN, copy of *The Raven and Other Poems* inscribed to, 281.

WHITMAN, WALT, his fame lasting, 274; esteemed abroad, 282; *Leaves of Grass*, 291, 293; photograph of, 306.

WHITTIER, JOHN G., copy of Holmes's *Memoir of Emerson* inscribed to, 281; mentioned, 274, 279.

WHITTINGHAM, CHARLES, uncle and nephew, 117.

WIDENER, HARRY ELKINS, his collection given to Harvard University, 31; at Hoe Sale, 193.

WIER, RICHARD, bookbinder, 152.

WIGGLESWORTH, MICHAEL, *The Day of Doom*, 73–75.

WILDE, OSCAR, 295, 297.

WILDE, WILLIAM, 371.

WILDER, THORNTON, *The Bridge of San Luis Rey*, 391.

WILDER AND CAMPBELL, publishers, 95.

WILKES, JOHN, 327.

"WILMINGTON (DELAWARE) LIBRARY AND YOUNG MEN'S ASSOCIATION," 88.

WILSON, FRANCIS, *The Eugene Field I Knew*, 286.

WILTSHIRE, Earl of, father of Anne Bullen, 139.

WINTERICH, JOHN T., 8.

WISE, THOMAS JAMES, collector, motto on his bookplate, 2; his catalogue, 188, 189, 250, 252; on forgeries, 222, 223; his "points," 232; his library, 250–253.

WISTER, OWEN, 386.

WITHER, GEORGE. *Abuses Stript and Whipt*, 82, 84, 234.

WOLSEY, THOMAS, 137.

WOTTON, SIR HENRY, 140.

WOTTON, THOMAS, bibliophile, 140.

WYSS, DAVID, author of *Swiss Family Robinson*, 63. See *Swiss Family Robinson, The*.

WYSS, PROFESSOR, son of David Wyss, 63.

YALE UNIVERSITY, Cochran books at, 31; Gutenberg Bible presented to, 97, 199.

YOUNG, OWEN D., 316.

ZAEHNSDORF, bookbinder, 156, 166, 174, 226.

ZAHN, MABEL, 112.

ZOLA, ÉMILE, English publisher of, arrested, 296; publicly entertained in England, 297.

THIS BOOK HAS BEEN SET ON THE
MONOTYPE MACHINE IN GARAMONT TYPE
AND PRINTED
(BOTH TEXT AND ILLUSTRATIONS)
BY THE AQUATONE PROCESS AT THE PRESS OF
EDWARD STERN & COMPANY, INC.
PHILADELPHIA, PENNA.